GORE

GORE

A POLITICAL LIFE

BOB ZELNICK

Since 1947
REGNERY
PUBLISHING, INC.
An Eagle Publishing Company • Washington, DC

Library of Congress Cataloging-in-Publication Data

Published in the United States by
Regnery Publishing, Inc.
An Eagle Publishing Company
One Massachusetts Avenue, NW
Washington, DC 20001

Distributed to the trade by
National Book Network
4720-A Boston Way
Lanham, MD 20706

Printed on acid-free paper.
Manufactured in the United States of America

10 9 8 7 6 5 4 3 2 1

Books are available in quantity for promotional or premium use. Write to Director of Special Sales, Regnery Publishing, Inc., One Massachusetts Avenue, NW Washington, DC 20001, for information on discounts and terms or call (202) 216-0600.

To Ken Juster,
a friend in need.

CONTENTS

ACKNOWLEDGMENTS

LET ME FIRST express my deep gratitude to colleagues and former colleagues who called or wrote to express their support after I left ABC News as the price for continuing to work on this book. I felt fortunate then, and even more fortunate now, to have been provided with so much moral support at a time when I dearly needed it.

Others helped in more concrete ways. President John Raisian and Tom Henriksen of the Hoover Institution came immediately to my "rescue" with a lovely office and a generous five-month fellowship, enabling me to complete the manuscript on schedule. They have my everlasting loyalty and gratitude. (The only problem, as always, is tearing yourself away from Palo Alto when the fellowship ends.)

Admiral Brent Baker, dean of the College of Communication at Boston University, then invited me to "teach a little journalism" at his fine school, which I have been doing since September. The experience has proven so pleasant that, at the dean's invitation, I have decided to "re-up."

I want to thank Al Regnery for his commitment to me and this project. Devin Schaumburg provided capable research assistance, as she did on *Backfire*, my first book. A second-year law student when we first met, she is now in private practice in Washington, DC. Greg Schultze, my other *Backfire* researcher, read an early version of

ix

this manuscript and offered many helpful suggestions. Professor Pat Michaels of the University of Virginia reviewed the chapters that deal with environmental issues and provided valuable advice.

My editor at Regnery, Harry Crocker, helped turn a lot of good information, insights, and analysis into a book. David Dortman performed ably as his colleague. Trish Bozell again showed herself to be one of the finest copy editors in the business. And a truly remarkable job was done by Lydia Yeh, a student at Wellesley College, who gave the manuscript a final "once over." If we are lucky, Lydia will choose to pursue a career in journalism.

My wife Pamela kept my spirits up through some difficult days and fed me a stream of Gore clips at a pace steady enough to prevent me from thinking I could ever relax. My daughter Marni, now at Dartmouth, remained alert long after her dormmates were sound asleep, ready to solve my insoluble computer problems.

I owe special thanks to historian James B. Gardner for providing me with copies of the best material—two research papers he wrote—on Albert Gore, Sr., and the Tennessee politics of his era: "Political Leadership in a time of Transition: Frank G. Clemment, Albert Gore, Estes Kefauver and Tennessee Politics, 1948–1956," a dissertation submitted to the faculty of the Graduate School of Vanderbilt University in partial fulfillment of the requirements for the degree of Doctor of Philosophy in History, August 1978; and, "State Politics and National Ambitions: Frank Clement, Albert Gore, Estes Kefauver and Tennessee Politics, 1948–1956," a paper for the session on "Tennessee Politics in State and Nation," presented during the 1982 meeting of the Southern Historical Association, November 5, 1982. Gardner's oral history sessions with Albert Gore, Sr., now housed at the University of North Carolina, Chapel Hill, were also helpful.

Albert Gore, Sr., also wrote two books about himself and his era: *The Eye of the Storm: A People's Politics for the Seventies* (Herder & Herder, New York, 1970), and *Let the Glory Out: My South and its Politics* (Viking Press, New York, 1972).

I also benefited from earlier studies of the younger Gore performed by others. When Al Gore, Jr., declared for the presidency in 1988, Hank Hillen, a former FBI agent, then sheriff of Nashville, slapped together an adoring book, *Al Gore, Jr.: His Life and Career*. Whatever its shortcomings, the book has valuable background on Gore and several interesting perspectives from people who knew him as a boy and young man, along with transcripts of several important statements from his early political years. In a few instances, quotes attributed to Eleanor Smotherman, Gore's second-grade teacher; young Gore himself, and his girlfriend, Donna Armistead, first appeared in Hillen's account.

There have also been a number of fine newspaper and magazine profiles of Gore over the years. Among the best: the Gore profile prepared by Nolan Walters for Knight-Ridder Newspapers (undated) prior to the 1988 primary campaign. Others include:

"Albert Gore, Jr.," by Otto Kreisher, Copley News Service, September 6, 1987.

"Al Gore," by Michael Kelly, *The Baltimore Sun*, December 13, 1987.

"Gore: The Son Also Rises," by Gail Sheehy, *Vanity Fair*, March 1988.

"The Boy Who Would Be President," by Sarah Booth Conroy, *Washington Post*, July 10, 1992.

"Al Gore's Double Life," by Alex S. Jones, *New York Times Sunday Magazine*, October 25, 1992.

"The Drama of the Gifted Vice President," by Katherine Boo, *Washington Post*, November 28, 1993.

"Gore's Dilemma," by Peter J. Boyer, *New Yorker*, November 28, 1994.

"The Chosen One," by Marjorie Williams, *Vanity Fair*, February 1998.

"The Gore Guide to the Future," by Richard L. Berke, *New York Times Sunday Magazine*, February 22, 1998.

Three articles in the *New Republic*, March 2, 1998: "Color Blind," by Jim Sleeper; "Tomorrow Never dies," by Jacob Heilbrunn; and "Uncovered," by Paul Glastris.

"After Elvis," by Louis Menand, *New Yorker*, October 26 and November 2, 1998.

"Blood and Gore," by Gore Vidal, *GQ*, December 1998.

Several books on the Clinton Administration also provided valuable information on Gore and his White House role. These include: *On the Edge: the Clinton Presidency*, by Elizabeth Drew (Simon & Schuster, New York, 1994); *Showdown: The Struggle Between the Gingrich Congress and the White House*, by Elizabeth Drew (Simon & Schuster, New York, 1996); *Whatever It Takes: The Real Struggle for Political Power in America*, by Elizabeth Drew (Viking, New York, 1997); *The Agenda: Inside the Clinton White House*, by Bob Woodward (Simon & Schuster, New York, 1994); *The Choice*, by Bob Woodward (Simon & Schuster, New York, 1996); and *Behind the Oval Office: Winning the Presidency in the Nineties*, by Dick Morris (Random House, New York, 1997).

Hundreds, if not thousands, of newspaper articles as well as interview transcripts, books, academic papers, and committee hearing records and reports were informative, as well as more than one hundred personal interviews. I flirted with using footnotes or endnotes but decided against both. Except for the mundane stuff of daily reporting, I have tried to cite the source of my information in the text of the book. I apologize in advance for any material oversights.

Early into the project, I was advised by the vice president's office that he had decided against cooperating with me and would personally resent attempts to contact his family, particularly his aged parents. I promised I would make no such attempt—not because I was intimidated, but because I have quaint, old-fashioned notions about honoring the privacy of home and family. As chance would have it, my daughter Marni and I did run into the elder Gore at the offices of the *Carthage Courier* in July, 1997, seventeen months before his death. But I made no attempt to interview him, simply exchanging idle chitchat during the fifteen or so minutes we spent together. Several former aides and associates of the vice president did choose to cooperate, and for that I am grateful.

GORE

DUTY BEFORE ALL

O N THE AFTERNOON of September 10, 1998, two black government vans cruised to a stop at the House entrance to the United States Capitol. As swarms of television crews squirmed and elbowed and cursed their way into favorable locations for the shots seen round the world, networks interrupted their regular programming to report that Independent Counsel Kenneth Starr had delivered thirty-six boxes of material he considered evidence of impeachable offenses committed by President William Jefferson Clinton. Within twenty-four hours the House Judiciary Committee would release Starr's book-length narrative of presidential misconduct, proving to most who read it that the president had lied under oath in denying a sexual relationship with former White House intern Monica Lewinsky, and may well have obstructed justice in engineering the false testimony of others.

The event would set in motion a political process infinitely more layered and complex than even the most sophisticated observers predicted in its earliest stages. Republicans were confident at first that a majority of Americans would be repelled by Clinton's dishonesty if not his predatory sexual conduct to the extent that they would demand, or at least accept, the sustained tribulation of impeachment and trial. So they dumped a garbage truck full of raw evidence—documents, interview transcripts, even the president's videotaped grand jury testimony of August 17—into the public domain, and moved briskly toward an October 8 House vote initiating an impeachment inquiry by the House Judiciary Committee. So quickly did the train gather momentum that not even clear polling indications that the public was not on board slowed it.

The standard wisdom at first was that the polls were misleading because those most likely to vote in nonpresidential years were disproportionately core constituency Republicans who supported the impeachment effort. But soon the "most likely voter" polls began to level off. There were clear signs that much of the public blamed Congress for putting out more graphic material than was necessary, and for allowing itself to become distracted from its legislative business to focus single-mindedly on Clinton's wrongdoing. By Election Day the approval rating for Congress was lower, and that for the president higher, than had been the case before the acute phase of the Lewinsky scandal had broken.

If Bill Clinton stood center stage during the unfolding drama, much attention was also focused on his hand-picked successor, the man who would instantly succeed him were he forced from office: Albert Arnold Gore, Jr., a man—to borrow Professor Henry Higgins's words—"of good character where women are concerned."

But, however pure his private habits, Gore, like Clinton, was also under investigation for possible crimes committed while in office. Since March 1997, when he acknowledged soliciting campaign money in nearly four dozen calls placed from the White House, the Justice Department had been trying to determine whether he had violated a century-old law prohibiting political fund-raising "in any room or building occupied in the discharge of official duties." For much of that period, Republican political opponents had been demanding that Attorney General Janet Reno appoint an independent counsel to conduct the investigation. Twice Reno had considered and rejected the idea, each time concluding, on the basis of disputed precedent, that the statute barred only "hard" money intended to affect the outcome of a specific federal campaign, rather than "soft" money intended to benefit the party as a whole. And she had accepted Gore's word, and that of several donors, that he had only soft money in mind when he placed the calls, thus seemingly laying the matter to rest. But when a campaign memo surfaced suggesting that Gore had been informed that hard money was involved, Reno initiated yet another inquiry, this time including the question of whether the vice president had deliberately misled Justice Department investigators.

The president's and Gore's problems had contradictory implications. On the one hand, Gore could become president nearly two years before Election Day 2000, perhaps short-circuiting the ability of potential Democratic opponents to mount credible primary campaigns, and greatly complicating the task of any Republican challenger. On the other, a full-blown independent counsel investigation of his fund-raising activity could spread to other far more serious areas of possible campaign misconduct, such as knowingly accepting foreign campaign contributions. "We're concerned that an independent counsel will start connecting the dots," conceded one Gore strategist in the wake of the late summer developments. "The picture he draws may not be the correct one. But politically, it could be very damaging."

With the Reno decision out of their hands, Gore and his team concentrated instead on how the vice president should comport himself during the House investigation of the Clinton-Lewinsky matter. Overnight, a group consisting of Gore, his wife Tipper, and a small core of loyalists in and out of government, which had been meeting regularly at the vice president's Naval Observatory residence to organize his presidential campaign, was transformed into a virtual crisis committee. The first order of business was to decide how Gore should respond to what was now convincing evidence of presidential misconduct. In January, when the Lewinsky allegations had first appeared, Gore, like many in the White House and cabinet, had told the public that Clinton had denied the charges and that he believed the president. At a closed-door session of the Democratic caucus on Capitol Hill, Gore had urged legislators to trust Clinton and battle to enact his agenda. And at a strange joint appearance at the University of Illinois, he had literally screamed his support for the president.

But he had stopped short of joining Clinton's attack dogs in their political assault on Kenneth Starr. Nor had he endorsed Hillary Rodham Clinton's charge of a "right-wing conspiracy." And he had said nothing about Clinton's character, declining in one interview to dismiss the relevance of presidential character, saying instead that the issue was "for the American people to decide."

Now, freshly back from a Hawaiian family vacation, Gore decided that both loyalty and a commitment to constitutional propriety demanded that he take a stand against impeachment. This did not mean embracing the convoluted argument of the president and his private counsel, David Kendall, that, however misleading, the Clinton answers in the Paula Corbin Jones deposition had been technically true and thus could not support perjury charges. And he still had no apparent appetite for an attack on Starr. So Gore's defense of his friend, while emphatic, was nevertheless circumscribed.

In his first, defining statement on the issue—strengthened from the draft prepared by his staff—Gore said about the Starr material, "I do not believe that this report serves as the basis for overturning the judgment of the American people in 1992 and again in 1996 that Bill Clinton should be their president." Then Gore added a strong personal endorsement of Clinton, but one that was limited to his public policies as president: "[F]or almost six years now I have worked alongside this president as he has led us toward unprecedented prosperity and toward solutions for the problems that we need to address in America. We have made tremendous progress under his leadership. He is doing a tremendous job as president and I look forward to continuing to work with him as he continues to address the issues that face this country."

In a revealing October interview with Ceci Connolly of the *Washington Post*, Gore amplified his approach. "I've defined my job in exactly the same way for six years now: to do everything I can to help him be the best president possible," he said. "That gives a clarity of focus to everything I do and serves to filter out a lot of the ups and downs." Gore could not, however, turn himself into a pretzel with every turn in Clinton's private fortunes. "Whether the news is good or bad, whether the roller coaster goes up or down means exactly the same thing for me."

Gore, in the first hours of the intensified crisis, struck the essential political theme Democrats would play with remarkable success in the weeks ahead—that however indefensible Bill Clinton's personal conduct, his offenses stopped short of an impeachable offense and should not distract Congress from needed tobacco legislation, campaign reform, a "Bill of Rights" for HMO subscribers, and more money for new teachers and school construction.

In subsequent days, both in appearances with Clinton and campaigning on his own, Gore was effusive in his praise of the Clinton record, claiming at one Boston stop that the president had offered the most creative approach to government since Franklin Delano Roosevelt. Gore affected a "business as usual" demeanor, delivering a previously scheduled address on the need to contain urban sprawl to the Brookings Institution in Washington. He traveled to Keene, New Hampshire, where he delivered a health care talk to a local college, declined to take a position on the merits of the House Judiciary Committee decision to release the tape of Clinton's four-hour grand jury testimony, and expressed disappointment only at the "partisan" division of the committee. While in the state, he acknowledged that the president's conduct was "indefensible," but he declared the grand jury tape to be "much ado about not much new."

Still, as Democrats—flush with favorable public opinion polls—accused Starr of everything from breaking grand jury secrecy rules to withholding exculpatory evidence in presenting his initial report to the House, and Republicans of conducting a "partisan witch hunt," Gore exercised considerable restraint. He would not become Clinton's hatchet man. He would not play with deep public emotions on the issue. He would not, Samson-like, tear down the pillars of the government he fervently hoped to inherit. He would do all within his power to demonstrate loyalty to Bill Clinton. But he would do it in a manner consistent with his own conscience.

As far back as January 1998, Gore had warned his staff, as he had already done after the disastrous 1994 midterm elections, that under no circumstances was anyone to say a word—publicly or privately—to indicate dissatisfaction with the president. Moreover, when members of Gore's extended political family were reported to have been wrestling with the question of the impact of a Clinton resignation or impeachment on his own chances in the year 2000, Gore let them know he wanted that kind of talk to stop. That has been his consistent pattern. In all the research and interviewing undertaken for this project, I've yet to document any instance where Gore has had so much as a single negative comment about a president who—for all his dazzling political intuition and success in moving his party toward the center—may well be as personally corrupt as any in the nation's history. Gore has had no "backgrounders," no off-the-record chats with favored journalists, no trusted aides to speak authoritatively on their boss's behalf offering derogatory information on Bill Clinton.

Yet as the campaign for control of Congress intensified with Gore as the lead Democratic campaigner, the vice president's aggressive, partisan style tended to blur the lines he had drawn between attacking Republicans and defending Mr. Clinton only to a point. His standard stump speech became more and more harsh. At times he would slide into the rhythmic cadence of a black Baptist preacher: "We say legislate," he would roar, "they say investigate. We say educate, they say interrogate. We say illuminate, they say instigate. We say unify, they say vilify. We make the tough decisions, they take depositions. We find real solutions, they launch prosecutions. We know our future's nearing, they want to hold more hearings." Here Gore seemed not only to be taking on the Clinton baggage, but exhibiting qualities about himself that start the juices flowing with opponents. "The vice president," wrote John F. Harris in the *Washington Post*, "approaches politics with a streak of intellectual and moral righteousness that lead him to frame issues— both in public and in internal White House deliberations—in starker terms than the accommodationist president he serves." After stumping for well over two hundred Democrats in 1998, Gore made many grateful friends, and many spiteful enemies.

The election returns seemed at first to smile on Gore. Democrats narrrowed the gap in the House and held their own in the Senate. Speaker of the House Newt Gingrich was in full retreat in the face of dissatisfaction from his own party. National sentiment against impeachment was running at roughly two to one. Surely the charge toward impeachment by zealot Republicans would be beaten back. Surely the new speaker designate, Robert Livingston of Louisiana, would accept compromise on censure, and move from there to legislative accommodation. Surely Gore would quickly resume his cherished role as "president in training."

But House Republicans, perhaps emboldened by a sense of earnest mission, perhaps by intuition that Clinton's numerical support lacked political intensity, or perhaps by a lemming instinct unparallel in 20th Century politics, moved forward toward impeachment. During the second week of December, the House Judiciary committee adopted four articles. And as its last act of meaningful business, the full House voted dramatically on December 19 to send two of those articles to the Senate for trial. In a political display widely condemned as tasteless, if not thoroughly repugnant, House Democrats, whose defeated motion of censure contained language almost as harsh as the GOP-sponsored impeachment articles, adjourned to the White House for what appeared to all the world a political pep rally. Gore used the occasion to declare that the impeachment vote "does a great disservice to a man I believe will be regarded in the history books as one of our greatest Presidents." The vice president, who had earlier in the month received good news when the attorney general once again decided against referring his case to a special counsel, could be excused for thinking, along with many others, "Events are in the saddle; they ride mankind."

For Gore, the political task ahead is not easy. His role in the Clinton administration has been so prominent and his allegiance to Clinton so complete that he will find it difficult to escape the taint of his benefactor—even though Clinton was acquitted on both articles of impeachment, with neither mustering even a majority. And lacking Clinton's roguish charm, Gore could find public outrage transferred to his shoulders where Clinton had been spared. Groomed since birth for the presidency, Gore's political destiny may now involve inheriting his party's mantle in circumstances that devalue the achievement.

There is, of course, another highly plausible scenario. It is that once out from under the Clinton shadow, Gore will be appraised and judged on the basis of his own record, his own words, his own character and personality. It is a record and background that received limited attention in 1988 when he first sought the presidency. And there have been material additions to the "Gore file" since then: the emotional trauma of a son's serious injury; a critical party-defying vote on the Persian Gulf War; an important book on the environment; two national campaigns; six years spent as "the greatest vice president in history"; and, in December, the death of his father and early mentor, Albert Gore, Sr., a longtime representative and senator from Tennessee.

Gore's political identity is now indissolubly linked to the man from Hope. But a truer measure of who he is begins with the man from Possum Hollow.

CHAPTER ONE

THE MAN FROM POSSUM HOLLOW

WHEN AL GORE'S FATHER, Albert Gore, Sr., first ran for the Senate from Tennessee in 1952 after fourteen years in the House, his supporters bragged, "The twang of Smith County is still in his voice and the steel of hard work is still in his muscles." When, in his 1988 quest for the presidency, Al Gore, Jr., sought to pile up primary states in the South, many saw him as a computer-age preppie programmed as a virtual Tennessean. They joked that in prep school and at Harvard he had taken "Southern" as a foreign language. Albert Gore Sr., who had never lost his roots in the yeoman hill country of Middle Tennessee, and who had tried to make sure his son didn't either, was not amused.

The ancestors came from England. A plaque in Jamestown, Virginia, lists one of the colony's original settlers as "Thomas Gore, Gentleman." When the thirteen-year-old Al, Jr., first saw the plaque on a visit with his father, he remarked, "Dad, we've slipped a little, haven't we?"

To reward their military service in the Revolutionary War, the government granted two of the Gore brothers, both privates, parcels of land in what is now Overton County, Tennessee. Middle

Tennessee is a hundred-and-forty-mile-wide basin that stretches from the middle of the Cumberland Plateau to the western loop of the Tennessee River. The area's small farmers have long grown strawberries, cantaloupes, and tobacco. According to the senior Gore, "[I]t was a rather rough terrain characterized by marginal clay soil, steep hills, shaded coves, and clear creeks. There was no river transportation; 'bottom land' was scarce." Albert Gore, Sr., has written that his search of the family history revealed not a single slave-owning Gore, a claim that could be made by many if not most of the hill country's small farm families. By the Civil War, the state was bitterly divided between the loyal Republican East and the planter-dominated pro-slavery West, a far cry from the unity of purpose of Mexican War days when the statewide call for 2,600 "volunteers" had been answered by 30,000 young men.

Sympathies in central Tennessee ran mainly toward the Confederacy, despite the paucity of slave owners, and the Gores were no exception. A grandfather of Albert, Sr., served in uniform, and Al, Jr., has told at least one friend of a Gore who peacefully worked his farm during the war until he was robbed, shot, and left for dead by two Yankee deserters. According to the tale, for which there is no documentation, a family servant nursed the wounded Gore back to health. He then set out after his attackers, found them both, and killed them.

While distant Mississippi cousins of the Tennessee Gores became part of their state's landed gentry, the fortunes of the Tennessee Gores were never great. Albert, Sr.'s, parents, Allen and Maggie Denny Gore, grew tobacco, feed, and vegetables, and raised cattle, hogs, and chickens on modest acreage near the town of Possum Hollow. One of Allen's boyhood chums, Cordell Hull, would later serve in Congress and, at the time Albert, Sr., was elected, had become Franklin Delano Roosevelt's secretary of state. The two young men would sometimes "run the river" together, rafting down the Cumberland as far as Nashville, returning via steamboat.

In many ways Albert Gore, Sr., loved the farm and rural life, yet both he and his dad always assumed that he would be the one to break the hold of the land over successive generations of Gores. He knew that "to get out, you had to get up." He attended a one-room schoolhouse, which also served as a social center. It was there that he became acquainted with some of the area's best fiddlers and became an accomplished fiddler himself. It was an avocation his father disparaged as a short-cut to a life of poverty.

Equally disparaging was Pauline LaFon Gore, Albert, Sr.'s, future bride, who viewed his playing at campaign events as both undignified and leaving him open to the charge of fiddling while Rome (or at least Carthage, Tennessee) burned. Years later, Pauline Gore, whose abundant virtues do not include a sense of humor, would halt her son Al's music lessons with the admonition, "Future world leaders do not play the violin."

Albert Gore, Sr., took a course out of high school in teacher training and soon secured a teaching certificate and a job. He earned enough money to enroll at Murfreesboro State, but was never able to afford more than two consecutive semesters in college. Still, he became principal of a three-teacher school before he graduated. Before long he campaigned for superintendent of Smith County schools. He lost that first political contest, but later won appointment to the job, after the man who beat him died. He followed that up with election to the full four-year term. He also found enough spare time to study law, and enrolled at an evening law school run by the Nashville YMCA.

The drive to Nashville was just under sixty miles on a serviceable two-lane highway. Gore negotiated the round trip three nights each week during the academic year and won his law degree after three years. After class, he would stop for coffee at the ornate Andrew Jackson Hotel. There he met Pauline LaFon. Tall, raven-haired, of Huguenot background, she was the daughter of a merchant whose business had failed in the Depression. Her soft-spoken manner and stoic appearance masked an inner drive that to this day has yet to stall. Pauline was attending Vanderbilt Law School—the second woman to do so—while waiting on tables at the coffee shop during the evening. "Pretty soon," Gore recalled, "there was but one girl whose coffee tasted just right." His consumption "increased dramatically." They courted, married, and passed the bar together. "By the slimmest, thinnest of margins, she made a grade of 84 on hers and I made $84^1/_2$. By that narrow position, I maintained a position as head of the household." Many who have known the family over the years argue that it would have taken considerable effort for Pauline LaFon to finish behind Albert Gore, Sr.,—or nearly anyone else—in a competitive academic exam. Pauline would be an extraordinary political partner throughout her husband's career and later a valued political confidant of her son. Frequent visitors to the Gore home recall that during the family's many political discussions, the elder Senator Gore would invariably focus on matters of policy while Pauline LaFon Gore would talk about constituencies and interest groups. "Albert Gore, Sr.," one noted, "had firm ideas on what *should* be done; Pauline always seemed to know what *could* be done." Their daughter, Nancy Gore Hunger, once said of her parents: "He just doesn't know how to gossip, how to make small talk. He doesn't like to pull off shoes, drink beer and shoot the bull. Mother will talk 45 minutes to a person, where Daddy will talk 10."

The senior Gore glided easily toward politics. He was appointed commissioner of labor in the state after backing the winning gubernatorial candidate, Tom Browning. In 1938, when the congressional seat in his home district became vacant, he ran for it and won, thanks in part to some inspired fiddle playing along the campaign trail, and a $40,000 contribution from cousin Grady Gore, a wealthy Washington, D.C., landlord. He moved to

Washington with his wife and their infant daughter Nancy. He would never again play the fiddle in public.

Gore, Sr., always self-conscious about his teachers college undergraduate study and YMCA law degree, worked hard to polish his prose and speaking style. Ultimately, Gore's southern hill country twang would subside in "respectable" company as he became one of the better public orators in the nation's capital, only to reappear miraculously on the stump in Tennessee. As time went by, he favored the imported knits and tweeds of the British aristocracy. Here the contrast with Tennessee's most famous political figure of the 1950s, Senator Estes Kefauver, was profound. Kefauver, the son of a prosperous hardware merchant and twenty-year mayor of Madisonville, was educated at Yale Law School and seemed always, in the words of David Halberstam, a former *Nashville Tennessean* reporter, "surrounded by an emotional moat." As he rose to national prominence, he affected a coonskin cap, and built a fair portion of Tennessee slang into his informal speeches. Comparing the two men, one political observer saw in Gore a self-made highbrow, and in Kefauver a self-made lowbrow. In later years, Al Gore, Sr., would take particular pride in the bearing and erudition of his son. "When Al, Jr., speaks, you can practically see the commas falling into place," he would brag to a member of the press.

Shortly after his election to Congress, Albert Gore, Sr., sought advice from the party's elder statesmen. Vice President John Nance Garner told him, "Young man, I never saw a congressman defeated for something he didn't say and didn't do." Cordell Hull told him to "stay on the floor and learn the rules," advice Gore took to heart. He was later designated by Speaker of the House Sam Rayburn as one of six Democratic "watchdogs" rotating on the floor to respond to any GOP assault.

Today, of course, a contemporary Cordell Hull would probably tell a young Gore that, other than ceremonial occasions, there are only three possible excuses for being on the floor: if you are speaking, if you are voting, or if you happen to have died there. And as for "learning the rules," the Albert Gore, Jr., method is much to be preferred. When he sought to learn legislative rules and procedures following his 1976 election to the House, young Gore sent for the best parliamentarian the Library of Congress could offer and received a series of briefings and written outlines on the subject.

The senior Gore enjoyed life in Washington and reveled in his duties as a member of Congress. He sat on the Banking and Currency Committee and held the chairmanship of a subcommittee overseeing the development of atomic energy. His wife Pauline LaFon Gore "retired" from law practice because the family regarded it as unseemly for her to be hawking clients in Washington while hubby passed laws a few blocks away. But, as was widely practiced during the period, neither spouse saw any conflict with Mrs. Gore accepting a position on the congressman's staff. Later she would serve as a delegate to the United Nations.

Nor did Gore chafe at participating in one of the crudest fictions of the World War II period. He ostentatiously waived his draft deferment as a congressman and "volunteered" for the armed forces, declaring his wife, Pauline, would run the office in his absence. That was the public story. But in fact President Franklin Roosevelt would, in the "national interest," summon Gore back to his civilian duties as soon as he was sworn in as a soldier. Years later, when Al Gore, Jr., decided to enlist during the Vietnam era, principally to spare his father political embarrassment during a tough reelection campaign, he engaged in no similar chicanery, signing on as an army journalist and serving seven months working out of an air base near Saigon.

After the war, politics in Tennessee underwent a dramatic change. In 1948 Estes Kefauver campaigned for the Senate against a candidate backed by the most powerful political machine in the state, run by "Boss" Edward Hull Crump of Memphis. Lacking Crump's professional organization, Kefauver campaigned relentlessly in most of the state's ninety-five counties. He employed radio and, for the first time, television to reach the mass electorate. He mobilized groups that had never before been politicized in Tennessee: women, veterans, and young people, as well as the more traditional constituencies of blacks* and organized labor. As chronicled by historian James B. Gardner, Kefauver's female supporters "enlisted a wide range of previously inactive voters in the Kefauver cause, including housewives, teachers, businesswomen, clerks, and factory workers." These constituencies would be a mighty factor in Tennessee politics in the years to come.

The year 1948 also saw the third party presidential campaign of South Carolina Governor J. Strom Thurmond, leader of the anti-civil rights "Dixiecrat" challenge to President Harry S. Truman. Thurmond was endorsed by Crump and ran a strong but losing race in the state. Still, the local effect of Thurmond's campaign was to pry an important segment of the state's Democratic constituency loose from its moorings, opening the door for its eventual shift to the GOP. Al Gore, Jr.'s, Tennessee would be a state with a heated two-party competition in nearly every region and at nearly every level of government.

In 1952 Al Gore, Sr., moved to the Senate, employing Kefauver's organization to defeat an octogenarian ally of the Crump machine, Senator Kenneth McKellar. That same year, Kefauver made the first of his two unsuccessful runs for the Democratic presidential nomination, and Tennessee gained a new governor in Frank G. Clement—a Bible-toting, mandolin-picking World War II veteran and former FBI agent, who would embellish many a political stump appearance with a chorus or two from his theme song, "Take my hand, precious Lord, lead me on, lead me on."

Kefauver, Gore, Sr., and Clement would dominate Tennessee politics for more than a decade, competing with one another, but holding together on key issues like civil rights and support for the

---

* Unlike many southern juridictions, which used a variety of tricks and tactics to prevent blacks from voting, the Crump machine would pay the poll taxes for black supporters ensuring that tens of thousands of them would back organization candidates on Election Day.

Tennessee Valley Authority (TVA) energy monopoly. While none of the three pushed the envelope on desegregation, each counseled adherence to federal court decisions. When, for example, a mob of white segregationists in Clinton, Tennessee, sought to prevent fifteen black students from entering a high school ordered integrated by the courts, Clement—like other southern governors—sent national guard troops to the school, but unlike the others, he sent them to enforce the court decree.

Albert Gore, Sr., tried to concentrate on other issues. As a member of the Public Works Committee, he was a sponsor of the $50 billion National Highway Defense Act of 1956, the largest public works undertaking in the history of the world. The system included 40,000 miles of limited access, toll-free roads—29,000 of which had to be built from scratch—that linked 90 percent of all American cities with populations of 50,000 or more.

Gore was also a reflexive, unwavering champion of the TVA. Created by special act of Congress in 1933, the TVA's basic mission was to enhance the navigability of the Tennessee River, improve flood control, help farmers with fertilizer and land use techniques, and develop an impoverished economy. The TVA was propelled by the vision and drive of David Lilienthal, an early director, into a taxpayer-subsidized, regional, monopolistic provider of cheap hydroelectric power, as well as coal, and eventually nuclear-powered energy. Despite its abysmal environmental record and its anachronistic state-subsidized monopoly power, Al Gore, Jr., the champion of environmentalism and of "reinventing government," has been as staunch and unquestioning in his support of the TVA as was his father.

But unlike his son, Albert Gore, Sr., was frequently at odds with environmentalists. In words that seem squarely contrary to the values his son came to represent, the elder Gore wrote:

"'Ecology is now a household word, but many of those who use it do not seem aware of the fact that by definition ecology is tied to economics, that man's *well-being* is tied to his *being;* that although preservation of an unsullied crystal stream, a purer atmosphere, a virgin tract of forest, or an unblemished landscape are noble goals, they are not the noblest: the noblest is to provide man with the basic stuff of his existence—food and housing, and meaningful work. Before we can recreate we must create."

But if Albert Gore, Sr., was on the side of economic growth, some of his business acquaintances were less than savory. One of them was Armand Hammer, an entrepreneur extraordinaire with a particular talent for buying or otherwise ingratiating himself to those who could help him befriend top government decision-makers. During the early part of his career, Hammer also served as an agent of the infant Soviet Union. In his extraordinary account, *Dossier: The Secret History of Armand Hammer*, Edward Jay Epstein documents how, during the 1920s and 1930s, Hammer—who lived in Moscow for many years—took his orders from the regimes of Lenin and Stalin. During a period when the Soviets had few diplomatic missions in the West, Hammer began by serving as a courier for the Soviets under the cover of normal business travels to and from Moscow. Hammer then graduated to more sophisticated assignments. He used his Allied American Corporation to launder Soviet funds, helped recruit Soviet spies and position them in the U.S. government, and became a key link in operations that financed Soviet espionage in London and New York. In what was perhaps his shabbiest venture, Hammer—working closely with Stalin's young aide Anastas Mikoyan—helped the Soviets sell communist-confiscated art and jewelry to the West by falsely proclaiming the items were "Romanoff treasure." In perhaps his ugliest venture, Hammer used his firm to provide a cover for the shipment of machine tools to the Soviet Union, which were then employed to help Germany circumvent Treaty of Versailles restrictions on military aircraft and weapons manufacture.

All of this was well known to the FBI, whose director, J. Edgar

Hoover, had kept track of Hammer for decades. But Hoover had some of Washington's most sensitive political antenna and was wary of moving publicly against Hammer so long as he appeared "protected" by powerful members of the executive or legislative branches. Hammer had enjoyed easy access to the Roosevelt Administration, but the Truman Administration, viewing him as a possible Soviet agent, kept him at arm's length, as did the Eisenhower Administration. So he developed a core of Capitol Hill allies led by Gore, Representative James Roosevelt, and Senator Styles Bridges, a conservative New Hampshire Republican. Thus insulated from FBI interference, he went about building his economic empire.

Through the 1950s and well into the following decade, Hammer counted on Gore as his principal link to the Democratic congressional leadership, and to defend his economic interests. In the early 1950s, for example, when Hammer's United Distilleries sought to lease the Army's ordnance works in Morgantown, West Virginia, in order to develop a fertilizer manufacturing operation, Hammer relied on Senator Bridges to run interference for him. When the magazine *Reporter* exposed Bridges' intervention, noting the irony of his alliance with a former Soviet booster, Gore took the Senate floor to defend both Hammer and Bridges. "This private citizen has had aspersions cast upon his character and his patriotism," he declared. "I could see no reason for that except as a means of attacking the senior senator from New Hampshire."

In the late 1950s Gore introduced Hammer to Senator John F. Kennedy. Hammer contributed to Kennedy's 1960 campaign and attended his inauguration as Gore's guest. During the following weeks, Kennedy discussed with Gore a report that the Soviets were employing slave labor to produce crabmeat for export. Kennedy felt he had no choice but to ban the commodity, and the controversy had become a minor irritant to already troubled U.S.–Soviet relations. Gore suggested Kennedy send Hammer to the Soviet Union to investigate the claim, which, given Hammer's background, was rather like dispatching a fox to investigate the disappearance of chickens. Nonetheless, less than a month after he took office, Kennedy had Commerce Secretary Luther Hodges name Hammer a roving economic emissary and organize an itinerary that included stops in the United Kingdom, France, West Germany, Italy, Libya, India, Japan, and the Soviet Union.

Gore wrote a letter "introducing" Hammer to Soviet leader Nikita Khruschev's deputy, Anastas Mikoyan, who had been Hammer's handler on the Romanoff art and jewelry scam three decades earlier. Mikoyan set up a February 17, 1961, meeting between Hammer and Khruschev, at which Khruschev quickly moved beyond the crabmeat issue to the general desirability of expanding trade between the two countries.

Upon his return to Washington, Hammer held meetings with both Senator Gore and Secretary Hodges. To no one's surprise, he reported finding no evidence that slave labor was used in the production of Soviet crabmeat. Even hardline Secretary of State Dean Rusk supported lifting the ban as a "tangible demonstration of our desire to improve United States–Soviet relations." Kennedy accepted the advice. In a March 17, 1961, letter to Hammer informing him of the action, Gore stated, "In the broad spectrum of the struggle to find a way for the East and the West to live in peace on one planet, this may not appear to some as a major item, but when one considers the dangers to mankind involved in war today, any step that moves toward better understanding and peaceful relations is important." By then, however, Hammer had all but forgotten the crabmeat controversy amid plans to export to the Soviet Union the machinery and know-how to begin production of massive amounts of phosphate fertilizer.

Al Gore, Sr., profited handsomely from his association with Hammer, even while still in office. By 1950 Hammer had ingratiated himself to Gore by taking him as a partner in his cattle-breeding business. He also supplied Gore with Christmas gifts of expensive silver. During the years that followed, Gore's herd of Aberdeen-Angus cattle was enriched by several bulls and heifers produced by Hammer's stock.

There is in Middle Tennessee much folklore about Albert Gore, Sr.'s, cattle business and its relationship to his political dealings. Residents will tell the inquiring visitor of how lobbyists and others with an interest in Gore's work would parade to Carthage during the fall auction period, bid outrageously high prices for Gore's stock, and sometimes not even bother to pick up what they had purchased. Proof of such de facto bribery is lacking. But what is not lacking are local press reports from the era which chronicle the many distinguished folks who came to buy Albert Gore's cattle. In the 1957–58 period, for example, the *Carthage Courier* reported that cattle purchasers included Senator Robert Kerr, the Oklahoma Democrat and oil industry point man, who owned a large herd of his own; Gordon Dean, a former chairman of the Atomic Energy Commission, some of whose Wall Street dealings now fell under Gore's legislative jurisdiction; and, most peculiarly, legendary baseball great Joe DiMaggio. In 1958 the "Yankee Clipper" showed up in Carthage and purchased ten calves from Gore on behalf of clients whose identities he declined to disclose.

Payoffs? Or good faith, arms-length business transactions? Even good friends of the Gore family retain their suspicions. Says former Governor Ned McWherter, one of Al Gore, Jr.'s, staunchest Tennessee allies, and the man who delivered the clinching arguments to Bill Clinton for putting Gore on the '92 ticket, "I've sold some Angus in my time too, but I never got the kind of prices for my cattle that the Gores got for theirs."

In the political world that Al Gore, Jr., would inherit, padding one's political war chest through the sale of black Angus cattle would seem a trifle quaint. Al Gore, Sr., tried to educate his son about the world of politics, hoping he would find it exciting and rise to the top.

But when it came to political fundraising, the time would come when the younger man would have been able to teach his father a thing or two.

CHAPTER TWO

A GOOD BOY

WHEN AL GORE, JR., was born on March 31, 1948, his father redeemed a promise. Months earlier, he had read on an inside page of the *Nashville Tennessean* of the birth of Estes Kefauver's new daughter, Diane. Gore thought his own offspring deserved more prominent treatment. He told a Washington reporter for the *Nashville Tennessean*, "If I have a baby boy, I don't want it buried on the inside of the paper. I want it on Page 1 where it belongs."

He got his wish. "A son was born to Mrs. Pauline Gore in Washington yesterday and the *Nashville Tennessean* hereby makes good on a long-standing promise to Rep. Albert Gore to give this good news Page 1 play." The report listed the baby's weight as 9 pounds 2 ounces and said, "The Gore's other child, ten-year-old Nancy, was at home calling up everybody in the telephone directory."

The senior Gore was overjoyed. He had all but given up hope for another child, let alone a son, as his wife entered her midthirties. Now at thirty-six she had delivered the heir he had wanted for years.

The Gores soon moved into a six-room, eighth-floor apartment of the Fairfax Hotel on Massachusetts Avenue in Washington. There they lived rent-free, compliments of cousin Grady Gore, who owned the establishment. To make certain his son would be more than a product of Embassy Row, Al, Sr., insisted the boy spend a fair chunk of his childhood on the family's 250-acre farm above the Caney Fork River, not far from Possum Hollow where he had lived as a young man.

Al, Sr., raised his son on stories about the hard-scrabble years of his own youth, of how his father had presciently divided the family's $8,000 in savings among three banks, only to have all three fail after the Crash of '29. Al, Sr., recalled full-time farmers who also worked twelve-hour shifts in coal mines to make ends meet. He told of seeing grown men break down and cry when their annual crop brought less than $100 profit, knowing it could not sustain their families or their farms. He remembered a beautiful young girl he had taught in high school who, beaten by poverty, showed a lined face, unkempt hair, and missing teeth in her twenties when he ran into her during a campaign stop.

Young Al would spend long weekends, summers, holidays, and his entire seventh year on the Carthage property. The senior Gore said it would build his character to live with the plain people who raised crops and livestock. He asked Will and Alota Thompson, the tenant farmers who leased his acreage, to open their home to the boy. It was a house with neither electricity nor running water. But Will was a gentle, kindly man and, from all reports, he and Alota, a nurse, genuinely loved Al, Jr., and treated him as one of their own. Gore hung out with the Thompson's son, Gordon, later a factory worker, and with boys like Ed Blair, a future highway cop; Terry Pope, who would enlist in the air force; and Steve Armistead, whose folks operated a country store. Gore went steady with Steve's sister Donna, from the time he was fourteen and she, sixteen, until the summer following his graduation from St. Albans. During that period, the Armisteads appear to have succeeded William and Alota

Thompson as Gore's surrogate Tennessee family. "What he didn't get from his family he picked up from my own," Donna Armistead has recalled. "I guess he kind of got a nurturing that he was lacking."

Some descriptions of life on the farm seem idyllic. Gore and his friends tended to the prize Angus cattle. They would build tunnels and fortresses of hay bales in the lofts and use them as shelter from which to zing shelled corn pellets at the field hands milking cows below. When he was eight his dad gave him a pony named Flame. Once he escaped injury when the animal reared and rolled on him. Years later, he flipped the family Studebaker station wagon and again walked away unhurt. The boys played pick-up touch football against the sons of livestock dealers and other visitors, refreshed themselves by plunging "bare ass" into the sulfuric waters of cattle troughs, ate cheeseburgers and fries at the B&B Drive-in, went to services and social dances at the New Salem Missionary Baptist Church, and made out with girls wherever they could. Gore has told interviewers he preferred Carthage to Washington by a mile. "[I]f you're a boy, and you have the choice between the eighth floor of a hotel and a big farm with horses, cows, canoes, and a river, it was an easy choice for me."

But the senior Gore remained in charge of his son's schedule, often *in absentia*. The senator urged his son to do push-ups "until you can do more than I can," a number that eventually reached about 120. The young Gore never arrived on the farm without a long list of chores assigned by Senator Gore. "I guess I was a little severe," recalled the senior Gore, "but I didn't want my son to have the easy tasks."

"In the summer I would have to get up before dawn and help feed the livestock," Gore remembered. "Then I would have to clean out the hog parlors. Then I would go back for breakfast. Then I would work the farm all day and feed the stock again at night before dinner." And there was always a special summer-long assignment. One year the senator instructed him to clear a field that was overgrown with trees and shrubs, with only a small hand-axe as his tool. "It nearly killed him, but he finished it that summer," Donna Armistead recalled. "It was backbreaking work, with a tool far too small for the job, but his father wanted him to learn work and the work ethic." On another occasion, the senior Gore ordered his son take a plow to a particularly steep slope. Pauline argued it was too dangerous but the Senator insisted.

"Yes," she conceded, "a boy could never be president if he couldn't plow with that damned hillside plow."

The senior Gore could also be emotionally remote, expecting obedience and good results on the farm, in school, and at home, but slow to offer praise when his son performed, simply issuing a new set of tasks for the boy to fill. By all accounts, Al, Jr., was a very good boy. Friends admired him. Adults treated him almost as one of their own. Eleanor Smotherman, who taught second graders in Carthage for fifty years, said, "Al Gore, Jr., was so mature and advanced I had to almost look at him to see whether he was a child or a man." But many who knew Al Gore, Jr., as he was growing up speak of tensions and contradictions that made it tough for him to figure out who he was. Was his father the ultimate role model, or had he simply established a benchmark the younger man was expected to surpass? Was he the farm kid from Carthage, or the Washingtonian? And why were his folks often far away and unreachable? Were they simply drawn by the duties and responsibilities of the United States Senate and the United Nations? Or was the distance a rebuke, a reflection of disappointment to be overcome by greater effort, ever more sparkling results? If he were more perfect would their love be more tangible? Some have speculated that his lifelong drive to excel, his "accumulation of achievement," represented an attempt to compensate for parental inattentiveness, or, in the words of one writer, "a blurring of the difference between the acquisition of admiration and the experience of intimacy."

"You remember Oedipus," was how Tipper Gore once described Al, Jr.'s, relationship with his father. And as an adult, Al, Jr., has long been interested in situations where, as he has written, "children in some families are deprived of the unconditional love essential for normal development and made to feel that something inside them is missing. Consequently, these children develop a low opinion of themselves and begin to look constantly to others for the approval and validation they so desperately need. The new term 'codependency' describes the reliance on another for validation and positive feelings about oneself." That quest for perfection as a vehicle for winning approval, for winning parental love, for achieving self-esteem, could explain Gore's later tendency to equate his policy choices with moral superiority. The man who must be perfect equates nonperfection with evil. Further, he can relax only in an environment where perfection is not demanded. In a 1992 *New York Times Magazine* profile, Pulitzer Prize-winning journalist Alex S. Jones suggested that to Gore the home of Will and Alota Thompson may have provided "a kind of emotional Citadel, a refuge from the larger world, where great expectations awaited him."

Gore has expressed anger at this line of analysis, even though it was cobbled together, mostly in sympathetic portraits, from his own writing and the insights of people who love him. In a remarkable letter to the *New York Times* appearing two weeks after his 1992 election as vice president, Gore said Jones had been guilty of "a glaring error of fact and interpretation that is hurtful and unfair not to me, but to my parents."

He continued: "I could never fully express in words the strength or depth of my feelings for my parents—nor could any child committed to such loving parents. And I suspect my parents would have the same difficult time expressing their feelings for me and my late sister, Nancy. Throughout my life—as a child growing up, as a teenager and young adult and even now, as a grown man with children of my own—I have always felt blessed to have such loving, caring, and involved parents. Their love and their lessons in life have sustained me and continue to sustain my family."

As a very young child, Al, Jr., had Nancy to provide care and companionship. Dark-haired and physically stunning from an early age, she played family rebel to Al's conformist. A bathroom smoker who wore make-up before her parents thought proper and sipped wine and beer in high school, she left only general indications of her comings and goings. Nancy Gore never met a curfew she liked. According to her mother, Nancy would figure out what her parents wanted in order to circumvent their will while Al would do so in order to obey it. Nancy loved and cherished her younger brother, often served as his baby-sitter, and doted attention on him. But as she grew older, she spent more time with her own friends and less with Al, Jr., By the time she enrolled at Vanderbilt, she was a viva-cious, politically sophisticated and liberal young woman who could hold her own with a band of intellectual and idealistic young men who thought they could change the politics of the South while keep-ing its charm. Those men—good friends of hers—included future Senator James Sasser, who in 1970 would run Al Gore, Sr.'s, last Senate campaign; Fred Graham, then a young Kefauver aide, later a prominent journalist with CBS News and Court TV; his brother Hugh Davis Graham, now a gifted Vanderbilt historian; and David Halberstam, then a highly respected young reporter with the *Nashville Tennessean*.

Hugh Davis Graham recalls idyllic summer days sipping lemonade or iced tea and discussing politics with Nancy and the oth-ers, swimming at the big lake near Carthage, and being hauled on water skis by the Gores' powerful motorboat. "The only bad thing I can say about her is how much she smoked," he recalls. "Most of us had either never smoked or started and quit. We used to tease her about it, but she never stopped." The much younger Al, Jr., would be baling hay or performing other chores on the family acreage while his sister enjoyed her friendships. "By then we wouldn't see them together too often," Fred Graham recalls. "My recollection is that Nancy had about as much interest in spending time with her brother as most twenty-year-old college girls have in spending time with their ten-year old brothers, and that's not much."

When Pauline was at the Carthage farm, she usually made certain that Al and his friends finished their work in ample time for a leisurely afternoon visit to the Carthage Pool. But when the senator visited, Al, Jr., could never sleep in and spent many a day working sunup to sundown with the field hands. Years later "Doonesbury" would remain unimpressed by this regime. In a "specially handicapped event" for just the Prince [Gore], the Veep [George Bush], and Pierre Lepete [Pete DuPont], Gary Trudeau had the Republicans claiming, "My Daddy made me scrape the boat!" and, "My Daddy made me roll the courts!" while Gore blew them away with the claim, "My Daddy made me shovel pig manure!"

Gore, of course, was not just one of the farm kids. Everybody knew that he was not destined to become a cop, a factory hand, or a career NCO. Nor would most of his pals by the Caney Fork River be his pals during the months he spent in Washington, or his confidants after he started St. Albans preparatory school and then Harvard. Young Gore was aware of his special status. Terry Pope once saw his dad, a farm worker, spank Al, Jr., for stinging him with corn pellets, only to have the youngster threaten, "I'm going up to the house and tell my mother. You work for my father. She won't stand for you spanking me." He changed his mind, but the message was plain.

Back in Washington, there were the periods when everyone was together in the apartment on Massachusetts Avenue. Then Pauline Gore would try to arrange things so that Senator Gore and his son could spend the better part of fifty-five minutes together before young Al left to catch the school bus that stopped at the Cosmos Club five minutes before eight. Some days he could keep his father company in what is now the Russell Senate office building, even walk with him to the Senate floor. He once sat on Vice President Richard Nixon's lap while the vice president presided over Senate business. And he attended major hearings on the highway bill and other important legislation. At home one day, Senator Gore motioned his son to eavesdrop on the second telephone as President Kennedy berated the steel industry for raising prices. The fourteen-year-old thought it odd that a president of the United States could find so few ordinary words with which to punctuate his profanity. As a senator, Kennedy had been an occasional visitor to the Gore apartment. Clark Clifford, the veteran Washington fixer, and Senator J. William Fulbright, came by more frequently.

The senator remained a figure of enormous inspiration to his son. Silver-tongued, yet folksy he fancied himself a populist. Though some found him pompous—Martin Peretz, Al, Jr.'s, long-time mentor, referees to Al, Sr., as "Senator Claghorn"—the senator enjoyed considerable respect and affection in Washington, which the young Gore could well have mistaken for power. Moreover, he was a man of strong principles, and his stands on issues provided object lessons in political wisdom and courage.

In March 1956 Senators Kefauver and Gore confronted the "Declaration of Constitutional Principles" or "Southern Manifesto," endorsed by nineteen southern senators and eighty-two members of the House, which called for southern legislators to support their states in defying Supreme Court decisions that struck at the legality of segregation. (Twenty-four House members from Dixie neglected or refused to sign it.) The document resurrected the discredited doctrine of "interposition" promulgated by Senator John C. Calhoun of South Carolina, perhaps the leading defender of slavery a century earlier, in which the states, by "all lawful means," were encouraged to interpose their sovereignty against the "unconstitutional" Supreme Court. Four states would ultimately pass "nullification" laws purporting to overturn *Brown* v. *Board*.

The ringleader behind the manifesto was Senator Strom

Thurmond, the South Carolinian who, over the course of the next forty years, would make a seamless journey from incompetence to dotage. Under pressure, Senator Walter George of Georgia introduced the declaration. Its Senate supporters would include Richard Russell of Georgia, Lister Hill and John Sparkman of Alabama, and J. William Fulbright of Arkansas. To avoid embarrassing the Senate's most prominent southerner, the group did not ask Majority Leader Lyndon Johnson to sign. Kefauver refused, saying, "The Supreme Court decision is the law of the land.... We cannot secede from the Supreme Court."

Gore examined the manifesto and concluded it was, as he would recall years later, "the most spurious, insane, insulting document of a political nature claiming to be legally founded that I had ever read." Not content with Gore's private refusal, Thurmond sought to embarrass him on the Senate floor, alerting the press corps that he planned to approach Gore during the afternoon of March 11, 1956. With the press gallery bulging with witnesses, Thurmond stepped toward Gore on the floor, handed him the document, and said, "Albert, would you care to sign our Declaration of Principles?"

"Hell no," said Gore, returning it to Thurmond.

The actions of Gore, Kefauver, and, at the state level, Clement, and their courage and decency on the civil rights issue, would be more a source of political trouble than benefit in Tennessee, though none of the three ever lost an election because of his position, at least until Gore's defeat in his 1970 campaign. Each reelection would be challenged and each man would be accused of being "out of touch" with sentiment in the state, or worse yet, a traitor to his region, his heritage, and his people. None of the three ever backed down. None ever engaged in racial demagoguery. None would ever require sympathetic chroniclers to explain that his conduct had to be judged in the context of his time and its political exigencies. Their courage would inspire later generations of southerners who sought to purge the region of its terrible racial heritage. After Al Gore, Sr.'s, death in December 1998 at the age of ninety, President Clinton said that Gore "helped to connect the South with the rest of America."

Albert Gore, Sr., liked to share with family and friends the story of a phone call received at his Carthage farm in the late 1950s. It was at 2AM and the well-lubricated voice at the other end of the line announced that he and his friends had decided to tell Gore exactly how they felt about "Nigras."

"Well, how do you feel about them?" asked the freshly awakened Senator.

"We don't want to eat with them. We don't want to go to school with them. And we don't want to go to church with them." The bluntness of the response helped clear Gore's grogginess.

"What about going to Heaven with them?" he asked.

There was a pause and some muffled conversation as the caller consulted with his confederates.

"No," he said, "We'd rather go straight to Hell with you, Estes, and the governor."

*   *   *

When Al, Jr., was eight, his father nearly won the vice presidential nomination on a ticket headed by Adlai Stevenson of Illinois, the latter making his second unsuccessful run against Dwight D. Eisenhower. Had Albert, Sr., pursued the nomination more aggressively he might have won it. But, after meeting privately with Stevenson, he thought he would be the choice and was caught unprepared when Stevenson decided to throw the nomination to the convention floor. The battle came down to a three-man contest between Senator John F. Kennedy of Massachusetts and two Tennesseans, Kefauver and Gore.

A third Tennessee contender, Governor Clement, had dropped from the picture after one of the more disastrous keynote addresses in convention annals. Even at the expected length of forty-five minutes his ranting ten-count "indictment" of the Eisenhower presidency would have been tedious. But after circulating the draft and receiving suggested inclusions, Clement showed little of the editor's skill and simply tacked one new paragraph upon another.

So when, late in the address, he thundered its signature peroration, "How long, America, oh how long?" one delegate was heard to mutter, "About one hour and ten minutes too long." Yet Clement lumbered on: "Your lands are studded with the white skulls and crossbones of broken Republican promises. How long, oh America, shall these things endure—how long, people of America, will you permit the welfare of this democracy to be danced on in the homeland and gambled on abroad?"

This sort of high octane gibberish was too much even for the serenely patient editors of the *New York Times*, who described Clement's speech as "a tub-thumping, breast-beating, roof-shaking example of campaign oratory at its worst," delivered by "an Evangelistic Elvis Presley." Another observer declared, "The Republican Party has been smote by the jawbone of an ass."

But Gore would not benefit from Clement's embarrassment. Slow to declare his intentions, he limped behind Kennedy and Kefauver in the roll call voting, dropping out during the third ballot and endorsing his fellow Tennessean to prevent a stampede to Kennedy. But Kefauver wasn't grateful. More than forty years later his daughter, Diane Kefauver Rubin, remembered, "He tried to snatch the vice presidency from my father, but played along as though he were a friend."

* * *

By the fourth grade, Senator Gore deemed his son ready for the sort of education a fine Washington prep school could provide. Like his work on the farm, this too would be part of his preparation for higher calling. In 1988, the year he first sought the presidency, the Senior Gore bragged, "If I may be a little proud, his grammar is as near perfect in extemporaneous speeches as you can come by." On another occasion, the elder Gore explained why he had sent both his children to fine private schools: "What I sought to do was compensate them for my own inadequacies." Another time he told an interviewer, "I was often embarrassed because I would be in conference with people who could switch to my language or another, while Tennessee hillbilly was all I could accommodate. So I undertook to provide for my children a better education than I had had." As with countless others—farmers, workers, immigrants—who pushed their way upward, tested each step of the way by hard times and hard knocks, Al Gore, Sr., was embarrassed by the "imperfections" that were in fact the greatest tributes to his ability and tenacity, and he strove to protect his son from having to overcome the very handicaps that had made him extraordinary.

The young Gore was enrolled at St. Albans. With its gray stone buildings, beautifully manicured athletic fields, and tradition of "muscular Christianity" symbolized by its "Cross and Torches" emblem—two candles on either side of a crucifix—the school has sought to leaven its education of the sons of the mighty with a deep sense of duty to the Almighty. For generations, Roosevelts, Kennedys, Jacksons, Bushes, and Grahams (as in the owner of the *Washington Post*) have trod its fieldstone walkways prodded by the words of Canon Charles S. Martin—the midcentury headmaster— to "choose the hard right over the easy wrong." Martin served as headmaster from 1949 to 1977. He died in 1997 at the age of ninety, confidant he had shown nearly three decades of St. Albans boys the true path to Heaven, and maybe even to Harvard.

It was the mission of St. Albans to sow certainty, not doubt into the minds of its students. Ferdinand Ruge—stocky but resplendent in his three-piece suit and gold watch chain—would see no hubris at all in instructing his class that Shelley's line, "Nothing beside remains," was the second greatest sentence in the English language. "Jesus wept," was first. After lunch in the refectory, one of ten student prefects—elected to reflect the highest St. Albans standards of conduct, spirit, and dress—would ring the big brass bell to claim attention and announce activities for the remainder of the day. Then he would step aside for Canon Martin who might, in the words of a former student, "find moral imperatives in everything from the U-T to the U-2." To Martin, there was a correct way to win at sports, suffer defeat, drive, even tie one's shoes. Alumni were signaled out for acclaim more for moral than economic or political achievements. College panty raids were denounced as victories for evil.

Alas, not all in the dining room maintained the comportment of the true believer during these daily mini-sermons. Table conversations often continued in whispers. Now and then a smirk could be seen or a snicker heard, not to mention the occasional passage of air worthy of Holden Caulfield. But no trace of derision or disrespect ever emanated from the bell-clanging prefect, at least not during the school year 1964–65 when the job belonged to Al Gore, then in his "sixth form," or senior year. Gore would pay respectful attention as Canon Martin spoke, vindicating the choice of his peers in entrusting him with this responsibility. Only by an eyelash had he lost the race for senior prefect to Daniel Woodruff, a superior athlete and promising intellect who would be the only person to administer an electoral defeat to Gore prior to the 1988 Democratic presidential primaries.

Until his senior year—when both his parents were busy campaigning in Tennessee—"Gorf," as the boys sometimes called him, had been a day student at St. Albans. He was part of a strangely disappointing class, one from which outstanding academic and athletic performance had been expected, but which had delivered neither. There were warning signs in the lower forms that this was a class of underachievers, but not even administration efforts to infuse the group with new talent by increasing outside admissions proved very helpful. Gore's senior yearbook lamented: "We've had a poor athletic season so far." The football team wound up 1-7 and the basketball team, 2-14. "We still enforce our reputation of being the class with the most potential and the least achievement—witness the number of those recognized in the National Merit Scholarship exams compared with the number of those recognized on the Head's List, or the failure's list, for that matter. We have no real leaders. We have a reputation of being good-time boys, but we are coming out of it all, we hope."

Gore was an exception. A good though not brilliant student, he was comfortably inside the top third of his class, ducking the tough calculus course his senior year, and joining the young poet, Phillip Rosenbaum, in winning early acceptance to Harvard. A disciplined if not gifted athlete, Gore played center on the football team, serving as co-captain his senior year but getting ejected for unsportsman-like conduct in losses his junior and senior years to arch-rival Episcopal. He was at one point interested in playing baseball, but after demonstrating to coaches that he would need radar to find a curve ball, he settled in as a so-so discus thrower on the track team.

Gore's best sport was basketball where his long-range shooting helped take pressure off the more talented Woodruff. But with average height, unexceptional speed, and modest ball handling ability, he was what today would be called a "role-player," a shooter not a scorer, able to help a good team but not carry a bad one. The brag of Donna Armistead, his Carthage girlfriend, that "he could have gotten a basketball scholarship to North Carolina or a bigger school"—this in the era of Billy Cunningham, Charlie Scott, and Larry Brown—seems far-fetched.

St. Albans conducted a sixth form government class that would meet each Thursday at 7:30 PM. The class of about twenty-five students was divided into "liberal" and "conservative" blocs. Each week, prior to class, the liberal and conservative leaders would meet with the teacher to prepare "legislation" for consideration by the class. In Gore's senior year he led the liberals while Brent Taylor, a Washingtonian appreciated more for his social than political skills, organized the conservative bloc. A businessman residing in California today, Taylor remembers Gore as an "awfully nice guy," who defended his positions strongly but fairly. "I wrote him after the Perot debate suggesting I deserved some credit for training him as a debater," Taylor recalls. In return he got a form letter signed by a member of the vice president's staff thanking him for his letter.

What positions did the young Gore take during those years? Classmates recall his backing Lyndon Johnson versus Barry Goldwater in the 1964 election, supporting civil rights legislation, opposing the dispatch of U.S. troops to block a left-wing power grab in the Dominican Republic, and urging new trade initiatives to unfreeze relations with Communist China. But while St. Albans maintains records for all legislation considered by the Government classes, including those immediately preceding and succeeding Gore's, the file on Gore's class is missing. A classmate calls the situation "strange." But there is, of course, "no controlling legal authority" preventing a former student from purging the record of his high school political views.

Gore lived on the third floor of the Lane Johnson dormitory his senior year as his parents campaigned in Tennessee. His roommate was a future Denver social worker named Geoffrey Kuhn. There was no lights-out rule for seniors. Two of his friends played the blues on guitars long into most nights. Gore tried to go to sleep by midnight but was never certain of sleeping through the noise. Often he would wake up at 2 or 3 AM, dress for class, and then go back to bed. Sometimes he would crash during the day. The blue-ribbed bedspreads would leave a deep imprint on his face, still visible at class or dinner. His classmates called it "Gore's disease."

Gore accepted challenges big and small. He was known as the fellow who could keep a broomstick balanced on the tip of his nose interminably. He was a "pre-wonk" and daydreamer. "If you sidled up to him you would be left with the sense he's aloof and his mind is someplace else," a friend recalls. Another member of his class says that "Al, then as now, was very self-controlled. There was always a very tight rubber band wrapped around his waist. He is not comfortable with mirth. He has to work at it." Diane Kefauver Rubin, who dated Gore's close friend Bart Day at St. Albans and Harvard, remembers Gore as "not really close to people. There is distance even between him and close friends. Al took himself pretty seriously. He could have some fun and be boyish, but he was very driven to succeed."

As a young man who excelled in academics, athletics, and extra-curricular activities, Gore enjoyed universal respect among students and faculty. Only rarely did his "perfection" inspire a note of satire as when his yearbook editors quoted Anatole France under his picture, "People who have no weaknesses are terrible," or when some "Albanians" compared him to "Ozymandias," the arrogant and ultimately tragic Shelley character who exalted, "[L]ook on my Works, ye Mighty, and despair!"

More typical was the yearbook description of Gore as "excellent at almost everything he does," with the prediction, "It probably won't be long before Al reaches the top. When he does, all of his classmates will remark to themselves, 'I knew that guy was going somewhere in life.'"

The boys at St. Albans liked to drink beer at "Tunes of Georgetown," "Bohemian Towers," "the Grog and Tankard," and the "Zebra Room." On Saturday night they would drive around Georgetown or suburban Maryland looking for parties. Geoff Kuhn had more social friends than he expected because the huge basement in his family's nearby home was excellent for partying. Gore would sometimes amuse himself and his friends by tossing plastic bags filled with water at passing motorists from the roof of his hotel. He celebrated graduation by driving around town in the big family Chrysler Imperial tossing cherry bombs into the street.

What is perhaps most stunning about this high school period is the extent to which Gore kept his two lives separate. Donna

Armistead has told several interviewers that he wrote her twice a day and phoned at least once a week during the entire period they dated. Yet not once did he bring her to Washington. And with the exception of a smattering of St. Albans friends who visited him in Carthage, few even knew about Donna. The couple broke up during the summer following his graduation. Donna claims she burned his love letters just prior to her own wedding a year later.

Several of Gore's friends at St. Albans had dated a stunning but deceptively self-conscious St. Agnes girl named Mary Elizabeth Aitcheson, known since early childhood by the nickname "Tipper," taken from a Spanish song. She lived in Arlington in a Tudor-style house built by her grandparents; her parents had divorced when she was three. Her hair was long and blonde, her eyes, blue. She played the drums for a rock group called "The Wildcats," partied hard but "knew when to say when" about all things, had a knack for complementing her date's personality, and, despite her beauty, seemed neither unapproachable nor threatening. If dates found anything at all about her annoying, it was her concern with making a good impression at all times and with all people. "Tipper could not bear to leave a room unless she was certain that everyone she had met liked her a lot," an acquaintance recalls.

Tipper went to the senior St. Albans dance as the date of Gordon Beall, whose passions included auto racing and the Rolling Stones, and whose life ambition, according to his yearbook, was to make a million dollars by the age of thirty-five. Gore and Tipper were introduced to each other during the evening. The following day he asked her out and, by all accounts, they have lived happily ever after. Convivial, warm, gracious, and outgoing, her social skills fill the gap in his own. "She greets you and she fills in conversation when Al goes to the seventy-third stellar galaxy," says a friend from St. Albans days.

Despite all this, a successful relationship was not inevitable. While Gore ended up at Harvard, Tipper started at a place called

Garland Junior College in Boston, before graduating as a psychology major from Boston University. Some of Gore's Harvard friends thought her less than their intellectual equal and treated her with barely concealed disdain, but she kept her eye on the prize. "I was always stuck by how protective she was of him," recalls Diane Kefauver Rubin. "She always seemed to be keeping him away from other people, jealously guarding him." By some accounts, Tipper spent enough time in Gore's Dunster House suite at Harvard to pass for part of the furniture. In *Coming Apart*, his lyrical memoir of the Harvard Wars of 1969, Roger Rosenblatt, a senior tutor at Dunster, recalls seeing Gore and Tipper leaving the dorm a full hour after the 11 PM evacuation time for female guests: "There was but one path connecting us and no escape for the future vice president. I saw the terror in his Boy Scout eyes, which might have read, 'There goes the presidency.' We passed each other quickly on the path. I greeted Al and Tipper, 'Good evening, boys.'"

Tipper also spent time visiting the senior Gores at the Carthage farm. Al, Sr., would chuckle at the fashion plate appearance of his future daughter-in-law as she would flutter in from her bedroom to join the family for breakfast. Early in their relationship, Tipper tended to take refuge in her physical beauty and instinct for style; gradually she would develop a more complete self-confidence.

The St. Albans Class of '65 was an insular lot. They had been stunned by the Kennedy assassination, but little else had penetrated their comfortable environment. Not a single member of the class had visited the Mall to hear the Martin Luther King, Jr., "I have a dream" speech of 1962. Peter, Paul and Mary were popular among the students; a few listened to Dylan. Blues and rock were big. "When we finished high school in '65 we were the same as kids who finished ten years earlier," recalls Matt Simchak, the son of a former Chicago mayor, and today, a powerful Washington lawyer. "Vietnam, drugs, the sexual revolution all lay ahead of us."

Harvard would provide a profoundly different experience.

CHAPTER THREE

HARVARD

WHEN THE DEAN'S committee that annually wrestled with such matters was considering men's housing assignments at Harvard for the academic year beginning September 1966, its members were troubled by the rather stagnant reputation of Dunster House. Among all the venerable three hundred- to four hundred-man dwelling places for sophomores, juniors, and seniors at Harvard—modeled on the academic community systems of Oxford and Cambridge—Dunster, built in 1931, seemed most to resemble the reprehensible "frat houses" of lesser institutions, or even the eating clubs at Princeton, dissected a few years earlier in a brilliant *Harvard Crimson* report, "The Search for the Cocktail Hour Soul." The resemblance was spiritual, not physical. Physically, in the words of Roger Rosenblatt, its senior tutor that year, Dunster's tower "looked like an Arabian tent mounted on a white gazebo." But in a nonselective system, where every effort was made to match the student with his choice of residence, Dunster had managed to attract a reputation as a pool-shooting, motorcycle-riding, poker-playing type of place that was a far cry from the sort of intellectual village intended by the administration.

So an effort was made to improve Dunster. The assignment of Rosenblatt, together with such fellow tutors as future historian, Doris Kearns and Martin Peretz, who would later run *The New Republic*, was certainly a start. But to really transform Dunster it would be necessary to "draft" a group of fellows who would have preferred other facilities. One such group quickly came to the attention of the school administration. It included men who had elected to live together but had listed Dunster as their third choice. Most were coming out of the Mauer freshman dorm, which had won intramural competitions in softball, football, and track. Each seemed promising in his own right. Collectively they could perhaps solve Dunster's image problem once and for all. The group included:

- Tommy Lee Jones, steely-eyed son of a Texas roustabout who combined a brilliant acting talent with fierce play on the gridiron. An offensive guard, he would be converted to linebacker, winning all-Ivy honors at a position he was supposedly too small and too slow to play.
- Michael Kapitan. Six feet, eight inches, but without a shred of athletic ability, this Michigan resident would become an outstanding wood sculptor. His family had such modest means that Kapitan came to school early to begin earning money as a member of the "dorm crew," mopping halls and cleaning johns.
- Al Gore, Jr., son of an important senator, who had seemed to regard his first year at Harvard as an extension of his "big man on campus" days at St. Albans. He won election as freshman class president and a place on the freshman basketball team. But class politics had lost its allure and college-level basketball meant collecting bench splinters. Gore had won a degree of local notoriety by driving his motorcycle back from Washington following winter break, arriving so frozen he could have been mistaken for a Kapitan ice sculpture.

• John Tyson, son of black well-to-do parents from Montclair, New Jersey, was a defensive back of sufficient skill to be drafted by the Dallas Cowboys. Serious, intellectual, and deeply idealistic, Tyson would shift from the ministry to entrepreneurial projects in Africa. Years later he would credit Gore with making him less antagonistic toward those of other races.

• J. G. Landau, a big, brash, street-smart Long Island Jew who brought a special charisma with him, not to mention a "great stick" (pool cue), which he wielded successfully during countless hours of combat on Dunster's elegant Brunswick table. Also a poker player who "was in your wallet in a hurry," "J.G." seemed to exert a particular magnetism on his more sober pal from Tennessee and St. Albans. Four years later, Landau would be best man at Gore's wedding. He would die after a massive coronary in 1997. Gore would serve as a pallbearer.

• Bob Somerby. Another would-be actor, he eventually turned his talents toward political humor. Years later, Somerby would become a regular at the "Improv" on Connecticut Avenue in Washington, D.C.

The group, despite having an avid cyclist and a poker-playing pool shark, did help transform Dunster's reputation to a place of sports, politics, and the arts. The dorm also became a campus center for the radical Students for a Democratic Society (SDS) that would tear college campuses apart with its political protests.

Among Gore's professors at Harvard were two whose influence would be lifelong. Roger Revelle was a geophysicist and oceanographer who—along with C. D. Keeling—was the first scientist to systematically measure the presence of carbon dioxide in the atmosphere. As part of the International Geophysical Year, 1957-58, he persuaded international scientific organizations to begin taking regular samples of carbon dioxide concentrations. Gore, like many Harvard juniors, took Revelle's course as a way of fulfilling his science requirement without undue intellectual strain. Revelle, however, captured young Gore's imagination.

Revelle's eight years of carbon dioxide atmospheric samplings had led him to believe that the concentrations were increasing rapidly every year. Revelle theorized that the higher carbon dioxide levels—attributable mainly to the great worldwide increase in the burning of fossil fuels—could produce what he called a "greenhouse effect" that could result in higher world temperatures. As early as his Harvard days, Gore took Revelle's studies and leaped to the "startling" conclusion—far beyond Revelle's own—that "if this trend continued, human civilization would be forcing a profound and disruptive change in the entire global climate."

Another lasting influence was the distinguished psychoanalyst Dr. Erik Erikson, from whom Gore also took a course. In the 1950s Erikson experimented by giving building blocks to groups of boys and girls. Gore recalled the girls tended to "build structures that seemed to define a space within the structure," while the boys tended to extend their structures from a base "outward and upward to penetrate the space around them." Gore would later translate this proclivity into the world of environmental values whereby women seemed more inclined to respect the world around them, while men tended to dominate nature. Gore concluded that civilization would benefit from "a healthier respect for female ways of experiencing the world."

Erikson was also a leader in describing the difficult developmental stages or passages of life that all experience. Gore would say he took Erikson's course at a point when "discovering and defining one's 'identity' is the primary psychological task." But after moving on to the work of "achieving communion and full mutual trust with another," Gore declared he was ready for what Erikson called "generativity," that stage where one achieves "the ability to care for many others and to establish and guide the next generation." And to Gore, increasingly obsessed with what he would see as the threat to the world's future posed by global warming, the solution would reside with an international commitment that made rescuing the world's environment the "central organizing principle" of relations among states. Once, when speaking of the need for international arms control, Gore said: "The possibility of species-wide destruction creates for the first time the necessity of a species-wide ethic." For Gore, the need for "a species-wide ethic" also spoke to the need for environmental protection.

But it was the war in Vietnam that transformed Gore's Harvard class, as it transformed classes in colleges and universities across the country. Students and—to some extent—faculties were radicalized by the notion of a superpower allegedly directing its bombs, napalm, and counterinsurgency tactics against a people struggling for self-determination. That America should wage such a war seemed terrible enough. That it should do so with an army of draftees seemed even worse. The eighteen- and nineteen-year-old boys scurrying to government class, or the Widener Library, or the chemistry lab, feared they would be sent to this "dirty little war," unless they maintained their deferment by going to graduate school, or criminally evaded the draft. Each evening the horror of their dilemma would be reinforced as they returned to their dorms to see Morley Safer report on the hootches burned and villages subjected to "tactical evacuation," while Chet Huntley or Walter Cronkite grimly announced the number of Americans killed during the previous week. By the late 1960s the number could be anywhere from two hundred to five hundred. "As time went on the foment on campus skewered everything," Michael Kapitan recalls. "Ours was the class that looked at television every night and saw body counts. The war colored our entire college experience."

At Harvard, the protests began slowly and would not reach their height until Gore's senior year. In the fall of 1966 a small band of students attacked a car transporting Secretary of Defense Robert McNamara from campus following a speech at Quincy House.

Demonstrators rocked the car and shouted anti-war slogans before letting it pass. Within days, 2,700 students had signed a letter of apology to McNamara.

During the following two years tensions slowly escalated. As chronicled by Rosenblatt, the membership and influence of the New Left group, Students for a Democratic Society, increased, as did that of the more traditional Progressive Labor faction, an offshoot of the Communist Party. Sit-ins and draft card burning became more frequent. In the fall of 1968, students in the Mallinkrodt Laboratory detained a recruiter from the Dow Chemical Company to protest the company's manufacture of napalm. A rule was adopted by the Student Faculty Advisory Committee requiring any company recruiting at Harvard to discuss its policies publicly upon the written demand of five hundred students.

That September, an AWOL Marine named Paul Olimpieri took refuge in the Divinity School. Students in the school chained themselves to him, but he was eventually forced to leave. In December the faculty tried to discuss the future of ROTC on campus at a meeting in Paine Hall, but about one hundred SDS-inspired students staged a sit-in. As a result, thirty-five participants were placed on probation; several had scholarships rescinded. In February 1969, following a faculty meeting attended by more than seven hundred students, ROTC faculty were denied Harvard Corporation appointments and the program was stripped of academic credit. In March about one hundred SDS demonstrators broke up a meeting on the ROTC question involving Harvard President Nathan Pusey and the Student Faculty Advisory Committee. At a huge outdoor rally, SDS leaders promised far more forceful action. On the evening of April 8 they occupied University Hall, an administration building, forcibly expelling several deans and triggering the confrontation that would define the senior year for the Class of '69, and for many, their future lives as well.

For Al Gore, Jr., majoring in government studies, many of the goings-on at Harvard could just as well have been occurring on another planet. His involvement on one side or the other was virtually nil. After playing big man on campus his first year, he left student government and university athletics, spending most of his time with his suite-mates and Tipper. Friends say he was something of a fixture on the Dunster lawn opposite the Charles River, often wearing bib overalls with a long blade of grass hanging from his mouth. Asked what he remembers of Gore during his sophomore and junior years, his friend and mentor, Martin Peretz, replied, "He played pool." He also began smoking marijuana during this period, a drug he used recreationally for approximately a decade, through his years in Vietnam and his period with the *Nashville Tennessean*. He would quit when he decided to run for Congress in 1976.

Gore would occasionally join Tommy Lee Jones, Bob Somerby, and others in brief excursions into "show biz." Somerby recalls an "Old Time Country Panorama" staged for the girls of Wellesley. A handbill prepared for the occasion highlights "TOMMY LEE JONES & the Ben Hill Country Boys in a musical program," and "DOCTOR ALBERT A. GORE of Carthage, Tennessee. Not only will Doctor Gore dispense his scientific TENNESSEE ELIXIR REMEDY, DESIGNED TO CURE WHAT AILS YOU (Dr. Gore tells us we may expect one healing with every five bottles sold)... but also... Dr. Gore has promised to favor us with readings from the society pages of the *Carthage Courier*, including news on Wilbur Gridley's recent trip to Bristol." Gore bought an old tweed jacket and top hat for the presentation. Somerby found a Wellesley girl at the performance whom he dated through college.

Gore stayed aloof from campus politics during this period. Those who knew him well employ such terms as "nice," "serious," "fond of music," "into Wallace Stevens," and "somewhat remote, because of the time he spent with Tipper" but never "involved." He is not known to have been active in any Harvard political organization. And while he served as head of "Tennessee Youth for McCarthy," his role there consisted of little more than attending the state Democratic convention, which met in late June to select delegates to the national convention, and urging consideration of Senator Eugene McCarthy, who represented the dovish wing of the party. "The processes by which the delegates are chosen don't square with the sentiment in the state," Gore complained. "I think there is no question but that in a choice between McCarthy and Humphrey, McCarthy would win in Tennessee." That proposition was, at the very least, debatable. Tennessee was no hotbed of anti-war sentiment, nor was it fertile ground for the likes of the cerebral Minnesotan. Even Al Gore, Sr., who opposed the war, supported Hubert Humphrey over McCarthy.

Gore did make it to Chicago during the Democratic convention. He was an occasional floor guest of his father, but did not participate in its deliberations. Instead he hung out on the streets with war protesters during the first day or two. Years later, as with other personal accounts of events that were charged with emotion at the time they occurred, Gore would offer a studiously dull, antiseptic account of his experience. Rather than cops with clubs and the dank and searing cloud of tear gas, Gore recalled "standing in one of the parks along one of the major streets with crowds of people. And there were army vehicles, jeeps, coming down the streets with movie cameras manned by guys in fatigues shooting primarily the crowd and capturing the faces on film."

Gore's sister Nancy was also in Chicago sharing a hotel room with her husband Frank Hunger, a Greenville, Mississippi, lawyer she had met following a post-college stint with the Peace Corps. An intelligent, low-keyed man, Hunger preferred pick-up trucks to cars and liked his beer straight from the bottle. A litigation specialist, he had a knack for communicating with people at their level rather than his, a wide circle of friends throughout the Fifth Judicial Circuit, and was appreciated in the family as having disarmingly good political judgment. Al, Jr., took to him at once and he remains to this day as close a personal confidant as Gore has in the world.

Running into an old southern acquaintance while the convention was still in session, Nancy confided that she had found her little brother wandering about the streets with a group that seemed to be on the borderline between demonstrators and sightseers. Nancy was concerned that Al could get in trouble. "So I got his young ass back to my hotel room and told him to stay there so he wouldn't get himself killed."

"And where does he sleep?" the friend inquired.

"In my bathtub," Nancy replied.

Gore would later have a similarly strange account of another protest, this one at Harvard. When the SDS crowd stormed Harvard's University Hall demanding, among other things, an end to the ROTC program, Gore was nowhere to be found. Nor was he on hand early the following morning, when three busloads of police ejected the demonstrators, making scores of arrests.

Hollywood producer Terrence McNally, a Gore friend at Harvard, was among those protesting at University Hall. "I was in the front line when we were routed out the next morning," he recalled. "I was scared shitless when the cops charged. They came in swinging and easily broke through the chains of students holding hands. I saw kids jumping out of windows to avoid the club-swinging cops." McNally remembers how many people found roles to play. "Chris Wallace [Class of '69] was reporting for the *Crimson*. Elliot Abrams [also Class of '69] organized a group against the strike. Al, though, tended to internalize things. He wasn't involved at all."

Gore later recalled "walking by University Hall during the occupation and feeling a swirl of emotions. I remember fringe statements on the Left that held that violence was justified, but I don't know that many of us were swayed to the Left. We had sympathy for the cause but not the tactics."

Gore's sympathy for "the cause" was made clear in a letter he sent to his father as the senator was preparing material for his book, *The Eye of the Storm*, a defense of his own career as a left-of-center southern populist. The letter was later quoted by Peter Boyer in the *New Yorker*. "We do have inveterate antipathy for communism—or paranoia as I like to put it," the young man wrote. "My own belief is that this form of psychological ailment—in this case a national madness—leads the victim to actually create the thing which is feared the most. It strikes me that this is precisely what the U.S. has been doing. Creating—and if not creating, energetically supporting—fascist, totalitarian regimes in the name of fighting totalitarianism. Greece, South Vietnam, a good deal of Latin America. For me, the best example of all is the U.S. army."

Gore has since explained the letter as the ruminations of an undergraduate who came to learn about and appreciate the army when he served in it. Certainly he was not the only left-wing college kid of the 1960s whose ideas evolved as he matured. But, accepting his sentiments as he stated them, if the U.S. army is the "best example" of a "totalitarian regime," which the country supports as part of its anticommunist "psychological ailment," then why not protest both against the war and the Harvard ROTC program that supported it? "I always thought there was something off concerning the students' choice of target," Gore said later. "I guess, if the university was the most convenient, then that was the target you chose."

Gore had good reason for keeping clear from Harvard disturbances. His father had weathered a tougher-than-expected challenge in 1964 and was clearly headed for an even more difficult contest in 1970. He was under attack for opposing the war in Vietnam, abandoning the South on civil rights, and lining up against an antiballistic missile system. Any left-wing antics by Al, Jr., at Harvard would have hurt his father. And young Gore had his own political ambitions to consider. The universal assumption among his Harvard friends, as among his St. Albans friends, was that "Al was heading for elective office."

Gore, moreover, was absorbed in his honors thesis, guided by presidential scholar Richard Neustadt. The subject was the impact of television—still a relatively new and developing medium—on the presidency. The paper Gore eventually produced was a credible piece of work, carefully researched, well sourced, and presciently argued. "I ended up doing more work on that than on all of my other courses combined," he would say of the thesis. Reading it today, however, and knowing the Gore of today, one is struck by his perhaps exaggerated belief in the ability of a new technology to change the character of the institution to which it is being applied.

No longer, wrote Gore, were White House press conferences in-depth, not-for-attribution briefings conducted by the president, with informed members of the print media taking the lead. Now they were often live with television correspondents asking one-sided theatrical questions, for which the president had prepared himself with briefing books. Television coverage was also a weapon for presidents to use against their adversaries. When Lyndon Johnson learned that Robert Kennedy was going to propose a halt to the bombing of North Vietnam, he responded with a Texas-sized media blitz, announcing a major nuclear arms control initiative from the Soviets, unveiling an education initiative, delivering a previously unscheduled speech at Harvard on civil rights, and revealing that his daughter Luci was pregnant with her first child.

Finally, Gore wondered whether a poor media performer— i.e., someone who hated television, like Harry Truman—could win, or whether future presidents would model themselves on John F. Kennedy. Ironically, Al Gore has now served with a president who has consciously modelled himself on Kennedy, and perhaps in the year 2000 Gore himself may be the one to prove or disprove the ability of a somewhat stilted personality to prevail in a television-dominated campaign.

*   *   *

In 1994 the Harvard Class of '69 convened in Cambridge for its twenty-fifth anniversary. The commencement speaker was Al Gore.

Gore's speech criticized the growing public cynicism he saw undermining confidence in government, business, the media, and other societal institutions. "Cynicism is stubborn, unwavering disbelief in the possibility of good," said Gore. "The skeptic may finally be persuaded by the facts; the cynic never, for he is so deeply invested in the conviction that virtue cannot prevail over the deep and essential evil in all things and all people."

Negative campaigning led the public suspicion about elected officials, and this, in turn, "feeds the voracious appetite of tabloid journalism for scandal." But Gore was not one to tread down such paths: "In the twenty-five years since my Harvard graduation, I have come to believe in hope over despair, striving over resignation, faith over cynicism." Gore believed "in the power of knowledge to make the world a better place. While critics may say, 'All families are confining and dysfunctional,' I know that is not true." Gore believed "in serving God and trying to understand His will," in "working to achieve social justice and freedom for all," and in "creating and celebrating beauty, for there is no better way to give back some of the miracles this world has given us."

"Cynics may laugh out loud and say that there is no utility in a work of art or a hillside where trees a thousand years old stand green and still in the summer air.

"I know that is not true.

"And finally, I believe in America. Cynics will say we have lost our way, that the American century is at its end. I say we are still the model to which the world aspires... I believe the American century is about to begin."

Gore's classmates loved it, as did the press. So did the man who wrote the speech, Harvard lecturer and native Tennessean, Richard

Marius, whose loyalty to Gore would soon be repaid with a crude act of betrayal.

Perhaps the most significant friendship Gore formed at Harvard was with his resident instructor, Martin Peretz, today the owner, chairman, and editor-in-chief of *The New Republic*. When the two first got to know each other, Peretz was a long-haired, bearded, left-wing, anti-war radical. One might say he was "deradicalized" by the seizure of University Hall.

Peretz drifted to the middle of the road, but would never become a "neo-conservative." While eclectic and independent, sometimes to the point of flakiness—he supported Eugene McCarthy for president in 1976—Peretz was, in his mature years, never very far from Al and his centrist Democratic Leadership Conference bloc. An avid Zionist, Peretz tolerated no criticism of Israel save his own. He might run a piece blasting the media for exaggerating the threat posed by the 1984 Knesset election of the late Meir Kahane, only to follow it up weeks later with his own assault on the racist rabbi. He would do the same with the notion of "land for peace," attacking the opponents of hardline Israeli policies only to emerge as an important diaspora voice in the "Peace Now" movement. His would be the most significant endorsement Gore would win during his 1988 run for the presidency.

Gore and Tipper were—and still are—frequent guests of Peretz and his wife Ann at their Cape Cod retreat. It was at Cape Cod after his graduation that Gore, consulting with Peretz and Richard Neustadt, wrestled with whether he should serve in the military.

Al Gore, Jr., would not endanger his father's political future or his own. He would volunteer for military service and take his chances in Vietnam.

CHAPTER FOUR

ALBERT Sr.'s LAST HURRAH

GORE'S CONSIDERATION of whether to serve in the military has become the subject of a rich mythology. Young Albert, the militantly anti-war dove, has been depicted as having gone through a crisis of conscience, weighing outright defiance of the law, even pondering flight to Canada. His mother, Pauline LaFon Gore—according to numerous reports—had expressed willingness to "flee across the border with her son," joining him in exile. Martin Peretz—who urged Gore to protect his political future by accepting military service—has told countless interviewers that his visitor to Cape Cod was in a highly emotional state as his time for decision neared. At last, Gore decided to accept military service. He flew to Newark, New Jersey, a location he considered "neutral and anonymous," reported to the army recruiting station, and, after a battery of tests, was assigned to duty as an army journalist. Then, the myth has it, the Nixon administration held up his orders to go to Vietnam, not wishing to do anything potentially helpful to his father's re-election campaign.

The Canada option has been convincingly denied both by Pauline LaFon Gore and by Gore himself, most elaborately in a

1988 interview with David Frost on the PBS series, "The Next President." Gore acknowledged that his decision had been difficult: "It really was a dilemma. Canada was not really a part of it. There were so many ways to not serve that I never considered that option. There were lots and lots of ways to find a pursuit that would get you a deferment, or some kind of exemption, and I did actively consider not serving." His friend, Tommy Lee Jones, would recall, "It is my recollection that Albert didn't want to kill anybody, and it probably bothered him quite a bit to make any contribution to the war."

The Cape Cod visit was no doubt important, but so had been a trip home to see parents and friends. Albert, Sr., and Pauline told him to make his decision without taking the coming political campaign into account. But his friend Steve Armistead offered advice predicated on a more distant future campaign. "Somewhere down the line you'll be in politics yourself, you won't have much choice," said his friend. John Tyson, Gore's Harvard roommate, recalled that "Al decided that he was going to enlist and he was helping the anti-war movement more or less by going and enlisting." The reason: "Well, in a sense I believe it would have helped his dad. He felt by helping his dad and campaigning with his dad that that was the greatest thing he as an individual could do to stop the war."

Gore knew that Tennesseans would take a dim view of his avoiding military service, regardless of the intensity of his convictions. Even kith and kin in the form of a West Tennessee uncle, had dismissed his religious protestations against Vietnam, saying, "I never knew there was anything in the Baptist religion against war." And, unlike the man from Hope, Arkansas, in whose administration he would one day serve, Gore seems to have been genuinely concerned about some other resident of Smith County being sent to Vietnam in his place should he not serve. This was, after all, not New York, Chicago, or Los Angeles, but Carthage, Tennessee, where, as Gore would later say, "it was no secret who was on the draft board, what the rough quota was each month, and if you didn't go it was no secret that one of your friends would have to go in your place." He could not see himself "walking down main street, which is called Main Street, and acting as if nothing had happened. It's a sense of duty that I think may be a little less abstract in a small community." So Al Gore enlisted.

The young soldier was also a young groom. Al and Tipper were married in the Washington Cathedral on May 19, 1970. Jerry Landau served as best man. Two cousins, other Harvard friends, and Steve Armistead, the sole Tennessee chum in the wedding party, served as ushers. After the wedding, Gore was assigned to work on the base newspaper at Fort Rucker, the huge army facility in the wiregrass section of southern Alabama where helicopter pilots and crews were trained, many just prior to assignment to Vietnam. Determined to live on Private Gore's army pay, the couple visited some of the more filthy trailer camps in the area. Tipper recalled examining one refrigerator "so infested with cockroaches you would not believe it. We opened the refrigerator door and it was black until they scattered, then it was white on the inside. I started crying at that point."

The Gores eventually found a more upscale trailer camp owned by Ewell and Vincille Horsley of Daleville, a few miles from the base. They rented an "Expando model" on Lot 10 and moved in. That first month, Gore was selected "Post Soldier of the Month," receiving a $50 savings bond and a letter of commendation from the commanding officer, Major General Delk M. Oden.

The charge, apparently originating with Gore himself and parroted by sympathetic journalists, that the Nixon administration held up his orders to Vietnam in order to avoid heaping a political windfall on his father's campaign, is baseless. As proof, one need go no further than a Page 1 story in the *Nashville Tennessean* dated September 27, 1970, which began, "Sen. Albert Gore's son, Albert A. Gore Jr., 23, stationed with the army in Alabama, has received orders to go to Vietnam, it was learned yesterday." Asked by the paper to comment, the senior Gore said, "I have not wished to bring my son's situation into the campaign and do not now. Like thousands of other Tennessee boys, he volunteered and has now received his orders for Vietnam."

Due partly to his military obligation, the younger Gore played only a small role in his father's campaign. On those weekends when he enjoyed liberty from his duties as a soldier, Gore would either campaign in uniform with his father, or speak at the fifth most important event on the schedule—Al, Sr., Pauline Gore, Frank Hunger, and Nancy Gore Hunger claiming the top four places. Before the campaign was over, the Gores, Sr. and Jr., would appear on horseback in a campaign commercial, the senator saying, "Son, always love your country."

Young Gore thus had the best of both political worlds: orders that would take him to Vietnam in December—thus blunting any issue of favored treatment—but meanwhile, enough liberty to permit him to campaign for his dad, often in uniform. Even Nixon haters must concede he could have managed a better conspiracy than that.

The last campaign of Albert Gore, Sr., would have a major impact upon Al Jr.'s own career path, discouraging him from entering politics in the short run, but, in the end, schooling him well on the pitfalls to avoid if he wished to practice Democratic politics successfully, either in a moderate-to-conservative border state, or as a national candidate.

The campaign was in trouble from the start. In 1964, running on the coattails of Lyndon Johnson, who defeated Barry Goldwater in Tennessee by 145,000 votes, Gore had beaten his Republican opponent, Dan Kuykendall, by 51,000 votes. Four years later, the strike of predominantly black sanitation workers in Memphis drew Martin Luther King, Jr., to town, and also his assassin, James Earl Ray. The murder spawned urban riots that cast a shadow over the 1968 presidential election in Tennessee. Richard Nixon won with

38 percent of the vote, George Wallace had 34 percent, and Hubert Humphrey 28 percent, his lowest percentage in the nation. To ensure his reelection in 1970, Gore would need a big chunk of the Wallace vote.

But in the August 1970 primary, Gore beat his principal opponent—a political lightweight named Hudley Crockett, press secretary to segregationist Governor Bufford Ellington—by only 30,000 votes, barely breaking 50 percent in a four-man field. That same day, the Republicans nominated three-term Congressman Bill Brock. Brock was a well-financed, solidly professional politician who had placed his election strategy firmly in the hands of Nixon's media men, Harry Treleaven and Kenneth Rietz. Their polling showed that Tennesseans thought Gore had fallen out of touch with his constituents and was a pal of Northeastern liberals like the Kennedys.

Al Gore, Sr., had voted for gun control, against amending the Constitution to permit prayer in the public schools, against Nixon's two southern Supreme Court nominees (Clement F. Haynsworth, Jr., and G. Harold Carswell), against a bill that would have banned busing to integrate the schools, for the Cooper-Church Amendment setting a firm date for withdrawal from Vietnam, and against development of an antiballistic missile system. Gore's record was tailor-made to be ground into mincemeat by the Nixon-Agnew team and its newly minted "Southern Strategy." While Brock campaigned in favor of small government, individual freedom, patriotism, and prayer, his media spots or guest speakers went for the jugular. Vice President Agnew, for example, said that Gore acted as though Tennessee was "located somewhere between the *New York Times* and the *Greenwich Village Voice*," and accused Gore of inspiring college-age men to say, "Hell no, we won't go." To emphasize Gore's estrangement from the values and beliefs of his fellow Tennesseans, Brock billboards proclaimed, "Bill Brock Believes," amending that to, "Bill Brock Believes in the Things that We Believe In" as the campaign progressed.

Race too was at least a contextual issue. David Halberstam, an unapologetic liberal who had worked for the *Nashville Tennessean* in the late 1950s, came back to write about the campaign for *Harper's* magazine. He saw "a code word for nigger" in virtually every Brock tactic. But as a keen observer, he also understood that white factory workers earning perhaps $7,000 to $9,000 a year and facing a tax bill of perhaps $1,500, were furious, and concluded that the money was going to blacks on welfare. As a Halberstam friend explained, "You can see them thinking, 'Where does the tax money go? Welfare. And who gets the welfare? The niggers. And who did I just see on my color TV raising hell and carrying on and burning some damn thing? The niggers.' And so they're angry as hell."

For all his vulnerabilities, which included only a skeletal political organization and an archaic style on the stump, Albert Gore, Sr., was no pushover. And Gore was determined. "If just my seat were at issue, I wouldn't run. I have had an honorable career and could retire with dignity. But a national party and ideology are at stake. If the right wing wins here and shows that the Southern Strategy works, no liberal or moderate in a border or southern state will dare raise his head again. That will be the death of the Democratic Party."

In one debate with Brock, Gore waved his finger in scolding fashion at his opponent. "Mr. Brock, yours is an honorable name. You come from an honorable family. If you don't repudiate this low road your campaign managers have taken in your name and denounce these smears and innuendoes, you will live the rest of your life in shame and regret."

But a last minute negative media blitz by Brock, hitting Gore on school prayer and gun control, did the trick. By 9:30 PM on election night, it was clear that Gore would not do well enough in middle Tennessee or with black voters in Shelby County to erase Brock's massive lead in the east. He would lose by 52 to 48 percent.

A weary Albert Gore, Sr., comforted his supporters from the stage of the Grand Ballroom at Nashville's Hermitage Hotel, while his son, according to friends, felt bitterness that voters could so easily be influenced by negative advertising—"subliminal slime," he called it—undoing forty years of public service.

The senator spoke briefly to his assembled supporters. "First I should like to express my faith in our system. We do not have a perfect system of government, but it is the best devised. It has been a very hard, very hard fight. We knew from the beginning that the odds were terrifically against us, but we had to make the fight.... I told the truth as I saw it. The causes for which we fought are not dead. The truth shall rise again."

As it turned out, Tennessee was the only victory for the Nixon-Agnew strategy that night. Even in Texas and Florida, Democratic Senate candidates won. But in the long-run, the "Southern Strategy" was sound. The South was drifting into the Republican column. The future balancing act for Southern Democrats would be combining liberalism on civil rights, to assure a large black vote, on the one hand, while being tough on crime, in favor of welfare reform, and hawkish on defense, in order to win conservative-leaning, southern white Democrats, on the other. None of this would be lost on Al Gore, Jr. If he were ever to compete politically from a southern base, he would have to be a different kind of Democrat. But, for now, he was disgusted by Tennessee politics, and wanted to be as far away from it as possible.

He would get his wish. He was headed thousands of miles away, to the rice paddies in Vietnam.

CHAPTER FIVE

VIETNAM

W HEN AL GORE went to Vietnam, it was to join the most demoralized army in American history, an army no longer interested in winning, but only in completing tours of duty and returning to safety. The reason for this state of affairs was the Nixon administration's policy of "Vietnamization," a passing of the baton to our soon-to-be-abandoned Vietnamese ally.

From the standpoint of Richard Nixon, Vietnamization made sense. It could reduce American casualties and buy time against domestic dissent. It could give talks with North Vietnam time to develop, possibly leading to the negotiated return of American POWs, essential to anything that could pass for "peace with honor." It would also remove a critical obstacle blocking the path toward détente with one of Hanoi's major allies—the Soviet Union—and normalized relations with another, the People's Republic of China.

Nixon began withdrawing U.S. troops at the rate of 12,000 to 15,000 per month. But for all its virtues, Vietnamization had one monumental defect: it was a thinly disguised formula for military defeat. No one understood this better than the combat-veteran "grunts" who knew their South Vietnamese allies could never hold off the North without a substantial U.S. presence on the ground. Compounding this problem was the shameless manner in which the U.S. Army used its draftees in the brutally dangerous game of front-line patrols while sending its regulars and "re-ups" to the relative comfort and safety of headquarters, supply, or logistical duty. With the enormous "tail to teeth" ratio of forces, perhaps four out of five could serve their time behind the lines afflicted by nothing worse than terminal boredom, while the remaining "grunts" carried the fantastically risky but strategically pointless combat load.

By the time Gore went to Vietnam, American troops were deserting at three times the rate of a few years earlier, when casualty rates were much higher. Distinguished *New York Times* military correspondent B. Drummond Ayres, Jr., offered this assessment: "The men themselves are fed up with the war and the draft, questioning orders, deserting, subverting, smoking marijuana, shooting heroin, stealing from their buddies, hurling racial epithets and rocks at their brothers."

Some troops refused to go out on combat patrols, defying direct orders. Officers who forced the issue risked being "fragged"— shot in the back or blown to bits by a hand grenade. Instead of "search and destroy," the operative term for combat sweeps became "search and avoid." Ordered to move one mile forward and sweep the terrain for enemy troops as part of a routine combat patrol, one grunt told a visitor, "What we did was go 100 yards, find us some heavy foliage, smoke, rap, and sack out." This sort of conduct became so predictable that often the troops were met on their sweeps not by the Vietcong but by South Vietnamese pimps, prostitutes, and purveyors of everything from refreshments to equipment, stolen from the mammoth U.S. supply "tail."

Courts-martial or even administrative punishments were rarely meted out. With troop withdrawals under way, draft quotas shrinking, casualties still high, and most soldiers guaranteed safe jobs, even recalcitrant combat troops were better than none at all.

Specialist 5 Albert Gore, Jr., arrived in Vietnam on December 26, 1970. He was no grunt. He was an army journalist assigned to the 20th Engineering Brigade headquartered at the mammoth Bien Hoa military base near Saigon. Most of the engineers were at Long Binh, not far away. The headquarters company handled personnel, press, communications, and other special services.

The engineers built roads, tunnels, airstrips, and ports. Occasionally they would undertake public works projects at nearby villages, missions left over from the days when the struggle was defined as one "to win the hearts and minds of the Vietnamese people." The engineers' morale was better than the grunts', but far from good. "It was clear this thing wouldn't end well," recalls Claude Page, who served with Gore in Headquarters Company. "The general feeling was that we were going to bail out. We had a contingency plan to break for the coast if things went to hell. The morale was bad. It gave people an attitude. The folks back home sent clips from the States. We knew there was no support for the war."

As the U.S. draw-down proceeded, Vietnamization meant that some duties previously performed by American combat troops were transferred to the South Vietnamese army. For the engineers working on construction and other projects, the task of securing the perimeter now belonged to the South Vietnamese. "They didn't do much of a job for us," recalls Brigadier General K. B. Cooper, commander of the 20th Engineers. "I lost my best young officer to a VC mortar. His colonel was goading him to get his men back and finish the road. If he'd have waited 10 minutes for the U.S. gunships to arrive and clear the perimeter, he'd be alive today."

"They'd harass the guys building the roads from time to time. And they'd plant mines along the roads into and out of Bien Hoa, just to let us know they were there," says Page. "But the VC didn't really try to stop us because they knew and we knew that we'd be out of there soon and that everything we were building would belong to them. The thing that got us was why we were sacrificing our lives to build roads and ports for Charlie."

More often than not the victims of enemy mines in and around the Bien Hoa base were not the Americans but the South Vietnamese youngsters who would bicycle onto the base to shine shoes, grub cigarettes, or sell items they had obtained through petty larceny. Page remembers seeing two Vietnamese boys hanging around outside the mess hall during lunch and then, minutes later, seeing medics collecting their remains after they had been blown up by a VC mine while bicycling home. It was the policy at the base to compensate the Vietnamese or their next of kin for accidental injuries or deaths suffered at the hands of Americans. The prices were set in consultation with the villages. "One kid, nine or ten years old, probably in the employ of the VC, tunneled into an arms bunker and stole some Claymores," recalls Page. "While he was trying to assemble them, one went off and blew him up. Even before he died, his mother was on the base demanding compensation. The villagers basically set the priorities. A water buffalo was worth more than a human being."

Headquarters Company for the 20th Engineers consisted of one single-story wooden structure with a tin roof, cordoned off with plywood into six to eight small living compartments, each with two small bunks and a footlocker. Soldiers trying to catch a nap came to expect a visit from the "rodent of the day." But the most celebrated member of the Headquarters Company was neither a soldier nor a rodent, but a giant python named "Moonbeam," who became the company pet. "Moonbeam" had a voracious appetite for rodents but far preferred chicken, and the soldiers would take turns purchasing birds from the villagers and presenting them to the snake. Like the others in Headquarters Company, "Moonbeam" would eventually make it safely home, finally taking up residence in a Minnesota zoo.

There was nothing pretty about Gore's new home. For much of the year Bien Hoa was dry, dusty, and dirty. An open sewage trench along the base provided the mess hall with a fragrance not even army cooking could overwhelm. And the First Air Cavalry, housed in the next section of the base, was an inviting target for enemy mortars, assuring members of Headquarters Company occasional excitement, if not danger.

For recreation the men had the "Bien Hoa Beach Club," an enlisted hang-out where gut-wrenching Miller's beer—alternately stored in the blazing sun or cool refrigerators—was bought by the pallet. Marijuana was available in abundance, and Gore smoked his share. Almost everyone had his own record collection and stereo bought cheap on the "Pacific Exchange," the name given to the local black market on which the Vietnamese sold items "diverted" from the U.S. military supply system. There was also a volleyball court laid out behind the headquarters building—two telephone poles and a net of half-inch cable strung so tight it left the most aggressive spikers with prominent bruises to show for their efforts.

Of greatest interest to Gore was the company basketball team, which practiced nightly on a steamy asphalt court. Michael O'Hara, now a sports writer for the *Detroit News*, remembers the games as being "the most important things in the world to us." He still recalls winning a game by making foul shots after the final whistle blew. Gore devised plays and won one game by tapping a jump ball to team-mate Andy Anderson who made the score. "Gore's out-coaching me," screamed player-coach Gary Bremer during the post-game celebration. "From now on, let him be the coach."

One match featured NCOs versus officers. Elbows and knees flew from the opening tap until the final whistle. "It made *The Longest Yard* seem like the Powder Puff Derby," O'Hara recalls. The team won the league championship in 1971.

The men liked Gore. According to Rick Ensor, the personnel sergeant, "He was there doing what everyone else was. You get your short-timer's calendar counting the days till you get out of Dodge. I was very much impressed by the fact that he was well spoken, intelligent. He had his shit in the bag. He was no snot-nosed backward hillbilly kid."

Lieutenant Clayton M. Ryce was Gore's company commander. "I was most amazed that he came over with only seven months to serve," he remembers. "He never complained. He just accepted it. But he made no secret of the fact that he felt Nixon had been responsible for the delay in his assignment." In fact, Gore complained often, to anyone who would listen, that Nixon delayed his going to Vietnam because the president feared a combat wound to Al, Jr., would mean votes for Al, Sr.

Gore tried to be "one of the boys," and Michael O'Hara remembers that "his special status lasted about 3 1/2 minutes. He pulled his weight like anyone else." O'Hara roomed with Gore, played basketball with him, pulled liberty with him, and traveled with him as photographer when Gore covered stories for the base newspaper. "We were so close, it was like being married," he recalls. He saw a good sense of humor in his friend and an encyclopedic mind when it came to rock and roll. "He knew the lyrics to every song, the names of every band member, who played what instrument." From Gore he learned that "Sky Pilots" was really about army chaplains—"How high do they fly."

O'Hara credits his friend for saving his life, not on the battlefield, but during a weekend of liberty spent at Vung Tau, the South China Sea resort. "I was body surfing when I got caught in a rip tide. I thought I was a goner. I called, 'Al, Al!' I remember him grabbing me. I might not have made it if he didn't."

The reporting assignments provided less adventure. Most were routine fluff pieces dreamed up at the company HQ. When Gore and O'Hara had a legitimate news story and their paths crossed those of the civilian war correspondents, their status as low level military functionaries quickly became apparent. For example, when they were assigned to cover the North Vietnamese invasion of Laos, military officers ignored them, and members of the working press dismissed them as "combat news." Gore was insulted, especially when a colonel offered to fly the visiting press corps to Khe Sanh for dinner, ignoring the military correspondents. "What is this shit all about?" Gore complained to his friend. O'Hara shrugged.

Gore and O'Hara covered the Laos operation from Quang Tri. The atmosphere was tense, but not because of enemy activity. There were lots of grunts there, and far more black soldiers than at Bien Hoa's Headquarters Company. The air was filled with racial hostility. Once Gore tried to photograph a Cobra chopper that was parked near a basketball court where black soldiers were playing. One of them approached him and said threateningly, "No pictures." "Hey man," Gore started, but the warning was repeated and Gore abandoned the photo.

According to O'Hara, the grunts at Quang Tri hated the visiting press, because they suspected combat operations were staged for their benefit. One afternoon the soldiers "accidentally" tear-gassed the press area. Gore got a good whiff of the stuff. "What the fuck is going on here?" he asked. Someone told him it was a variation of the "frag the friendlies" game.

The Gore-O'Hara team got another taste of anti-military discrimination by the military when they tried to cover the first plane landing at an expanded and resurfaced Khe Sanh airstrip. Officially, they were told nothing, but from NCO sources they learned the arrival time and staked out the location. Then, as if on cue, trucks carrying more than a hundred members of the civilian media pulled up on a road recently built to accommodate heavy equipment. "Al and I just looked at each other and shook our heads," says O'Hara. "We were shit."

Gore talked a lot about home and Tipper. "I felt I knew her," O'Hara recalls. "The way he described his wedding, it sounded like the *Blues Brothers* with all these guys with long hair and bikes." O'Hara thought his friend had a great sense of humor. Once they were at Quang Tri when Gloria Emerson, the *New York Times* correspondent, came calling. Knowing Gore had worked as a copy boy at the paper one summer, O'Hara asked whether he had ever met her. "No," replied Gore. Pause. "But I saw her in the newsroom." Pause. "Actually, I knew her slightly." Pause. "Well, we dated." Pause. "We had an affair." Pause. "In fact, we were married and divorced."

"It must have been a very bad marriage," said O'Hara, "because she's acting like she doesn't even recognize you." By this time, the two were laughing so hard, tears streamed down their faces.

A piece Gore wrote, "Fire Base Blue Is Overrun," ran in *Stars and Stripes.* The article described an enemy attack on a U.S. outpost several days before Gore arrived on the scene. Gore sent the article home to Tipper, who contacted John Siegenthaler, editor of the *Nashville Tennessean*, which ran the piece. Very few newspapers of national standing would have been tempted to print a rambling story like this by a journalist who had missed the action. Gore began the article:

"'Overrun' is a fairly explicit military term, but its full meaning is known only to those who live through it.

"It describes the most nitty-gritty conflict that a soldier ever sees."

Gore is right. "Overrun" does have a precise meaning. It means to take control of an opponent's position. But Fire Base Blue was not overrun. Not even close. It was merely infiltrated by several enemy soldiers who did some damage before they were killed or expelled. Five Americans, out of the 135 at the base, died repelling the attack by a dozen or two dozen enemy soldiers. So aside from being poorly written and outdated, the lead was inaccurate. But Gore had the kind of celebrity status the *Tennessean* loved to put on display.

Gore has spoken sparingly and to some extent inconsistently of his experiences in Vietnam. He wrote to one buddy from Fort Rucker about seeing women and children cut in half by Huey helicopter gunships and told his friend that when he got home, "I'm going to divinity school to atone for my sins." Another army journalist who worked with him recalled of those days, "We were basically conscientious objectors while in the army. But we felt the military was an obligation, even though we disagreed with what was going on."

By 1988 Gore had a somewhat different perspective on how he had felt about Vietnam at the time he was there, saying, "I don't know why, but during the debate before I went over I never really had an emotional appreciation for the fact that there were people in South Vietnam who desperately wanted the United States to win and to keep them away from this loss of freedom." More recently, Gore told the *New Yorker*, "When I actually went there and got to know some of the South Vietnamese, who were genuinely terrified of what would happen to them if they lost their freedom in a takeover by the North, my easy assumptions about the nature of the conflict were challenged by the reality of it."

It is strange that these insights were so long in incubation, that they run counter to the recollections of his fellow officers and NCOs—the men who, at the time, knew Gore best—and counter to nearly all contemporary accounts of his feelings upon returning home.

Even longer developing was Gore's recollection of the wrath he felt as a soldier returning for a visit to Harvard Yard. "My hair was cut short and I wore my uniform. I walked through the streets of Cambridge, and I became so angry at the presumption of those who instantly shouted epithets and sneered," which sounds suspiciously like retrospective emotion for what is politically correct now, but which no one remembers him saying then.

When he ran for president in 1988, Gore told Gail Sheehy, who was writing a *Vanity Fair* profile of him, "I took my turn regularly on the perimeter in these little firebases out in the boonies. Someone would move, we'd fire first and ask questions later."

O'Hara has a different recollection. "We never pulled guard duty in the field because we weren't part of those units. The only place we stood guard was back at Bien Hoa, first in bunkers and later in some guard towers they built," he says.

To Michael Kelly, reporting for the *Baltimore Sun* during the 1988 campaign, Gore recalled, "I pulled my turn on the perimeter at night and walked through the elephant grass and I was fired upon, but I never saw the kind of conflict that a lot of people did." But when asked by David Frost whether he had seen "the ugliness of war in action," Gore replied, "No, I never saw it the way... when you use that word... I did not see the kind of ugliness of war, to use your phrase, that a lot of people in the infantry saw, no. I never had to come face-to-face with someone that I had to either kill or be killed by." In fact, in seven month's duty he had never witnessed an American casualty.

Michael O'Hara, who often pulled guard duty with his friend at Bien Hoa, recalls that the base was in a very secure area. "It was the equivalent of being a crossing guard. I know guys that didn't even take their rifles with them. Sometimes, just to make sure we were alert, they'd ask us to lock and load two grenades and fire off. But no one was out there."

Without question, Gore spent plenty of time in the field covering the engineers as they built roads or airstrips. While not nearly as dangerous as the activity of the grunts, it was a decent and honorable way for him to discharge his obligation to his country during a period of great domestic turbulence and moral ambiguity. It was also far more dangerous than the post-graduate courses and "essential" jobs to which flocked many future hard-liners whose reverence for interventionist military policies would grow in direct proportion to their personal distance from the threat of military service. Further, it was a choice that showed far more integrity than his dad's phantom military career in World War II.

Both O'Hara and Clayton Ryce finished their tours before

Gore. "Morale tailed off while I was there," O'Hara recalls. "You did whatever you had to do to get you home." He remembers getting a call from Gore on one of the vice president's visits to Detroit. "He asked me to meet him at the airport. I did. We embraced. We talked. It really wasn't very different from seeing any other old army buddy. For four months, I was his closest friend."

Gore's commanding officer Ryce saw little redeeming value in his Vietnam experience. "It was clear no one's heart was in it. Mine certainly wasn't. I just think of it as a wasted year of my life. The handwriting was on the wall. I think what happened in '75 shows how bad things really were there."

As Lieutenant Ryce was completing his tour, Gore asked him to call Tipper when he got back to the States. Ryce said he would. He made similar promises to other soldiers. He broke them all. "I didn't call Tipper or anyone else. I was just glad to be done with Vietnam. I wanted to purge it from my memory."

Contrast these stark and candid recollections of the men who served with Gore with those of Gore himself. Gore's descriptions have such a bland, emotionally neutered quality as to lead some observers to conclude that his stiff exterior is a fair reflection of the man inside. Or it may be that Gore believes Vietnam remains a political minefield, as it was for his father.

When Al Gore, Jr.'s, own tour was up, he returned to Nashville and his thoughts turned to redemption.

CHAPTER SIX

THE REPORTER

RELEASED FROM THE ARMY following seven months in Vietnam, Gore decided to reside with Tipper on the family property in Carthage and attend Vanderbilt Divinity School in Nashville, fifty miles away. Friends have described him as being at loose ends, angry at the way his father's public career had ended, and wondering whether for political reasons he had participated in a war that was brutal and wrong. No one from the period remembers the Al Gore self-memorialized in 1988 who saw both sides of this wrenching conflict and who resented the arrogance of the Harvard Square dissenters cursing their uniformed visitor. Rather, friends speak of a young man angry with his country, bitter over the carnage it was inflicting indiscriminately on a people defined as the enemy, and tormented by guilt for having participated—however reluctantly—in that effort.

Years later, Gore would offer a more elaborate if not convoluted explanation for his divinity school decision to the *Washington Post:* "I think a lot of people who have faith in this day and age try to find ways to reconcile their faith with what initially appear to be challenges to that faith.... The best known are Galileo, which displaced the Earth as the center of the universe; Darwin, which places us in the animal kingdom; Freud, which displaced consciousness as the sole process of thought; Einstein, which destroyed the concept of solidity and matter. And today the existence of massive starvation and prospect of nuclear holocaust side by side with the whole idea of progress and civilization makes one question where we are going. But the answer is within ourselves."

Tipper Gore would have a more concise explanation for her husband's decision to enter divinity school after Vietnam. "It was purification," she said.

The senior Gore wanted his son to attend law school as a prelude to a career in Tennessee and national politics. But the choice of divinity school seems in keeping with Al Gore's way of addressing problems. Having attended a fine prep school and a great university, he had an exalted if not exaggerated respect for a structured learning environment. Feeling troubled to the depths of his soul, his catharsis was to take courses in spirituality rather than, say, wander off into the woods to commune with nature, or simply proceed with the daily grind, figuring "this too shall pass." Later, when troubled by the nuclear arms race, he would take lessons on strategic theory from leading experts on Capitol Hill and then develop a proposal he felt would remove any incentive by one side or the other to launch a preemptive nuclear strike. And when he wanted to have a son following the birth of three daughters, he would read a book on ways to determine the sex of one's baby, apply every detail to his own marital bed, and become a leading dinner table proselytizer for its methodology.

Gore received a scholarship to the Vanderbilt Divinity School from the Rockefeller Foundation, which at the time was seeking to attract talented people to study religion, even if not to take a Doctor of Divinity degree. Gore would skirt the degree-track, preferring to take courses that interested him and directed him to see how a social and political agenda could serve God's purpose.

The Vanderbilt Divinity School was at the time a hotbed of political liberalism and activism on both racial and environmental issues. Its dean was the revered Dr. Walter Harrelson who had established himself as a moral force on the race question in the South as early as 1960 when a black divinity student from Masilon, Ohio, James Lawson, announced at a breakfast meeting of black ministers that his anti-segregation campaign was about to escalate from peaceful and orderly street demonstrations to civil disobedience. The law, he said, was "a gimmick" to oppress his race. This action drove *Nashville Banner* publisher James G. Stahlman apoplectic. Stahlman branded Lawson a "flannel-mouthed agitator" and demanded his expulsion from Vanderbilt, declaring, "The sooner both Nashville and Vanderbilt are rid of the presence and the baneful influence and tactics of Mr. Lawson, the better." After the student newspaper echoed the call for Lawson's ouster, the school's predominantly conservative administration capitulated. When Lawson refused to withdraw voluntarily he was expelled, promptly assuming leadership of the freedom riders.

Dean Harrelson organized a strike by the divinity school faculty, but the university administration held firm. So Harrelson approached representatives of the medical school, who promptly announced plans to join the strike. The doctors carried more weight than the preachers, and the administration backed down. Lawson was readmitted to Vanderbilt, and Dean Harrelson was celebrated with playing an indispensable role in the victory.

"That's pretty much what Dean Harrelson was all about in those days, and his passionate intellect informed the entire school," recalls Roy Herron, a Tennessee state senator and minister who attended the school a few years after Gore. Dean Harrelson lectured on the prophets of ancient Israel, and about the rage and godly cry of Amos, Isiah, Hosea, and Micah. "The prophets were outraged by the oppression of eighth-century (B.C.) Israel," says Herron. "They proclaimed comfort for the afflicted and affliction for the comfortable." Their message was that one couldn't truly worship God unless one is committed to justice. If one's life isn't just, one's religion isn't true, it is idolatry. "When Micah instructed on how to worship God, he declared, 'What is required is to do justice and to have mercy and to walk humbly with your God.'"

Gore would take these lessons seriously. Beginning a few years later he would sometimes tell friends of a "special relationship with Jesus Christ." On a visit to San Francisco in the early 1980s, he told Diane Kefauver Rubin that God sometimes talked to him. "That frightens me in a political person," she said. "They have power and direction enough from the people without feeling a mandate from God as well." Herron takes a more sanguine view of the way Gore internalized the teachings at Vanderbilt. "Part of the divinity school heritage is that we ought to fix our problems. We live in a fallen world, a world in which no part escaped the fall, no part is perfect. I know Al Gore is idealistic. But I also know he is realistic. And part of his realism is grounded in the eighth-century prophets."

Gore also took a course on ethics taught by Professor David Ogeltree and one entitled "Theology and the Natural Sciences" taught by Professor Eugene TeSelle. Ogeltree said the purpose of his course was to "dispute the strong tendency of the human sciences to explain human behavior and to make moral behavior irrelevant." Man, in Ogeltree's teaching, has a responsibility to make a moral choice, where necessary to overcome his passions and desires. TeSelle saw his course as providing a religious basis for man to care for the earth's environment. He saw his teaching as a continuation of seminal works written as early as 1875 on the way human beings change the surface of the earth. He assigned books on Darwin, Teilhard de Chardin's *The Phenomenon of Man,* and the 1940 work, *Our Plundered Planet.*

"The course was strong on environmental responsibility," recalled Herron. "It rejected the interpretation of Genesis as giving man dominion over the environment. Rather stewardship was emphasized. The earth is the Lord's. It is never really ours. We don't ever really own it. We are stewards."

While those thoughts would find almost perfect expression in Gore's later book, *Earth in the Balance*, over the coming years Dr. TeSelle would also develop many points of contention with his former star pupil. "My bridges with Al have gotten pretty well burned," he recalls. They had one serious confrontation over Gore's willingness to provide humanitarian support for the contras of Nicaragua while TeSelle remained an anti-Reagan, pro-Sandinista liberal. And, in something of a stretch, TeSelle looked upon the Clinton-Gore taste for "soft" corporate money during their reelection campaign as a logical outgrowth of their involvement with the moderate, pro-business Democratic Leadership Conference. "With the DLC pandering to corporate money, why should anyone be surprised at Clinton and Gore's soft money solicitations?"

TeSelle's reading list also included the Club of Rome's famously pessimistic 197-page analysis, *The Limits to Growth*. Based on a massive computer study designed by an MIT economist able to simulate the critical ecological forces at work in the world, the study pointed to population growth and industrialization as the two critical factors which, by depleting the world's resources and polluting the earth, would, by around the year 2020, "cause the end of the civilization enjoyed by today's contented consumer."

The process could be calculated with mathematical precision. Growing populations demand more food. But with most of the best lands on earth already under cultivation, food production can increase only through the use of polluting tractors, fertilizers, and pesticides, all industrial products. Growing industrialization consumes resources, which must be replaced. That in turn means more money spent on procuring raw materials and less on investment in new plants and facilities. Eventually, population outstrips food and industrial supplies. "Investment in new materials falls behind the rate of obsolescence, and the industrial base begins to collapse, carrying along with it the service and agricultural activities that have become dependent on industrial products...." Thus, each technological advance "consumes scarce natural resources, throws off more pollutants and often has unwanted social side effects, like creating huge and unmanageable unemployment."

The Club of Rome team suggested that the solution was zero population and industrial growth, to be achieved by an all-out effort commencing in 1975. *Time* magazine offered the following summary: "Investment in new non-polluting plants must not exceed the retirement of old facilities. A series of fundamental shifts in behavioral patterns must take place. Instead of yearning for material goods, people must learn to prefer services like education or recreation. All possible resources must be recycled, including the composting of organic garbage. Products like automobiles and television sets must be designed to last long and to be repaired easily."

TeSelle remembers that Gore was moved by the Club of Rome report. It reinforced his disenchantment with an insane society that built mighty armies, killed innocent women and children in Vietnam, fell for the "subliminal slime" that had finished his father's political career, and was now, fueled by obsessive consumerism, careening out of control toward environmental disaster. The cure was not some petty trifling at the margins of the problem, but a fundamental reordering of human behavior, stopping population growth in its tracks, and meeting the industrial behemoth head-on.

Years later, when he would finally put pen to paper, every Malthusian tremor captured in the Club of Rome report would reappear as an earthquake in his own *Earth in the Balance.*

*   *   *

On his first day back in Nashville, Gore placed a call to John Seigenthaler, editor of the *Nashville Tennessean* and an old friend and supporter of his father. Seigenthaler promptly offered him a job.

Seigenthaler was one of Nashville's giants, a socially prominent Catholic and two-fisted journalist. He had met Bobby Kennedy while a Neimann Fellow at Harvard and served as Kennedy's aide at the Justice Department, where he was a point man in desegregation battles.

Back home, Seigenthaler was no less a crusader. With the same vigor he had shown urging recalcitrant southerners to accept integration, he threw his and the paper's energies into the battle for reapportionment that would benefit black and other urban voters, and was cheered when the Supreme Court chose a Tennessee case, *Baker* v. *Carr*, to begin that critical journey. Seigenthaler also backed metropolitan government for Nashville to prevent the evolution of a core inner city, predominantly black and poor, surrounded by affluent white suburbs whose tax base remained out of reach. "For him and the other [liberal] white southerners it was the civil war of their time," wrote James D. Squires in his book on midcentury Nashville politics, *The Secrets of the Hopewell Box*, "a mission to free black Americans, the modern American city, and the political process itself from the imprisoning inertia of the last hundred years."

Nor was Seigenthaler averse to a little gentle nepotism. The by-line of Andrew Schlesinger, the son of historian Arthur Schlesinger, Jr., often graced the pages of the *Tennessean*. So did those of Kaycee Freed, the daughter of a prominent NBC News executive; baseball great Hank Aaron's daughter; Judge John Sirica's son; and a scion of the Newhouse newspaper dynasty. A few months after enrolling at Vanderbilt Divinity School, Al Jr. called to set up an interview with his new boss, City Editor Frank Ritter.

Ritter would remember Gore as a poor but educable writer who never met a deadline he liked. From the first, though, he had high regard for the young man's integrity. This grew out of Gore's response to the "Ritter Question," put to all job applicants of the period. The question was, "What would you do if your editor asked you to write a story you knew to be untrue?"

Gore's response, according to Ritter was, "I can't imagine that my editor would ask me to do that. But if he did, I'd resign. I would never violate my conscience." Ritter calls Gore's response "the best I had ever heard from a job applicant," which is hard to fathom. Certainly it is a sensible and appropriate answer, but also a pretty fat pitch. If Gore's response were that much better than anyone else's, one wonders what others may have said: "I'd write the story but never use my by-line," or, "I'd only use the false information if I could confirm it from a second source," or, "I'd try to persuade the editors to put it on the Opinion Page."

Ritter formally offered Gore the job. Gore was ready to begin work. He and Tipper returned to Nashville where, after a series of moves, they wound up in the fashionable subdivision of Belle Meade. While Gore worked nights at the paper, Tipper enrolled at Nashville Tech and studied photography, eventually landing her own job on the *Tennessean*. With the exception of offering to recuse himself from state political coverage—an unnecessary gesture, because those choice assignments went to far more senior journalists—Gore was just one of the boys.

*   *   *

When Al, Jr., told his father about his new job, the elder Gore expressed dismay. He wanted his son in law school, preparing for a career in politics. Thanks to his growing relationship with Armand Hammer, Al, Sr., had both the time and the resources to devote to any quest for office his son might undertake.

In February 1967—three years before the senior Gore's election defeat—Hammer had bribed his way into two lucrative Libyan oil concessions for his previously modest Occidental World Wide Corporation. A year later, he bought the European marketing and refining operations of Signal Oil.

Gore accompanied Hammer to Libya where Hammer "dedicated" Occidental's oil fields in festivities that included a $1 million feast in honor of King Idris. Shortly thereafter, the King was over-thrown by Colonel Muammer Qaddafi, who began pressuring Occidental on ownership and the power to establish prices. Faced with similar local pressures in the past, the so-called "Seven Sisters"—the consortium of major oil companies that dominated operations in the Middle East—had stood firm. But when an inde-pendent like Occidental agreed to increase Libyan participation in oil revenues from 40 to 55 percent, and to give Qaddafi effective control over pricing, the giants caved as well, setting the stage for the quadrupling of oil prices throughout the area a few years later.

With Occidental oil revenues now flowing, Hammer began to diversify, purchasing more than a dozen companies, the largest of which was the Island Creek Coal Company, the nation's third largest coal producer. Following Gore's 1970 defeat by Bill Brock III, Hammer named Gore president of Island Creek and executive vice president of Occidental. Gore's annual compensation package, esti-mated at $500,000, was extremely generous by the day's standards. Chided by an old Washington friend for rushing to cash in on his lengthy public service career, Gore replied, "Since the voters of Tennessee have chosen to send me out to pasture, I intend to graze in the tall grass."

In 1969 Hammer had purchased the Hooker Chemical Company at a cost of $800 million. House majority leader Hale Boggs accused Occidental of violating insider trading rules when buying Hooker, but a Securities Exchange Commission (SEC) investigation proved inconclusive. One friend of Hammer's to profit handsomely was Albert Gore, Sr., who was then still a senator. In 1969 he sent Hammer money to cover the purchase of a thousand Hooker chemical shares at $150 each, far less than the stock was worth.

The Gores, father and son, were also involved in a three-way real estate transaction involving the Occidental Minerals Corporation owned by Hammer. Included were two parcels of land on the Caney Fork River, which would become Al, Jr.'s, farm. In the late 1960s the land had been owned by local residents W.A. McDonald and his wife, Belle Gresham McDonald, the latter inheriting it under the terms of her husband's will.

In a will filed with Smith County on May 25, 1972, Mrs. McDonald left the land to the Cumberland Presbyterian Church.

On September 15, 1972, the Cumberland Presbyterian Church sold the two parcels to the Occidental Minerals Corporation for the sum of $160,000. The price was steep for a bit over 88 acres, but in the late 1960s, a substantial zinc deposit had been discovered under many of the area's properties, including the McDonald parcels.

On September 22, 1973, a warranty deed filed in Smith County records the transfer of the land minus subterranean minerals rights from Occidental to Albert Gore, Sr., and Pauline Gore for $80,000. That same day a separate transfer of the mineral rights between the same parties was recorded for another $80,000. Continental also leased the mineral rights from the senior Gores for the stated price of $1.00 "and other good and valuable considerations," a standard, unedifying clause. And two separate deeds were recorded transferring the ownership first of the surface and then of the subsurface rights to Albert Gore, Jr., and Mary Elizabeth Gore for the sums of $80,000 and $60,000 respectively.

Al, Jr., took out a mortgage of $100,000 on the property, which he paid in full over a period of ten years. The terms of payment between Albert Gore, Sr., and Hammer or his company were not recorded. The property provided a bonanza for Al Jr. when, in 1987, germanium was discovered in addition to the zinc. Following a 1992 lawsuit against Union Zinc, Incorporated, which had been operating the mineral concession, the Gores, who insisted they were entitled to 4 percent of the germanium's worth—about $482 per pound in the early 1990s compared to 82 cents per pound for zinc—a three-member arbitration panel found in their behalf. Mineral profits per month soon exceeded the cattle profits, or even those from tobacco.

By this time, of course, Hammer's early days as a Soviet agent were all but forgotten and his political tastes tended toward the ecumenical. In a career that included many legal risks, the only blight on his criminal record grew out of illegal contributions to the 1972 Nixon campaign.

A footnote to the relationship between Hammer and the senior Gore would be written in May 1989, when an investment advisor named Alan Hahn initiated a class-action lawsuit on behalf of Occidental's shareholders. Kahn alleged that the company's $30 million contribution to build the "Hammer Museum" and its purchase of a $36 million endowment annuity to run the institution was a waste of corporate assets. Other shareholder groups soon joined the litigation. Hammer had told the press that only his personal assets had been used in the project, but company transcripts indicated that a special committee consisting of sympathetic directors had covertly voted to establish a "special appropriations fund" to finance the museum. When this information became public, Occidental moved speedily to settle the litigation. The presiding judge, criticizing much of Occidental's activity, specifically reprimanded the "independent group of directors" that had voted to spend millions of shareholder dollars without consulting independent counsel.

The chairman of the "independent group of directors" was Albert Gore, Sr.

*   *   *

The newsroom where Gore began work in the autumn of 1971 bore a close resemblance to the one from the mid-1960s described by James Squires in *The Secrets of the Hopewell Box*: "The newsroom itself was a pigsty of scarred old metal desks strewn with paper and clusters of half-filled coffee cups, floating cigarette butts and other indistinguishable lumps, sitting around on the desks like so many putrid little ponds. Here and there a big green trash can overflowed with snarls of old typewriter ribbon and wadded copy paper. One back corner had become a junkyard of maimed and invalid chairs; in another, the huge world map on the wall was so close to the back row of desks that its equator was clearly denoted by fist-sized black smudges from the hair grease of reporters who'd leaned against it."

Gore set to work on the sort of general assignment pieces familiar to every rookie journalist. He checked with the cops for arrests and potential features. He wrote about a grand jury investigation of alleged drug dealing by the police, efforts by the Socialist Workers and Communist parties to get on the November 1972 ballot, and the visit of a man named Gene Darcy, who had become a millionaire selling memorabilia from *HMS Queen Mary*, *HMS Queen Elizabeth*, and other great ocean liners of the recent past.

Gore kept his hair long and parted in the middle. He often wore jeans to work. Reporters at the paper came quickly to like their new colleague. To this day they describe him as smart, hard-working, unpretentious, and sincere. Frank Sutherland, a colleague who worked nearby, recalls Gore poring over old clips on a subject before he went out to do his own investigation. He usually got his facts right. Foreshadowing his less than Epicurean tastes while in congress, Gore's daily lunch would often consist of nothing more than a Tab and an apple. Still, most on the paper thought he would eventually find his way into politics. A few prognosticated a Gore race for the presidency circa 2008, but Gore dismissed such talk curtly.

Once Tipper joined the staff as a weekend photographer, she not only proved herself talented and professional but quickly showed how her friendly, outgoing personality complemented her far more reserved husband. "I think Tipper could have won a Pulitzer Prize if she stayed with it," recalled Ritter, only half in jest.

"I've voted for Al many times over the years, but really I was voting for Tipper."

Jerry Thompson, a working-class native of Nashville who scrambled his way to prominence on the paper, remembers Gore as "an energetic and enthusiastic reporter with insatiable curiosity." Thompson concedes that Gore wrote slowly and not all that well. "But at least among recent vice presidents, he was not the worst speller."

Thompson and Gore would often drink beer after work at "Tootsie's Orchid Lounge" near the Grand Old Opry, sharing the atmosphere with the likes of Opry stars Tom T. Hall and Roy Acuff. In all the conversations they had, Thompson never once recalls Gore discussing the war in which he had so recently served, or even mentioning it. But Geoff Kuhn, Gore's old St. Albans roommate, dropped in one night at the couple's Belle Meade home and waited until his friend got home from work. "He talked a lot about Vietnam that night," Kuhn would recall. "Mostly I remember him saying how sick it was to kill so many people in that kind of fight."

Gore would also sip a few at "Tommy's Pub," with Fred Seedahl, a UPI reporter, and other journalists like Craven Growell, Seymour Alan Carmichael, and, sometimes, Jerry Thompson. Often the group would adjourn to Carmichael's house for a night of poker, which might last until sunrise. Seedahl remembers Gore as a "fair player" who sometimes stuck with losing hands too long, but who had "a good poker face; you could never read him." He considered Gore "good company," but never the life of the party. "Unlike his father, he never struck me as a remarkable person. And in fact, he was a pretty pedestrian journalist."

It was traditional at the *Tennessean* to hoodwink each new reporter by summoning him to the phone to "take an obit" which would turn out to be a fictional decedent whose name was merely the reporter's name spelled backwards. Newcomers who were slow to catch onto the ruse would thus carve their names into newsroom lore, none more so than Albert Gore. With Ritter disguising his voice, Gore was told that the decedent was a Scandinavian gynecologist from Carthage named Trebla Erog. As Gore jotted down the vital statistics, his caller added that the ambulance had crashed en route to the hospital. "Hold on," Gore called to his editors across the newsroom, "this story is more than an obit." Then Ritter added that Erog's wife had suffered a heart attack while waiting at the hospital. "Oh my God, this is Page 1," shouted Gore to his colleagues, now convulsed with laughter.

Finally, they could take it no more. "Al," they told him, "Trebla Erog is no Scandinavian gynecologist, he is simply Al Gore spelled backwards."

"All right," protested Gore, "but it's still a darn good story."

With Seigenthaler himself leading the chorus, there has been some tendency by colleagues from the *Tennessean* to portray Gore as a young man of considerable journalistic talent who would likely have been "drafted" by a television network, or at least have followed the paper's most distinguished alumnus, David Halberstam, to the *New York Times*, had he not finally opted for politics. The hundreds of clips from Gore's years on the paper present a mixed picture. Much of the writing is dull. The narrative plods to a wooden cadence with neither pace nor anecdote to invite the reader along. Rarely does Gore enliven the copy with examples to illustrate the point at issue. When he does, they are usually buried like wildflowers under a compost heap.

For example, a wonderful story about a decorated Vietnam veteran fired by the local fire department for wearing his hair too long is told with such mechanical balance as to raise questions about whether Gore feared inspiring emotion in his readers. Fourteen paragraphs into the story the acting chief is finally quoted, revealing himself to be the social bigot one might have expected: "'We don't want any hippies in the fire department. That hair is a hazard to their health.' He claimed sideburns prevent a tight seal on a fireman's smoke mask and long hair is not a 'good seat' for a helmet. 'Plus him looking ridiculous,' Quinn added."

A potentially riveting account, datelined Summertown, Tennessee, describing the results of the decision by a conservative rural church to engage a dope-smoking hippie commune of 450 souls in biweekly debate begins, reasonably enough, setting the scene: "A barn decorated with Oriental rugs and bleachers made from straw has become the unlikely meeting ground between members of Steven Gaskin's commune near here and a Church of Christ congregation." But twenty-one paragraphs and one jump-page later, journalist Gore is still setting the scene for us and providing background on the decision as though he were discussing a bill on eminent domain. We never get a true sense of clashing lifestyles, physical description of the event, or the tension within the hearts of individuals on both sides between tolerance and repugnance.

At least in his similarly unmemorable account of the activities of a "Death Angels" motorcycle club, Gore is helped by a five-column photograph of the motley group hanging out with their bikes at an abandoned gas station. But Gore's prose could just as well be describing the new chapter of a horticultural society: "Two former members of the 'Hell's Angels' motorcycle club in California have organized a new club in Nashville—the 'Death Angels,' Gore begins.

"The organization has grown rapidly since it was founded last month, gathering together bikers who used to ride with such clubs as 'Satan's Slaves,' 'The Head-Hunters,' 'The Outcasts,' and 'The Saints'.

"It isn't difficult to recognize them on the road. Just look for a denim jacket with the sleeves cut off and a skull on the back. Swastikas, iron crosses and leather boots—and, of course, a monster-size motorcycle." Pretty ho-hum stuff.

There is, in short, little passion, humor, calculated irony, or human insight in Gore's journalism. Instead one finds a studious, relentless dullness at the core of his work, much as some would find it at the core of his public personality years later.

Ritter would later acknowledge that at the beginning Gore was "awfully green" as a writer and that his "messy copy resembled nothing so much as a hen scratching where he had penciled in numerous corrections and additions." According to Ritter, "Al, we gotta have that story now!" became a familiar refrain in the *Tennessean* city room as a deadline neared.

Seigenthaler nonetheless continued working with his protégé, discussing current affairs during long sessions in his office, working with Gore on his writing. Seigenthaler tapped him in December 1972 to attend a two-week Columbia Journalism School seminar on investigative reporting. With the recent Watergate reporting of Bob Woodward and Carl Bernstein for inspiration, many in the print media were convinced that the complexities of investigative reporting gave them an inherent advantage over their television colleagues. Here was an area to be studied, nurtured, and developed. And it was an area Seigenthaler treated as important. He had himself come to prominence investigating the Teamsters. Jerry Thompson had all but gotten himself killed infiltrating the Ku Klux Klan. Another reporter had written poignantly about conditions in a public insane asylum after having gotten himself committed.

Late the following year Gore got the opportunity to apply his new expertise. By then he was back-up Metro Council correspondent. Working that beat, Gore was told by a developer named Gilbert Cohen that Councilman Morris Haddox wanted a $1,000 bribe in return for granting the developer a relatively minor zoning variance. Gore told Seigenthaler, and together they contacted Nashville District Attorney Tom Shriver. With Cohen wired for sound, Shriver, Gore, and Seigenthaler secretly watched as Cohen offered Haddox a $300 "down-payment" on the bribe.

"Oh, you don't have to count it for me, Gibby," said Haddox.

"Okay, well there's three hundred here, that's all I got, okay?" said Cohen.

"All right, I'll take care of it."

The $300 had been provided by the *Tennessean*. Three of the paper's photographers took pictures of the transaction.

The *Tennessean* didn't report the incident until Haddox was indicted and—the same day—arrested in the Metro Council chamber.

Gore had obviously found his niche as an investigative reporter. Here, in contrast to his other work, his writing was clean, logical, and strong. And he was coming up with good stories, most related to zoning. In February 1974 he broke a story alleging that council member Jack Clariday had changed zoning ordinances to benefit two companies in which he held stock. A third legislator, reported Gore, required that a petitioner hire his father at a $3,000 consulting fee if he wanted zoning help.

In his 1988 presidential campaign, Gore would brag to the *Des Moines Register* that his investigative reporting "got a bunch of people indicted and sent to jail." Challenged by reporters who reviewed the record, Gore would later admit that no one had been sent to jail on the basis of his *Tennessean* investigations. The box score included one hung jury followed by an acquittal (the Haddox case), and one suspended sentence (the Clariday case).

Moral disillusionment with Vietnam had propelled Gore to divinity school and a structured search for repentance. Now, disillusionment with reporting that could find corruption but not punish it led Gore to law school and a structured search for more practical skills. "It was an outcome that amazed me," Gore would tell the *Washington Post*'s David Maraniss twenty-five years later, claiming he had been struck by the "unusual power of some words and phrases thrown around in a courtroom." He recalled telling himself, "I need to know more about that." Gore took a leave of absence from the *Tennessean* and began studying at Vanderbilt Law School that September. He returned later as a part-time editorial writer, but effectively, his three-year career as a full-time civilian journalist was over.

That career certainly helped bring closer to the surface traits already evident in the Gore personality. As Maraniss noted, "His fascination with the big story, his determined sense of mission, at times spilling over into self-righteousness, his conviction that if he is doing something it must be ethically correct, his competing impulses of daring and caution, his reverence for information above intuition—there is a clear line between these traits in Gore the journalist and Gore the politician."

His brief coverage of local politics may also have infected Gore with what might be called "political journalists' disease," the barely concealed notion that any idiot—including, if not especially, oneself—could do the job better than the idiots one is covering. Gore has indicated as much, telling one journalist, "I felt intensely frustrated about policies and decisions I was writing about because I felt they were often dead wrong. But as a journalist I could do nothing to change them."

Two years after taking his leave to attend law school, political opportunity knocked. Gore seized it even before its knuckles were off the door.

The knock took the form of a telephone call from Seigenthaler in late February 1976. "Joe Evans is going to announce his retirement from Congress tomorrow," Steigenthaler said, "The story just came across my desk." With a rush of adrenaline, Gore dropped the phone and threw himself to the floor beginning a long set of push-ups. By the time the weekend was over, he had quit the paper, withdrawn from law school, put his house up for sale, trimmed his hair, changed his part to the conventional left side, and outfitted himself in the attire—blue suit, red tie, scuffed shoes—that would become his political uniform. For a short period, Winifred Dunn, the GOP governor at the time, remembers Gore identifying himself as "a

Nashville home builder," reference to his brief partnership in a construction venture in which his father also invested.

Several of his Vanderbilt Law School professors, led by James F. Blumstein, who taught local government, offered to let Gore satisfy their requirements with research papers rather than having to take exams in courses he skipped. This would have permitted him to come to Washington needing only one more year of classes to earn his degree. Gore agreed in principle, but was far too distracted by other matters to submit anything. For years afterward Gore would smilingly greet Blumstein with the words, "I owe you a paper."

Gore would be the first candidate to declare for the open House seat. He chose the steps of the courthouse in Carthage for the occasion. He was so nervous that before speaking, he retired to the men's room and threw up.

With Tipper at his side and the couple's first child, two-year-old Karenna, dancing on the courthouse steps, Gore said the central issue of the campaign would be which candidate could be a "force in getting this nation moving in the right direction again." Mixing populism with liberalism, he called for bringing down interest and electric rates by imposing price controls on coal and all basic energy fuels, "and moving to reduce tax incentives, which encourage energy monopolies." He would also "close many of the tax loopholes that allow many of the wealthy to go without paying any taxes while the working men and women, farmers and teachers shoulder the burden." Proving that he—or a speechwriter—had a talent for the one-liner, he called the tax system "a national joke that hurts when you laugh."

Asked whether his name would be an asset in the contest, Gore replied, "I don't want the people to vote for or against me because my name is Albert Gore. I want to speak on the issues, and the people of the Fourth District are perfectly capable of judging me on this basis."

Gore was, of course, acutely conscious of both the good and ill that his father could bring to the campaign. Clearly there was access to people with money and political veterans ready to serve the younger man out of allegiance to the older one. On the other hand, the Brock campaign had successfully painted the elder Gore as a captive of the Eastern Liberal Establishment, out of touch with the voters of Tennessee on many bedrock issues. So Al, Jr., reluctantly asked his father to remain in the background, neither stumping nor speaking for the candidate.

The older man accepted the decision, but watched as his son's campaign manager decided that Pauline LaFon Gore could help. She was sent on the campaign trail. Often, in the presence of her husband, she would brag, "I trained both of them, and I did a better job with my son." Twenty-three years later, she would still be using the same line at the vice president's political gatherings.

Gore's principal opponent was Stanley Rogers of Manchester, the speaker of the state house. A seasoned politician, Rogers proved a tough opponent, moving from early attacks on Gore's youth and inexperience to his life of "silverspoon" privilege, noting his opponent's stated net worth of $273,000. Rogers also hit the senior Gore's ties to the Island Creek Coal Company and other business and energy interests.

Rogers was from the conservative wing of the Democratic Party. He was a vigorous opponent of gun control and sought to paint Al Gore, Jr., as a liberal in his father's image. This may have been a long-term blessing in disguise because it encouraged Gore to establish moderate credentials. Gore proved he was tough on crime by calling for mandatory criminal sentences. He also called for military strength "second to none" and suggested that America's experience in Vietnam should not dissuade the United States from military involvement in other conflicts. He suggested a "sunset law" so that federal agencies would have to justify their existence to congressional oversight committees or be abolished after five years.

"We've got to stop throwing money at every problem," Gore said. "Because once a bureaucracy is set up, we can't get rid of it."

According to Federal Election Commission figures, Gore collected $197,363 in his race and spent $188,560, both figures above average for that year's House campaigns. He was, in addition, one of only ten House candidates to give his own campaign at least $100,000 from his own pocket, providing loans of $50,000 and contributions of $75,150. More than 40 percent of Gore's net worth was at risk in his first congressional race.

Of special note to reporters covering the campaign was that Gore, never the most effusive of personalities, adopted the sort of slow, stiff, almost painfully measured way of addressing groups of voters that would become familiar to Americans in the years ahead. Perhaps the young man was awed by finally starting down the long road his distinguished father had traveled before him. Or perhaps, as a twenty-eight-year-old student who had smoked pot and worn his hair long, Al thought it necessary to project a wholly different image.

Gore polled less than a third of the total vote in the multicandidate field primary, but it was enough to win, and with the GOP declining to field a candidate in November, Gore was home free.

The family moved into the Tudor-style Arlington, Virginia, home built by Tipper's grandparents. With three generations of Gores on hand for the occasion, the new congressman was sworn in January 4, 1977. Asked what advice he had given his son, Albert Gore, Sr., replied, "I told him what Cordell Hull told me. Stay on the floor and learn the rules. They will come in handy."

That was not exactly what Al Gore, Jr., had in mind.

CHAPTER SEVEN

THE HOUSE

A L GORE, JR., was the prototype of a late twentieth century Democratic congressman: a businesslike practitioner of government, media-smart, service-oriented, with an eclectic legislative agenda, a full court press on issues important to the folks back home, and a muted ideology.

Nowhere was this more evident than in the way the new congressman worked his Fourth Tennessee District. He maintained a full-time staff in Carthage. He would generally hold a town meeting in the Nashville area on Friday night, sleep at the farm, and start out early Saturday morning for a schedule that would not break until dinner. Again he would stay overnight at the farm before heading home Sunday morning, usually meeting Tipper and the children in time for services at the Mt. Vernon Baptist Church near the couple's Arlington, Virginia, home. On many of these weekend trips he would pay a call at the *Tennessean* to check the wires and catch up with former colleagues, one of whom—his Harvard classmate and former *Tennessean* colleague, Ken Jost—had become his press secretary and legislative assistant.

Gore quickly established himself as a political fixture in the district. By the time he moved on to the Senate in 1985 he had conducted an estimated 1,200 meetings in the Fourth District. He would hold nearly four hundred more statewide as a United States senator.

Gore was anxious to avoid the traps of doctrinaire liberalism. He immediately branded himself a "screaming moderate," and searched for opportunities to display his proclaimed moderation. During his House years, he would refrain from knee-jerk opposition to U.S. military involvement in Lebanon or Grenada. Later he would back limited support for the anticommunist Contras in Nicaragua and endorse an American naval presence in the Persian Gulf. He would support controversial weapons systems like the MX nuclear missile. And he would be prudent in his approach to fiscal policy—for example, voting against the Reagan tax cuts. Until presidential politics forced a more orthodox "pro-choice" position on him, the former divinity student took positions on abortion that delighted "right-to life" advocates—positions that would deepen their later sense of betrayal.

Gore's congressional Class of '77 arrived in Washington with a new Democratic president, Jimmy Carter. The Watergate scandal had temporarily interrupted the run of Republican presidential victories and had inflated Democratic congressional strength. The Democrats now held a 289 to 146 majority in the House and a 62 to 38 edge in the Senate. But the numbers failed to translate into real legislative advantage. One reason was Carter himself. So magnificent has Carter been as a *former* president that the four-year debacle that was his presidency is occasionally forgotten. Determined to end the "disharmony and total separation" that had characterized White House relations with Capitol Hill, Carter instead stumbled on obstacles big and small, real and artificial, his own and others' making.

He won ratification of the Panama Canal treaties, but at the cost of protracted debate that evaporated congressional goodwill.

The glow following a brilliant success in bringing Anwar Sadat and Menachem Begin together at Camp David proved ephemeral. The fall of the Shah; the seizure of U.S. hostages by student supporters of the Ayatollah Khomeini; soaring inflation, interest rates, and oil prices; the Soviet invasion of Afghanistan; and a primary challenge by Ted Kennedy combined to doom the Carter presidency. Senate ratification of the SALT II accord reached with Leonid Brezhnev was out of the question. Substantial parts of the president's energy package, which he called "the moral equivalent of war," could not be passed. Cabinet shakeups and grumbling about a "malaise" of the American spirit proved poor substitutes for a strong leader in the White House. And with no such leader in view, Democrats on Capitol Hill did their own thing.

The trend toward individuality was reinforced by developments in the House itself. As Gore began his first term as a representative, Thomas P. "Tip" O'Neill, Jr., began his as Speaker. His predecessor, Carl Albert, like those who came before him, was a man of the institution, barely visible outside, whose definition of leadership was to steer the right bills to the right committees and bring them to the floor under the right rule. But by 1977 real power was becoming diffuse. The seniority system had already been reformed, the prerogatives of committee chairmen weakened, and subcommittees and their staffs had proliferated, enhancing the power of relatively junior members. Albert rarely addressed matters of policy; his idea of a press conference was to meet with a handful of reporters in the well of the House to disclose the day's legislative schedule.

At first, the septuagenarian O'Neill was expected to continue this tradition. "He was," said the *Congressional Quarterly*, "a rank-and-file Massachusetts Democrat who arrived in Washington on Tuesday mornings, returned home Thursday afternoons, and conducted his congressional business over poker, golf and dinner at Duke Zeibert's restaurant at Connecticut Avenue and 'L' Street in downtown Washington." But where Albert all but ignored television as a medium of political communication, O'Neill actively embraced it, both for himself and, by backing televised House floor proceedings, for the entire membership of 435. After suffering through the Carter years, O'Neill came into his own during the presidency of Ronald Reagan. His barbs directed at Reagan initiatives became news events, shown in bite-sized chunks on the evening news. The Republicans responded by turning him into a caricature in two national congressional campaigns.

As they saw the Speaker gaining national prominence, members realized this was a game any number could play. Gore made sure he was the first member to speak on the opening day of televised proceedings, March 19, 1979, a stunt he would repeat as a freshman senator. As his closest House friend, Tom Downey, said, "If you want to reach your colleagues, sometimes the best way is to let them see you on TV or read your name in the paper."

Some old-timers were disturbed by the change. Henry J. Hyde complained about "a bunch of verbalizers who have a smattering of the jargon and who have natural media ability." The Illinois Republican added, "A lot of them have been touched by the aphrodisiac of seeing their name in the papers or going on the evening news. It's a heady experience for them." Chris Matthews, the O'Neill press aide who masterminded much of the Speaker's approach, understood that the new media age was producing a new species of politician. "You ask these guys why they like to be on TV," he said, "and it's like asking a moth why he likes a light bulb. It's why they're here."

Gore was assigned to the smallish Room 1725 in the Longworth House Office Building. But he fared considerably better in the far more important game of committee assignments, winning appointments to the Committee on Interstate and Foreign Commerce, together with its important Oversight and Investigation subcommittees, the Committee on Science and Technology, and later, the Select Committee on Intelligence.

The assignments did not come by accident. For days Gore had hung around outside the door of the room where the Committee on Committees was wrestling with names and vacancies, buttonholing members as they entered and left. There he encountered another freshman Democrat as anxious as himself not to be overlooked, David Bonior of Michigan, the future Democratic Whip.

Bonior's relationship with Gore over the years would be typical of many Democrats who came to Congress about the same time. Initially he viewed his fellow newcomer with skepticism if not downright hostility. There was, to begin with, Gore's pedigree. Bonior was a tough kid from a blue collar family whose ticket to a better life came in the form of a football scholarship to the University of Iowa, where he played quarterback. He was suspicious of this silver-spooned son of a senator, who had gone to St. Albans and Harvard, and who—to Bonior—still looked like a post-graduate preppie. "It was a class thing," Bonior recalls. "I was always more comfortable with people who made their own way in life, not by family connections." In Bonior's view, from the first day, Gore seemed to act as though he were destined for bigger things and was interested in the House only as a way station. Moreover, Bonior feared Gore's connections on the Hill would get him better assignments. Then there was Gore's "raging moderate" business. Bonior was wary of Democrats who sought to distance themselves from the progressive traditions of their party.

But Gore proved sensible enough to surmise that talking sports was a pretty good way to break the ice with a former Iowa quarterback. So he talked sports till he was blue in the face. Then the pair started going to the House gym together for pick-up basketball games. Bonior was the better athlete, but Gore impressed him with an assortment of trick shots, including one where he would carom the ball off the rear gym wall toward the basket, and another that Gore executed lying on his back, near half-court.

Bonior enlisted Gore in his effort to inaugurate a Vietnam

Veterans caucus. The two became charter members. Most other members of the group, which included such heavy hitters as John Murtaugh, Jim Jones, and Les Aspin, believed that this "different kind" of veteran was being ignored both by the leading veterans groups and the government. Benefits were often poorly computed, checks were frequently late, claims of illness possibly attributable to exposure to Agent Orange were rejected without investigation, and the red tape seemed worse than ever.

Bonior probably did as much as anyone to reverse this situation over time, and he would remain grateful for Gore's work. But he never completely got beyond the notion of "class conflict" with Gore. Nor would he develop much sympathy with what he regarded as the anti-labor orientation of Gore's ideological compatriots at the Democratic Leadership Conference. Still, twenty-two years after their first awkward meetings, Bonior would view Gore as the most formidable man the Democrats could nominate in the year 2000. He did not look forward to a Gore-Gephardt battle and hoped that the Minority leader, Gephardt, could content himself with the Speakership if and when the Democrats recaptured the House.

Though he landed good committees, Gore did not pay excessive attention to committee business, save for his own policy frolics. Colleagues from the period did not see him as a "team player." He was no back-slapper, horse-trader, or, in the modern idiom, "networker." He built no institutional power base, because he did not see his long-term future in the House. Some saw Gore as a "loner," or a "self-promoter," or, in the words of one senior Republican staffer, "a Rosie Ruiz type who showed up for the splash and hype and for the last minute glory."

That seems unfair. For one thing, although like most members, he picked and chose those items from the committee menu he found most appetizing, once he took his seat in the committee room, he made certain he had a good feel for the subject at hand. Ron Wyden, a Democratic colleague from Oregon who would endorse

Gore rival Richard Gephardt in the 1988 primary campaign, still told one interviewer, "You could be certain when you walked into a hearing that Al Gore would be the best briefed, best prepared." Of greater importance, Gore seemed to appreciate two crucial political realities:

First, with the budget already in substantial deficit and the political mood totally inhospitable to the social welfare mentality of the Great Society years, a Democrat seeking to make a national reputation had to search for issues that used government power more to protect the life, health, and safety of all Americans and the amenities available to them, than to initiate new programs for the least well off, particularly those not gainfully employed.

Second, the most efficacious way for a young representative to advance was to capture the attention of the media rather than to build his way painstakingly up the seniority ladder or, as the late Sam Rayburn recommended, "to get along by going along." For Albert Gore, Sr., it was fine to "stay on the floor and learn the rules." For Al Gore, Jr., the object was to use his committee assignments as a "bully pulpit" where possible, and, where necessary, to push forward his ideas through the media even without a committee or subcommittee to work with. Invariably he would choose areas that required the mastery of technical or scientific detail but which had practical consequences for a great many Americans.

There are dozens of examples of this approach from Gore's early years, but none better than his work on the nutritional quality of infant formula. Through his position on the Oversight and Investigations Subcommittee, Gore was able to chair hearings on the events leading to the recall of "Neo-Mull-Soy" and "Cho-Free," two adulterated infant formulas manufactured by Syntex Corporation. He found that after reformulating their products for the purpose of reducing the sodium content to enhance long-term health, the company had failed to maintain optimum levels of chloride, a major electrolyte in blood and tissue and a key nutrient for infants. Further, although the Food and Drug Administration (FDA) had received recommendations from the American Academy of Pediatrics on appropriate formula composition, it had not acted on them. In effect, under the law then prevailing, "anything can be marketed in the United States as a sole source nourishment for babies.... Legally, anyone can mix up any mixture and call it infant formula as long as it was produced under sanitary conditions."

Gore later testified, "The tragic, catastrophic result was that thousands of infants were fed a formula that had dangerously low chloride levels. A number of children suffered from metabolic alkalosis, a chemical abnormality caused by deficient chloride intake." Afflicted children could suffer apathy and listlessness, muscle seizures, hyperventilation, ventilatory failure, potentially even death.

The legislation Gore passed required minimal nutrient standards in infant formula and gave the FDA the right to demand changes in nutrient levels as additional information came to light. Products would be tested rigorously and the FDA would be granted full access to all results. Gore noted that since the end of World War II, the percentage of American babies dependent on infant formula had gone from near zero to 60 percent, something he called "the most significant adjustment in the diet of human beings since the introduction of cooking." A penchant for understatement would never be a Gore hallmark.

Without question Gore could do impressive work with his committees. Once alerted to a problem, he would learn all he could about it, often working in shirt-sleeves at his desk, a computer to one side, the ubiquitous Tab bottle at the other. An irrepressible student, he sought instruction from experts and used the committee hearings to acquire hard information. He also, of course, used hearings to create a record to support legislative action. And his contributions were not frivolous. For example, when the manufacturers of children's pajamas that used a chemical agent known as TRIS to make them nonflammable—fulfilling a mandate by the Federal Product Safety Commission—got stuck with large inventories after the chemical was found to be carcinogenic, Gore pressed for legislation that banned TRIS but also compensated the innocent manufacturers.

Gore also investigated insurance companies that bilked the elderly through costly "medi-gap" policies, and brought to public (and grand jury) attention influence peddling in the contact lens industry. From time to time critics would say that Gore's singular ability involved little more than identifying potentially glamorous issues that carried little political risk and running with them to the plaudits of an easily manipulated press.

But most colleagues who worked with Gore saw in him a special talent. "Most of us in Congress are preoccupied with what's on our plate right now or with the next election," said California Democrat Henry Waxman in assessing his young colleague. "Al Gore anticipates problems down the road—and then it turns out they're not as far down the road as we thought."

But Gore also had a mind that could run in stubborn ideological channels, sometimes impeding the results of his work. He was most motivated when he could play the "white knight," galloping to the rescue of those victimized by an evil industry or a disdainful bureaucrat, and his solutions were often punitive.

Gore was the driving force behind the National Organ Transplant Act of 1984, which directed the secretary of health and human services to establish a private nonprofit United States Transportation Network to provide a central registry linking donors and potential recipients. The act also brought the program under Medicare and Medicaid coverage so long as the work was performed at certified medical centers and included coverage of the drugs needed to prevent rejection of transplanted organs.

But the most critical problem in the area of organ transplants was, and to this day remains, a shortage of donors. Gore's old law professor at Vanderbilt, James Blumstein, tried to persuade Gore to permit donors to receive financial compensation. He argued that countries that allow such payments have more donors. But Gore was unimpressed by Blumstein's advice. "They had locked into a national approach and treated everything else as an effort to undermine their plan," Blumstein recalls. After fifteen years, the shortage remains deadly to many in need of transplants.

Gore was also the prime mover behind the so-called "Superfund," a trust fund administered by the Environmental Protection Agency to clean up the most urgent toxic waste problems. The program was supposedly a short-term project, $1.6 billion over five years to clean up four hundred sites. Gore's committee held fifteen hearings on the problem, rallying public support for action with such high visibility cases as the disposal of chemical pollutants near New York State's Love Canal. The question was: Who should pay for the clean-up in situations that occurred long before passage of the act where the companies involved had violated no federal, state, or local law? Gore was adamant that the companies should pay, rejecting even a 50/50 split with government. "Industry not only created the risks but also enjoyed the profits derived from the sale of products whose prices did not reflect their true costs," he insisted.

Gore ignored those who argued that penalizing on an *ex post facto* basis businesses that had at all times acted lawfully set a bad precedent. Others warned that there was no need to federalize the clean-up effort. But Gore wanted anti-pollution efforts coordinated at the national level. To gain political support his initial legislation declared that every state would be entitled to at least one Superfund project, a standard that in practice came fairly close to one per congressional district. This effectively ensured immortality for the program, which is still quite alive at $30 billion and counting.

Predictably, too, the anti-industry provision has provoked years of litigation. About one-third of the $30 billion spent by 1998 has gone to fight lawsuits against companies challenging their assumed clean-up costs. Further, designated polluters often spread the liability, drawing in other businesses that were arguably involved with the problem. Meanwhile, many hazardous waste issues remain unaddressed, new industries are encouraged to pick pristine rural sites where there is no potential liability, and urban areas that need the jobs are left begging.

But Superfund rolls on. A March 1997 General Accounting Office report concluded that the time required to complete cleanups had increased from 2.3 years in 1986 to 10.5 years in 1996. Also, the "hazardous" wastes tapped for cleanup are often less hazardous than the cleanup operation itself. One economist concluded that the driver of a dump truck used in the cleanup operation is at substantially greater risk of death through an accident than are residents from exposure to unremediated sites. That would certainly appear to be true for the area around Love Canal itself, where recent studies have debunked earlier claims of a high incidence of cancer and other disease among area residents. These "victims" of chemical dumping appear to be about as healthy as the population at large.

Sometimes Gore's suspicions of business could have ironic results. When the Iran crisis of 1979 tightened the oil market, Energy Secretary James Schlesinger pushed for price deregulation to cut demand and restore competition. Gore was opposed, claiming that oil companies had artificially tightened supply to drive prices up, actions that "are normal for an oligopoly." Deregulation, he said, would make things worse. "Sharply higher prices risk simultaneous recession and double-digit inflation. The poor would be devastated; those barely making it now would be pushed beyond their limits. Yet once again, as in 1973–74, the oil companies would thrive, their profits inflated in direct proportion to the crushing economic burden on the country as a whole. In my opinion, our policy should reflect a greater concern for equity and a greater effort to avoid further drastic price increases."

In fact, deregulation led to sharply *lower* energy prices and eliminated shortages, developments that Gore later lamented because of the alleged link between fossil fuels, "greenhouse" gases, and "global warming."

Other issues caught Gore's interest. As a member of the House and later the Senate, he had many occasions on which to express his views of abortion. The 1973 Supreme Court decision in *Roe* v. *Wade* holding that abortion within the first two trimesters of pregnancy is a constitutionally protected right caught both liberals and conservatives by surprise and, in many cases, "out of position." For example, Ronald Reagan, as governor of California, had signed one of the nation's first laws legalizing abortion, and George Bush favored decriminalizing abortions. But there came a time in the careers of both men when political necessity—a.k.a., fresh moral insight— induced change. Both, however, had the integrity to admit that their later positions differed from their earlier ones. Not so Al Gore, Jr.

In 1977, Gore's first year in Congress, he voted for the amendment offered by Representative Henry J. Hyde banning the spending of federal funds on abortions unless necessary to save the life of the mother. Three times that year Gore voted against amendments that would have extended federal funding to cases of rape and incest. In 1979 he voted against a similar amendment offered by Democrat Henry Waxman of California. He also voted against permitting the District of Columbia to use its own funds on abortions, and voted to prohibit federal employee health insurance plans from financing abortions.

These positions appear to reflect the views Gore genuinely held at the time. Frank Ritter, his editor at the *Nashville Tennessean*, recalls a conversation with his young reporter in which Gore said, "I know many here will disagree with me but I simply don't believe the government ought to be spending tax dollars on abortions." His opinion was based partly on the belief that government should do nothing that could be interpreted as endorsing abortions, and partly that people morally or religiously opposed to the practice should not have their tax money spent paying for it.

In 1984 Gore supported a radical pro-life amendment offered by Republican Representative Mark Siljander of Michigan, which would have defined "person" to include unborn children from the moment of conception. Three years later he supported a pro-life amendment by Republican Representative Henry J. Hyde that declared, "abortion takes the life of an unborn child who is a living human being," and that "a right to abortion is not secured by the Constitution of the United States." In a letter to a constituent that year, Gore explained that his goal was "to reduce the outrageously large number of abortions which currently take place." He added, "During my eleven years in Congress, I have consistently opposed federal funding of abortions. In my opinion, it is wrong to spend federal funds for what is arguably the taking of human life."

By 1992 Gore had already reversed his opposition on the right of Washington, D.C., to finance abortions, and after his selection as Bill Clinton's running-mate, he endorsed the inclusion of abortions in national health insurance. Yet the 1992 debate with Vice President Dan Quayle includes this exchange:

Quayle: "At one time, and most of the time in the House of Representatives, you had a pro-life position."
Gore: "That's simply not true."

The issue was raised again as he campaigned as Bill Clinton's running-mate four years later. In an interview with David Frost, Gore denied that he had flip-flopped and said, "Then and now, I support a woman's right to choose and oppose the overturning of *Roe* v. *Wade*. Then and now, I support federal funding only in some circumstances." He did concede that he would no longer employ the term, "arguably the taking of human life," in discussing the issue because "I think the phrase is itself so loaded with political charge that it... one cannot be oblivious to the impact of phrasing like that."

As a loyal partner of Bill Clinton, Gore would later become a cheerleader for the pro-choice position, including the widely deplored late-term procedure known as "partial birth abortion." He would dutifully recite the administration's mantra that abortions should be "safe, legal, and rare," the term "rare" utterly devoid of policy content.

Gore's description of his zigs and zags on the issue has a bit of an Orwellian tone. What many find most objectionable about Gore's record on abortion is not his position *per se*, but his attempt to have it both ways, every response calculated to appeal to his audience *du jour*.

Still, Gore's early years in the House were filled with productive activity and the promise of more. In addition to his work on infant formula, industrial waste, organ transplants, and insurance fraud, he had begun to explore areas like robotics and supercomputer technology. With Democrat (later Republican) Billy Tauzin, he became one of the original House "dishheads," successfully leading the fight to prevent cable TV operators from denying programming to operators of direct satellites, a cause to which he gravitated after being impressed by the number of dishes he observed on a political tour of rural Tennessee.

Gore successfully sponsored legislation to toughen the warning labels on cigarette packs. Further, he began to build a good and intensely loyal staff who saw in their boss an ability to target interesting subjects, to master all kinds of technical detail, and to capture national attention without courting national controversy. Ken Jost helped get him off to a good start. Peter Knight, a savvy political operative, stayed on staff for more than a decade and chaired the 1996 Clinton/Gore reelection campaign. Roy Neel, an affable, "down home" consensus-builder, developed a fine feel for the legislative process and followed Gore from the House to the Senate to the West Wing of the White House. So did Leon Fuerth, a career foreign service officer who had worked at the State Department for such luminaries as Helmut Sonnenfeldt, Leslie Gelb, and George

Vest, and on the House Permanent Select Committee on Intelligence, specializing in nuclear arms control. His boss, Chairman Les Aspin, later became chairman of the Committee on Armed Services, and still later, secretary of defense. Fuerth was ten years older than Gore, but had long since become expert at subordinating his own ego for the delights of educating and influencing those who wielded political power. He formally joined the Gore staff in 1982 after helping Gore formulate his strategic views. Years later, a plaque graced the wall of his West Wing office with the words, "He who is able to give credit away can do unimaginable good."

That Fuerth would find his way onto Gore's staff reflected the latter's realization that while the kind of work he was doing on his committees had been splashy, it was not the stuff of which national reputations were built. Nor did these kinds of issues—many of which made him popular with his party's liberal activists—sufficiently denote the ideological niche he sought to establish. To achieve the kind of prominence that Gore was beginning to covet and a place in the center of the Democratic Party, it would be necessary to learn about national security, to contribute meaningfully to the great debate on East-West relations, and to become *un homme serieux* capable of holding his own with diplomats and with political leaders.

Gore staked out one "moderate" position by bucking the majority in his party and supporting, if not military aid, then occasional limited humanitarian assistance of food and medicine to the Contras in Nicaragua. His position gave him national exposure as a Democrat modestly to the right of his party in foreign affairs. But in terms of higher policy, Gore's position was virtually irrelevant. After all, the war in Nicaragua was a battle of bullets, not a food fight.

Gore needed something bigger than Nicaragua to forge his way into the front rank of national Democrats, something that really mattered, a life-and-death issue for the nation if not mankind. The issue he picked for self-definition was nuclear arms control.

CHAPTER EIGHT

GORE AND NUCLEAR ARMS CONTROL

IN PICKING NUCLEAR arms control as his proprietary issue, Gore was tapping into one of the most theological games in town, a game rich in arcane doctrine, liturgy, and vocabulary.

Gore would later claim his interest had been ignited by a speech he made to the Girls' State convention in Murfreesboro, Tennessee. At one point, he asked the delegates whether they expected to see nuclear war in their lifetimes. Most raised their hands in the affirmative. "How many believe we can change that if we really try?" he asked. Only a handful raised their hands. Thus another "road to Damascus" moment in the life of Al Gore, Jr.

True or apocryphal, Gore's new issue vaulted him to national prominence. As an extremely junior representative with no expertise in the field and only a tangential committee base from which to work—Gore was appointed to the Intelligence Oversight Committee at the start of the Ninety-seventh Congress—it was a daring move. But without his centrist foreign party credentials and his eagerly developed expertise in arms control, it is doubtful he would have had the *chutzpa* to declare for the presidency in 1988.

Fuerth set up the kind of structured learning program Gore

117

found most rewarding. The congressman devoted at least six to eight hours each week for a full thirteen months to studying the subject, often through lectures by Fuerth. Sometimes a "guest lecturer" would drop by. One week it might be Larry Smith, a former arms control staff expert for Senator Thomas McIntyre and later for Les Aspin. Or it might be James R. Woolsey, who would eventually have a brief, unrewarding stint as Bill Clinton's CIA director.

Woolsey recalls visiting Gore in his dingy Longworth Building office. Gore was in shirt-sleeves surrounded by more charts and graphs than a Super Bowl coach. Fourteen years earlier—in the mid-1960s—Woolsey had worked with Pentagon intellectual Alan Enthoven on a highly classified project called "Code 50," which sought to "game" various nuclear exchanges between the United States and the USSR in order to determine the optimum size of America's nuclear arsenal, and therefore, what arms control positions America should take. Woolsey noticed Gore had been punching away at some of the old "Code 50" scenarios on his IBM computer.

Prior to the 1960s there was little talk of placing mutual limits on nuclear weapons; the U.S. lead was so wide, policymakers could talk glibly about "massive retaliation," the automatic resort to nuclear weapons in response to a conventional Soviet attack in Europe. But in the years after President Kennedy stared down Nikita Khrushchev in the Cuban Missile Crisis, the Soviets had accelerated their weapons production and begun deploying ICBMs with very large warheads. Both sides had missiles that could release three warheads at a time, and the United States was close to deploying multiple warheads that could be targeted independently (the soon-to-be famous multiple independently targeted reentry vehicles, or MIRV). Before long it was possible to foresee the large Soviet missiles carrying ten MIRVs apiece. And with improving accuracy, the missiles would acquire a "counterforce capability"—

destroying not only citizens but some of America's retaliatory missiles as well.

The burgeoning Soviet missile force, together with the greater size and accuracy of Soviet missiles, put at risk the theory called "Mutual Assured Destruction" (MAD) which had grown out of the mid-1960s Pentagon war-gaming. To serve as a deterrent, particularly during a crisis, enough nuclear forces of either side had to be able to survive a first strike in order to inflict "unacceptable damage" on the other in return. For MAD to work, both sides had to be vulnerable and stay vulnerable, but not so vulnerable as to be unable to respond if they were hit first. In the service of MAD, the U.S. developed a so-called "triad" of strategic weapons—Intercontinental Ballistic Missiles (ICBMs), Submarine Launched Ballistic Missiles (SLBMs) and long-range bombers, thus ensuring the survival of retaliatory weapons even if one or more legs of the triad became vulnerable. Under MAD, it was fine to try to protect one's missiles by diversifying one's force, sheltering them, or making them mobile, because their survivability was the essence of deterrence. But trying to protect one's population centers was tampering with the essence of MAD. For that reason, in 1972, when he negotiated SALT I with the Soviets, placing limits on ICBMs and SLBMs, Henry Kissinger successfully insisted on a separate treaty limiting the deployment of antiballistic missile systems, thus assuring the preservation of MAD.

But now, many reasoned, even though the Soviets would still not have a "first strike capability" to take out America's entire arsenal, the potential vulnerability of America's land-based missiles was bad enough. With that capability, some thought the Soviet advantage would be so great they might be tempted to fight or at least threaten to fight a nuclear war causing the United States to back down in a crisis. In this concept, MAD became old-fashioned. The new term of art was "crisis stability."

There was much that was nonsensical about the entire nuclear theology. The theoretical vulnerability of one's weapons rested on the highly questionable assumption that they would be kept sitting patiently in their silos even after a confirmed launch by the other side. Many skeptics also wondered, what was the importance of one leg of the triad becoming theoretically vulnerable? After all, the ability to kill an aggressor with a missile launched from an invulnerable submarine, or a B-52 bomber that would have taken off before the first salvo of missiles landed, was just as much of a deterrent as a surviving ICBM. That was the purpose of having a triad in the first place. And in fact, the theoretical vulnerability of American ICBMs meant relatively little. Only 25 percent of America's firepower was devoted to land-based missiles, while for the Soviets, it was 80 percent. Much of what passed for U.S. "vulnerability" during the period was little more than the sort of asymmetry of forces one would expect between a continental superpower (the Soviet Union) and a naval superpower (the United States).

Nonetheless, the revisionists pressed their case. In a January 1976 essay in *Foreign Affairs*, Paul Nitze, one of the deans of arms control, condemned the 1975 Vladivostok accords signed by U.S. President Gerald Ford and USSR Communist Party Chairman Leonid Brezhnev. The Vladivostok agreement was meant to rectify one of the imbalances of the SALT I treaty, which had provided the Soviets with numerical advantages in land- and sea-based missile launchers. The Vladivostok accords changed that in favor of an equal number of "nuclear delivery systems" for both sides. But the changes did not come close to satisfying Nitze, because he believed the Soviets were no longer interested in mutual deterrence or crisis stability. "On the contrary, there is every prospect that under the terms of the SALT agreements the Soviet Union will continue to pursue a nuclear superiority that is not merely qualitative but designed to produce a theoretical war-winning capability. Further, there is a major risk that, if such a condition were achieved, the Soviet Union would adjust its policies and actions in ways that would undermine the present détente situation, with results that could only resurrect the danger of nuclear confrontation or, alternatively, increase the prospect of Soviet expansion through other means of pressure."

Nitze's recommended cure was for the United States to undertake a sizeable civil defense effort, as the Russians were already doing, while developing mobile missiles that would be harder for Soviet weapons to hit. He also urged agreements that would force the Soviets to reduce the size of their missiles. Unless the United States acted promptly, he said, the Soviets would soon come to enjoy a "window of opportunity," whereby their superiority would become so evident they might be able to force the United States to back down in one crisis or another.

Ronald Reagan would campaign on a promise to close this "window of opportunity" no matter what the cost, and to that end he reversed President Carter's cancellation of the B-1 Strategic Bomber and made building the MX missile—a mobile ten-warhead monster with the accuracy to hit Soviet missiles—his Number 1 priority.

As Gore began to grasp the intricacies of strategic theology, he became convinced that it was possible to deploy forces in a way that could produce permanent "crisis stability." Quite simply, it involved eliminating multiple warhead missiles altogether. Said Gore, "I suggest that they be replaced by a new, lightweight ICBM specifically designed to carry just one warhead." Since the nation contemplating a first strike would always have to spend at least one of its own single-warhead missiles to destroy one of its enemy's, there would never be any theoretical advantage in striking first. That is what Gore called "the key to a successful agreement in the age of parity...." Further protection could come from reinforcing launch sites or making missiles mobile, both steps making it harder to destroy the protected missiles.

The air force, which regarded the new missile as a nuclear cap pistol, termed it the "small ICBM missile." In popular parlance it became known as "Midgetman."

There was nothing particularly new in Gore's idea. As Larry Smith recalls, "It had been kicked around for years at Lawrence Livermore and other Western think tanks." In 1981, a year before Gore's epiphany, Jan Lodal, Kissinger's National Security Council expert on nuclear weapons, publicly proposed the concept. The Pentagon brass, which prized "bang for the buck," hated the idea. But Gore promoted it and found a key ally in Les Aspin, the new chairman of the House Armed Services Committee. A defense intellectual and an eclectic moderate frequently threatened with demotion by his party's liberal caucus, Aspin thought Midgetman a warm and cuddly nuke all Democrats could love.

Of course, having developed "the answer" to the most intractable problem of his age, Gore became a passionate salesman. Lamar Alexander, then governor of Tennessee, recalls a flight to Nashville with Gore. "Before we were off the ground, he had his papers out and was drawing charts to prove his plan was stabilizing," Alexander recalls. The governor was awed, but not impressed. In Alexander's view, "He [Gore] knows things in more detail than it is necessary for a decision-maker to know, although what he knows would be valuable for a staff man."

What gave Gore's idea real clout was the Reagan administration's need to gain Democratic support for the MX, the mobile missile no one wanted in his own backyard. Air force plans for hauling the MX on trucks across the Western deserts, carrying it on railroad tracks, and other mobile schemes, had all been rejected. In December 1982 Congress also voted down an alternative basing mode called "densepack." The idea was to crowd missiles together in reinforced silos in the hope that attacking Soviet missiles would crash into each other and commit "fratricide." What Democrats really wanted was not the MX, but arms control and a "freeze" on nuclear testing and deployment.

Gore was one of a few Democrats to oppose a nuclear freeze. For one thing, argued Gore, it would stop the development of more stable systems, like his Midgetman.

By the spring of 1983 former Air Force General Brent Scowcroft, then heading a defense committee for President Reagan, figured that if moderate Democrats got their Midgetman, the president could get his MX. "It might work, let me run the traps," House Democratic leader Les Aspin told Scowcroft. The key was winning over Al Gore. "Gore was the guy we needed," recalls James Woolsey. "He was one of the few in the House to have read the literature and learned the theory. This is a guy who rolls up his sleeves and masters the technical details the way almost nobody else does."

Gore had one demand before signing on to Scowcroft's plan— that the administration commit itself to a new arms control push. Some of Gore's closest friends thought he had been suckered into backing the MX by an administration with no commitment to arms control. Tom Downey, the Long Island congressman who was perhaps Gore's closest Washington friend, said the problem with the Reagan administration was that "they believe that real men don't control weapons, real men build them." But Gore replied, "Do we want to give up on the chance that this administration for the next two years, or possibly the next six years, can achieve an arms control agreement with the Soviet Union? Do we want to throw away the chance to build a bipartisan approach that might make some sense and might achieve an arms control agreement?"

Still others would find Gore's obsession with nuclear arms control in general and Midgetman in particular a piece with his fascination with organ transplants, and later, supercomputers, and depletion of the ozone layer—fine subjects all, but not the sort of stuff that translates into mass political appeal.

Reagan, of course, had done something in 1983 that would in time render much of the debate over both Midgetman and the MX moot. By embracing the Strategic Defense Initiative (SDI)—a space-based system of sensors and interceptors designed to thwart a nuclear attack long before the weapons ever reached U.S. territory—Reagan had drastically changed the terms of the debate. No longer was mutual vulnerability to be prized. No longer was the Anti-Ballistic Missile (ABM) Treaty sacrosanct. Indeed proponents of SDI urged withdrawal from a treaty calculated to leave both sides defenseless.

Gore was skeptical that SDI would work, and he was sure the Soviets would massively increase their offensive missiles to overcome it. As late as 1991 Gore, now working from the Senate, argued against deploying SDI systems, "until we know what system we want to deploy, until we know what changes are feasible and desirable in the ABM Treaty, until we know what the technology is capable of doing."

MX became a budget casualty of SDI. And Gore's Midgetman became a philosophical casualty, as few wanted to waste money on an undersized single warhead missile when the eventual need might be to overwhelm the Soviet Union's strategic defenses.

Albert Gore saw the USSR as a permanent partner in managing the peril of nuclear arms. But Ronald Reagan sensed that the USSR was ready for "the ash heap of history." Ultimately, President Reagan's endorsement of an unproven technology helped drive the Soviets to "perestroika" (restructuring) and "glasnost" (openness) in order to compete with American technology and defense spending. In fact, the Soviets' liberalization ended up undoing the entire Soviet Empire, as the reform, once begun, couldn't be stopped.

The irony for Gore is that on nuclear arms control, the issue that turned him from a mildly interesting and promising Tennessee representative to one of his party's premier voices on national security, he was brilliantly, studiously, imaginatively, responsibly, and valiantly wrong. To Gore, the nuclear issue was part of a relationship with the Soviet Union that had to be managed. To Reagan, it was part of a struggle that had to be won.

*   *   *

By 1983 Majority Leader Howard Baker had decided against seeking a fourth term in the U.S. Senate. The Senate was a poor place from which to campaign if he ran for president in 1988. But as the first Republican senator from Tennessee since Reconstruction, he had a proprietary feeling about his seat. He wanted to bequeath it to his former aide, Governor Lamar Alexander, but Alexander wouldn't leave his governorship.

So when Baker announced his retirement, the Republicans nominated Victor Ashe, a Yale-educated Knoxville lawyer and state senator with an acerbic wit and a low tolerance for fools, traits which failed to endear him to his colleagues in the Tennessee legislature. "I started way behind and never laid a glove on him," Ashe, now mayor of Knoxville, concedes.

"Nothing I tried worked," recalls Ashe. Assuming that Ronald Reagan would bury Walter Mondale in a landslide victory, Ashe tried to link Gore to the doomed Democratic presidential candidate. But Gore "stayed away from Mondale, though I tried to smoke him out in six face-to-face debates." In one debate, a frustrated Ashe offered Gore $5 on the spot if he would so much as state the name "Mondale." Gore promptly obliged, praised Mondale's "compassion"—and then went on to compliment Reagan for his commitment to a strong defense. He also took the $5, but donated it to charity.

If Gore's campaign was easy, his personal life was not. His sister Nancy had moved to the family's farm in Carthage after being diagnosed with lung cancer, the apparent result of a lifetime of smoking.

"Nancy thought she would recover. She never lost her confidence," says Jerry Futrell, a longtime friend of Albert, Sr. Futrell owned a drug store in Carthage where the Gores would have Nancy's prescriptions filled. Al, Jr., "would walk in here to buy drugs for Nancy," Futrell recalls. "It was very sad. He often seemed to be on the verge of tears. And it was easy for me to see why. The pre-scriptions were for pain killers. You can't cure cancer with painkillers."

Al, Jr., won his race easily, becoming the new senator from Tennessee, but his sister Nancy lost hers, dying in Vanderbilt Hospital, just as the campaign was moving into high gear.

CHAPTER NINE

TIPPER AND PORN ROCK

A S A SENATOR, Gore remained quintessentially Al Gore, the wonk. Former colleagues at the *Tennessean* still chortle about a call Gore placed to the newsroom early in his Senate term when he said to the reporter who answered the phone, "Charlie, what do you know about the relationship between consciousness and quantum physics?" But his wonkishness could sometimes take a purely personal turn.

The Gore's first daughter, Karenna, was born in August 1973. In June 1977 the Gores had their second daughter, Kristin, and in January 1979, their third, Sarah. Al wanted a son fervently, but it seemed unlikely to happen, and he and Tipper discussed various sterilization options. Then Gore learned about a book called *How to Choose the Sex of Your Baby*, which describes a method of gender selection developed by Dr. Landrum B. Shettles, a former member of the medical school faculty at Columbia University. Gore's most personal experience with structured learning was about to begin.

Shettles claims his method is 75 to 80 percent effective. It is based on the fact that male-produced Y chromosomes, which result in male babies, are faster but smaller and weaker, than the X chromosomes, which create female babies. The Y chromosomes also tend to thrive better in the high alkaline environment closest to the female period of ovulation rather than the more acidic environment further from that critical moment.

The key to success in the Shettles method is for the female partner to identify the precise time of ovulation by monitoring such indicators as daily temperature and the color and consistency of cervical mucous, and for the couple to have intercourse at that optimum moment.

Dr. Shettles offers other advice to further improve the odds of conceiving a male. While intercourse is permitted during the early part of the cycle, condoms must be used or the result could be a girl. "When you believe you are within four days of your time of ovulation, *abstain entirely* from any sexual activity that results in male ejaculation. It is important to increase sperm count as much as possible—a factor that favors male conceptions."

Shettles cautions males wanting a son to "avoid jockey shorts, jockstraps, and other tight-fitting clothing" or risk "raising the temperature within the testes to the point where sperm count is reduced."

Also, "drinking a couple of cups of strong caffeinated coffee fifteen to thirty minutes before having intercourse, on the try for the boy, may impart some extra speed to the male-producing sperm."

Further, since female orgasm increases the flow of natural alkaline secretions, "The woman trying to conceive a boy should try to experience orgasm during the critical intercourse," or, even better, multiple orgasms "at the same time as or, better yet, just *before* the male orgasm."

"The man should try for *deep* penetration at the time of his climax," since this will deposit sperm closest to the cervix where the most alkaline secretions occur. In addition, Dr. Shettles recommends "vaginal penetration from the rear when trying for the boy.

This may sound odd, but, in fact, this position helps ensure that the sperm are deposited near the opening of the cervix...."

In October 1982 the Gores' son, Albert Arnold Gore III, was born. Frank Gibson, an old Gore chum from the *Tennessean*, called to congratulate him. "Now that you have a boy do you intend to quit?" he asked. "Dammit, Gibson," Gore replied, "I believe I'll discuss that with Tipper before I discuss it with the *Nashville Tennessean*." "It was the only time I ever heard him curse," Gibson maintains. The Gores had no more children.

As with much of his acquired knowledge, Gore's mastery of the technique for determining the sex of one's child became something he delighted in sharing with friends. In early 1988 he was the guest of honor at a presidential campaign fundraising dinner at the Maryland home of his great financial backer Nate Landow. Gore was seated next to Landow's daughter, Harolyn, who is married to Michael Cardozo, an assistant White House counsel in the Carter administration and, later, the chairman of the Clinton Defense Fund. During dinner conversation, Gore learned that the Cardozos, who had two daughters, were discouraged about having a son, and were thinking of stopping their attempts. "Don't do it," offered Gore. "At least not until you've tried the Shettles method." He then waxed eloquent about the success he and Tipper had experienced with *How to Choose the Sex of Your Baby*.

"I felt like I was practicing witchcraft, drinking two cups of coffee before sex and all that other stuff," Cardozo would later recall. "But damn if we didn't have a son. So the next thing, I recommended it to my friend Zoe Baird, and it worked for her too."

Cardozo says that whenever Gore runs into Harolyn, his first question is always, "How's my son?"

*　　　*　　　*

Kristen Erwin was the Gore's weekend babysitter for three

years in the mid-1980s. Now an aspiring actress in New York City, with red-brown hair and dark brown eyes, Ms. Erwin recalls the job fondly. The Gores paid her one dollar per child, per hour, and she loved all four little Gores. She recalls one particular night when Al and Tipper had dinner guests. Karenna, then ten, proposed, "Let's sneak over to the top of the stairs and listen to Daddy talk." Why? "Because the guests are all from Tennessee tonight, and when Daddy has people from Tennessee his accent gets very thick and it's fun to listen to."

Once Kristen was changing the infant Gore when Albert Gore, Sr., stumbled into the room. "He started harumphing and seemed to turn color," she recalls. "I was afraid he was going to faint. I guess he hadn't changed many diapers in his time."

Al Gore, Jr., had no similar problem. Kristen has good memories of the senator. "When he drove me home, he would stay parked by the driveway until I was safely inside my house. Always."

But Tipper was her favorite. She found her "very, very friendly, warm, and comfortable," and a superb artist. "Everyone knows of the fantastic photos she took of the whole family— swimming, diving, trying on Mommy's wedding dress, everything. But people don't know how well she painted. She made magnificent portraits of Kristen and Sarah." What about Al's taste in art? "He kept a poster promoting one of Reagan's movies in the basement. He thought it was funny."

Al and Tipper enjoyed rock music. They listened to the Beatles and the Grateful Dead, among others. But they were unfamiliar with the way a part of the genre had evolved in the eighties. Kristen Erwin played a role in their sudden education. "I was the cause of PMRC," she remembers, "the group Tipper formed to pressure the record companies to label their records with explicit lyrics. Karenna was just starting to get into music. So one day I brought over my Prince album, *Purple Rain*. Our favorite song was 'Let's Go Crazy.'

I can still remember little Al—one year old—jumping up and down on the bed screaming 'Let's Go Tazy.' But the last song on the album refers to masturbation."

Knowing only that Karenna liked "Let's Go Crazy," Tipper bought the *Purple Rain* album in December 1984. In the final number, "Darling Nikki," Prince sings:

"I knew a girl named Nikki.

"I guess you could say she was a sex fiend.

"I met her in a hotel lobby masturbating with a magazine."

Tipper didn't know at the time that in concert Prince's guitar would sometimes spray the audience with water to simulate a woman's body fluid, but what she heard on her daughter's album was gross enough. "I couldn't believe my ears!" Tipper would later write. "The vulgar lyrics embarrassed both of us. At first, I was stunned—then I got mad! Millions of Americans were buying *Purple Rain* with no idea what to expect. Thousands of parents were giving the album to their children—many even younger than my daughter."

Then the two younger girls started asking Tipper about things they had seen on MTV. Soon, with her daughters, she was watching Van Halen's "Hot for Teacher," in which a teacher performs a striptease act for her male students, and Motley Crue's "Looks that Kill," with "scantily clad women being captured and imprisoned in cages by a studded-leather-clad male band." The more familiar Tipper became with "porn rock," the angrier she got. Some weeks after her introduction to Prince she had occasion to discuss her concern with Susan Baker, the wife of James Baker, Ronald Reagan's Treasury Secretary. Mrs. Baker was the mother or stepmother of eight. Her concern antedated Tipper's—she had already discussed the possibility of concerted action with Sally Nevius, the former chairman of the District of Columbia City Council, and Pam Howar, a Washington businesswoman.

The three women took the lead in establishing the Parents' Music Resource Center, or PMRC, as a nonprofit organization. Its initial agenda was ambitious. The group published a call for albums to be rated in one of four categories depending on how explicitly they treated sex or violence—a system similar in theory to the one used for years by the film industry. In addition the group wanted songs with offensive lyrics or graphics not to be displayed on album covers or inserts, and music videos showing graphic sex or violence not aired.

In mid-May PMRC enlisted rock musician turned youth minister Jeff Ling to narrate a slide show at St. Columbia's church in Washington. The show's purpose was to warn adults about the worst excesses of rock lyrics and videos available to their teenage children. The meeting was attended by about 350 people, considerably more than the organizers had expected. The media had also become conscious of the issue. *Newsweek, USA Today*, and *Good Morning America* had all run pieces on the subject, even before the May event. The only music industry insider to attend was the wife of Eddie Fritts, president of the National Association of Broadcasters. Mr. Fritts had already circulated one letter alerting his members to the growing concern about rock lyrics. Later he would write to the heads of forty-five major record companies asking that copies of lyrics accompany all recordings made available to broadcasters. The head of Warner Brothers Records, Lenny Waronker, rejected the request. "It smells of censorship," he complained.

Stan Gortikov, head of the Recording Industry Association of America (RIAA), was among those who criticized PMRC. Associating his warbling pornographers with past artistic giants, he claimed that artists from Cole Porter to the Beatles had faced complaints their music was "dirty," and claimed such history "is telling us it would be unrealistic for us to expect to attain any level of 'purity' that can satisfy all those who choose to critique music." He rejected as unreasonable the demand that record companies "rate" their new releases arguing that the process would be far more cumbersome for the record industry than for films, given that the record industry was then producing 25,000 songs and 2,500 albums each year, far more than the number of new films.

PMRC intensified its efforts to obtain media support; and a number of prominent journalists responded. The *Boston Globe's* Ellen Goodman, for example, offered this account of the evolution of rock: "The outrageous edge of rock and roll has shifted its focus from Elvis' pelvis to the saw protruding from Blackie Lawless's codpiece on a WASP album. Rock lyrics have turned from 'I can't get no satisfaction' to 'I am going to force you at gunpoint to eat me alive.'"

David Gergen, taking a punditry interlude between stints in the Reagan and Clinton administrations, struck a similar theme, saying that "the difference between the music of yesteryear and that of today is the leap one makes from swimsuits in *Sports Illustrated* to the centerfolds in *Hustler*."

From the right, George Will wondered whether the music would in its own way crush the developing spirit of youth: "The concern is less that children will emulate the frenzied behavior described in porn rock than that they will succumb to the lassitude of the demoralized—literally, the de-moralized."

A more enterprising critique was offered by gifted *Esquire* columnist Bob Greene, whose experience suggests that despite protestations of outrage, many parents are accessories to their children's self-degradation. While traveling through Texas, Greene heard a disc jockey on KISS-FM San Antonio offer free tickets to a Motley Crue concert to whoever sent in the best response to the question, "What would you do to meet the Crue?" Among many comparable responses was one from a sixteen-year-old girl who wrote: "First I would tie you up, spread-eagle and naked, with leather straps. Then I'd shave all the hair off your chest, and if I should nick you I'll suck up all the blood as it slowly trickles over your body. Next I'll cover your body with motion lotion to get things really heated up. When it gets *too* hot, I'll cover your body in crushed ice and lay on top of you to melt it down and cool you off."

Greene interviewed the girl's mother who first read the letter and then delivered it to the station. "I guess I was shocked in a way, but I'm sure she didn't mean anything by it," she said. "She's a very Christian girl."

Like the tobacco companies, the record industry targeted an audience of young teens, or even preteens. But unlike tobacco ads, their pitch was explicit. Take, for example, the press release by Electra-Asylum Records for the Motley Crue album, *Shout at the Devil*: "Dripping with impure and adulterated lust and take-no-shit-and-grab-some-tit attitude, *Shout at the Devil* is a call to arms for American youth."

With the public now engaged, the uncoordinated, sometimes ludicrous nature of the early industry responses seemed to play into the hands of Tipper Gore, Susan Baker, and their allies. For example, the then middle-aged (now deceased) rock star, Frank Zappa, labeled the group "cultural terrorists," and complained that "no person married to or related to a government official should be permitted to waste the nation's time on ill-conceived housewife hobby projects such as this."

In September 1985 Chairman John Danforth convened his Commerce, Science, and Transportation Committee for hearings on the issue. Tipper Gore was one of the witnesses. Al Gore, Jr., while a relatively junior member of the committee, was already considering a run for the presidency in 1988. His genuine concern about the issue and natural instinct to support his wife were to some extent mitigated by the knowledge that Hollywood had in recent years emerged as a vast source of money for Democratic campaigns.

The September 19 hearing in Room 253 of the Russell Senate Office Building proved to be one of those marvelous Washington events that combined confrontation, cowardice, and kitsch.

Danforth began by noting that while the music under scrutiny "deals very explicitly with sexual subjects... glorifies violence in various forms," and "advocates the use of drugs, I do not know of any suggestion that any legislation be passed."

That led Senator James Exon of Nebraska to wonder why any hearings at all were being held in the absence of any legislative purpose.

Senator Fritz Hollings of South Carolina was less restrained. "I would tell you it is outrageous filth," he fumed, and "if I could find some way constitutionally to do away with it, I would."

No one at the hearing had to guess what Senator Hollings was referring to when he used the words "outrageous filth." The event included a pause while some of the most explicit records and videos were played. Committee members, witnesses, and the press all got to appreciate Quiet Riot's *Metal Health:*

> "I'm gonna find a mama
> "That makes me feel alright
> "Wanna kiss your lips
> "Not the ones on your face."

And Great White's *On Your Knees:*

> "Kickin down your door
> "Gonna pull you to the floor
> "Taking what I choose
> "Never gonna loose
>
> "Gonna drive my love inside you
> "Gonna nail your ass to the floor..."

Still, Mrs. Gore seemed less outraged than some of her earlier statements would have suggested. She chose to emphasize the voluntary nature of her group's proposed remedy: "We do not want legislation to remedy this problem. The problem is one that developed in the marketplace. The music industry has allowed the excesses that you saw and we believe the music industry is the entity to address those excesses. We would like them to do this voluntarily. We propose no legislation whatsoever."

But Tipper's assurances failed to mollify Frank Zappa and his supporters. The belligerent Zappa told the committee, "The PMRC proposal is an ill-conceived piece of nonsense which fails to deliver any real benefits to children, infringes the civil liberties of people who are not children, and promises to keep the courts busy for years dealing with the interpretational and enforcement problems inherent in the proposal's design."

Betraying a healthy reservoir of vintage 1968 student paranoia, Zappa suggested an ulterior motive for the actions of Susan Baker and Tipper Gore: "While the wife of the secretary of the treasury recites 'Gonna drive my love inside you' and Senator Gore's wife talks about 'bondage' and 'oral sex at gunpoint' on the *CBS Evening News,* people in high places work on a tax bill that is so ridiculous, the only way to sneak it through is to keep the public's mind on something else: porn rock."

Zappa called PMRC "a cult" and launched a direct attack on Senator Gore. "Is it proper that the husband of a PMRC nonmember/founder/person sits on any committee considering business pertaining to the blank tape tax or his wife's lobbying organization? Can any committee thus constituted find facts in a fair and unbiased manner?"

Gore's response to Zappa's savage assault on his wife was—to put it mildly—restrained. He allowed that while he disagreed with some of Zappa's statements, "I have been a fan of your music, believe it or not. I respect you as a true original and a tremendously talented musician." Then, in what had become the ritual disclaimer,

Gore assured his tormentor that "the PMRC says repeatedly no legislation, no regulation, no government action."

That drew an unusual type of comment from a committee colleague, Republican Slade Gorton of Washington: "Mr. Zappa, I am astounded at the courtesy and soft-voiced nature of the comments of my friend, the senator from Tennessee. I can only say that I found your statement to be boorish, incredibly and insensitively insulting to the people that were here previously.... [Y]ou could manage to give the first amendment of the Constitution of the United States a bad name, if I felt that you had the slightest understanding of it, which I do not."

The record industry was actually in a mood to bargain because it needed more aggressive government enforcement of copyright protection against "pirating" of its product. Finally, a deal was struck. PMRC agreed to stop its media campaign in exchange for a promise from the Recording Industry Association of America to put a label on controversial music reading "Explicit Lyrics-Parental Advisory." The accord was announced at the National Press Club on November 1, 1985.

But Tipper's opponents continued to attack. Vulgar lyrics circulated purporting to describe her own sexual antics. The New York Chapter of the National Association of Recording Arts & Sciences invited Tipper to a "debate" at which rock stars and other recording professionals spent the better part of three hours berating her. Tipper, clearly set-up, had nowhere to hide. The proceedings reached a low point when singer Wendy O. Williams (who has since taken her own life) asserted that Tipper feared her own child would masturbate because of offensive rock lyrics.

After the "debate," bad weather canceled Tipper's flight home. She spent the night alone in a hotel. "This was one of the worst nights of my life," she would recall.

The relentless criticism was getting to Tipper. Once babysitter Kristen Erwin found her sitting on her front lawn staring off into the distance. "What do you think of what I'm doing?" Tipper asked.

"I told her it was a good thing to give parents control over what their kids were listening to and that the attacks on her had been blown out of all proportion. One of the things I loved best about Tipper was that she never was down for very long. A few minutes later she was bubbly and happy again and ready to go on with the fight."

Soon Tipper's spirit had so recovered that she was able to undertake a book on the issue, *Raising PG Kids in an X-Rated Society*. The publisher was Abingdon, a Nashville outfit that specialized in books on religious subjects. She hit the tour circuit in the spring of 1987, appearing on the *Oprah Winfrey Show*, *The 700 Club*, and *Good Morning America*, just about the time Al, Jr., was ready to declare for the presidency. Tipper would later tell interviewers the timing of his decision had created one of the few professional conflicts during their marriage. She, of course, abandoned much of her book tour to help him campaign. As a result, she said, her book wound up selling 50,000 copies when, with her full-time involvement, it could have sold 250,000. But she was good-humored about it. Asked once why her husband was spending so much money on media consultants, she replied, "We're trying to get his name recognition up to mine." They also needed to square the circle of Tipper's anti-porn rock campaign with the Democratic Party's core constituency of civil libertarians.

October 1987 was a defining moment. Early that month, PMRC sponsored a symposium in Washington at which a number of health officials and experts, including Dr. C. Everett Koop, the surgeon general, warned that the graphic sex and violence depicted in music videos could contribute to adolescent suicide, Satanism, and drug and alcohol abuse. Koop said many videos "are a combination of senseless violence and senseless pornography to the beat of rock music."

But as PMRC notables pressed the attack, candidate Gore was trying to set up a meeting with Hollywood record producers to "clear the air." His intermediary was Mickey Kantor, an old Tennessee friend whose legal practice included many Hollywood clients. Finally, an October 28 meeting at the MCA executive dining room was organized by the chairman of MCA Records, Irving Azoff, television producer Norman Lear, and Don Henley, a former drummer with the rock group the Eagles. Both Gores were there as were thirty to thirty-five representatives of the recording industry. The meeting was closed to the press, but a covertly recorded tape was leaked to *Variety*, which published a lengthy account in its edition of November 3.

Both Gores sought to ingratiate themselves to the group by apologizing for the Senate hearings two years earlier. Mrs. Gore termed the hearings "a mistake... that sent the wrong message" to the entertainment industry. "We sent the message that there's going to be censorship and that's clearly not the case," she said. "In my testimony I said that I am not for government intervention, I am not for legislation. I understand that the hearings frightened the artistic community; if I could rewrite the script I certainly would."

Senator Gore agreed that the hearings were "not a good idea." He was opposed to them, he said, but as "a freshman minority member of the committee," he could not block the wish of the majority. "I did not ask for the hearing. I was not in favor of the hearing." The statement seems another example of Gore's penchant for rewriting history. At the hearing, when Chairman Danforth indicated it was Gore's turn to speak, the first words out of Gore's mouth were, "Thank you very much, Mr. Chairman. I would like to thank you and commend you for calling this hearing."

Next, Gore distanced himself from some of the more "extreme" measures his wife's activities had inspired. "I disavow the actions of many who are extreme. I don't agree with the Wal-Mart decision," he said, referring to the chain's removal of all rock magazines, including *Rolling Stone*, from its stores. "Any action that's ever a violation of the First Amendment, I will be there to say I disagree."

The rock heads would not let the Gores off so easily. Azoff said that if the Gores really opposed the actions of Wal-Mart, and anti-porn rock legislation in San Antonio (which banned "obscene" concerts) and elsewhere, it was not enough to whisper that at a luncheon. "[W]e blame you for all of it," he said. "If you can learn anything from what I'm saying, it's that just doing an interview and saying 'I don't agree with San Antonio' isn't enough. You need to get on a plane and go to San Antonio. If you can get on national television for a Senate hearing, someone from your organization's got to go to San Antonio and stand up before the City Council and say this is wrong. People are riding your coattails."

"Irving, just so you know," interrupted Danny Goldberg, the head of Gold Mountain Records, "in her book she praises San Antonio."

Goldberg would later blast the Gores for "posing as moderates trying to woo people whose livelihood they were attacking forty-eight hours before."

IRS Records chief Miles Copeland warned that the Gores were on a course that "is very destructive and stupid."

"If I was an advisor to Gore I would say, 'Get your wife off this and quick because she's a liability,'" he said.

Others were more charitable. Entertainment lawyer Lee Phillips, for example, said Mrs. Gore had been "very sensitive to points made by the artistic community."

Variety treated the meeting as an attempt by the Gores to appease the record industry, while, in the paper's trademark language, "polishing showbiz apple." After the get-together, Tipper, choosing her words carefully, continued to urge disclosure by record companies if the lyrics or the accompanying video material contained graphic sex or violence. She later included television programming and video cassettes as well. Years later, as vice president,

Gore would become involved in the V-chip effort permitting parents to block out programming they considered inappropriate for their children.

It is difficult to assess where all of this left the Gores in the eyes of Hollywood. During his own presidential race in 1988, Gore got precious little help from the record or film industries, but his late entrance and middle-of-the-road positioning were probably as responsible as his wife's anti-porn rock campaign.

In one campaign incident that must have left his rivals chuckling, Gore sought to organize a series of "Rock 'n' Roll Fundraisers for Gore" in his home state, but was embarrassed when several bands declined to play for the events. A member of the campaign press staff admitted, "They're afraid of alienating the record industry."

The controversy undermined Gore's campaign attempt to present himself as the John F. Kennedy of 1988—young, Harvard-educated, a war veteran, married to a beautiful woman, a former reporter who went on to serve in the House and Senate. But the buttoned-down Gore never connected with the baby-boomers. *The New Republic*'s Hendrick Hertzberg suggested the reason was that "the fuss over porn rock has turned this into a Tipper-ware party." The political pundit Michael Kinsley memorably called Gore "an old person's idea of a young person," and indeed, Gore's greatest strength was among voters in the forty-five and over category.

In a December 1987 interview with Marvin Kalb at Harvard, Gore said that his wife's "effort" was "to ask the entertainment industry to use its own standards to elevate its own products in recognition of a trend that has been speeding up whereby younger and younger children are exposed to increasingly explicit material." He suggested it was legitimate to raise questions about what Tipper had called "the strip-mining of our culture." He noted that a child growing up in the late 1980s would see 18,000 murders on television by the time he or she graduated from high school, and restated his concern about "the effect on very young children of messages that glorify brutality against women and violence throughout the society."

Of his wife's work, Gore said, "I am very proud of what she has done. I think we as a society ought to ask questions about how we raise children in this culture and pay more attention to elevating the awareness of us all about the messages that young children get."

But throughout the controversy Gore was never able to maintain that consistent theme. He again diverged from Kennedy in that he hardly showed the stuff of which "profiles in courage" are drawn. From the start, strong statements defining the stakes of the battle— like the Kalb interview—were juxtaposed with expressions of excessive deference to those exploiting the emotions, immaturity, and hormones of their target audience, insensitive to the tragic human and social consequences described by Dr. Koop, among others. However pernicious the adversary, Gore always seemed more concerned about mitigating the political backlash from Hollywood.

In recent years, Gore's relationship with Hollywood appears to have improved, but that clearly has been influenced by the fact that as vice president he has ridden the coattails of Mr. Clinton, whose relationship with Hollywood has been mutually admiring. By 1995, when Frank Zappa's widow, Gail, sought to contribute to the national Democratic campaign, her attorney advised her to deal directly with Peter Knight, Gore's former aide who was serving as national campaign manager. Through Knight, Mrs. Zappa donated a total of $240,000 to the DNC. The *Washington Post*'s Bob Woodward reported that when Mrs. Zappa met Gore during the campaign, she thought his suit made him "look stiff like a policeman." With her next $50,000 check to Knight, she included a note, saying, "Peter, can Gore get a new suit now?"

In another effort to ingratiate himself to Hollywood, when ABC's Ellen DeGeneres acknowledged on one of her weekly sitcom programs that she was a lesbian, Gore practically tripped over himself in his haste to praise her action, cooing, "And when the character Ellen came out, millions of Americans were forced to look at sexual orientation in a more open light." Within the year, however, Ms. Degeneres' "courage" had degenerated into a vulgar weekly spectacle that failed to rescue her sinking ratings—about the only "sin" recognized in the network creed—and ABC dropped the show.

As could easily have been predicted, neither the mild measures advocated by PMRC nor the Clinton-Gore V-chip to block offensive programs from one's television set has had the slightest impact on the nature of the material produced. The evidence to date suggests that use of these devices has failed to restrict in any meaningful way the access of impressionable minors to this inappropriate material. Porn rock and its various rap progenies continue to flourish. Exploitative sex and violence are omnipresent on television. And pornography has become so powerful that serious news journals marvel at its rising respectability and political clout, wondering only when the blue chip conglomerates of our era will find the courage to plunge into the field. Some business analysts predict that by the year 2000 pornography will be America's leading export.

If there is a way to halt or even reverse this trend it almost certainly includes the consistent, reasoned application of moral pressure directed at both the producers and consumers of pornography. A dozen years ago, if only for a fleeting second, and following his wife's leadership, Al Gore, Jr., acted as if he knew that. Now, with his heralded V-chip, he has taken refuge behind his all-purpose remedy: the technological fix.

CHAPTER TEN

THE CAMPAIGN OF "PRINCE ALBERT"

A L GORE, JR., wanted to be president. He thought 1988 would be a good year to run. But his ambition prompted no uncalculated leap in the dark. There were many things he did not know about running for president, but the one thing he did know was that it took a lot of money. He asked his friend, insurance millionaire John Hay of Hendersonville, Tennessee, to assess the prospects of raising enough to get a competitive race for the nomination under way.

Gore believed the Democratic field, headed by Gary Hart, Michael Dukakis, Richard Gephardt, and Jesse Jackson, was overloaded with doctrinaire liberals and vulnerable to attack from the political center which he—Gore—represented. The second tier—Paul Simon, Joseph Biden, and Bruce Babbit—were an unfrightening lot, while such potential heavy hitters as Sam Nunn, Bill Bradley, and Mario Cuomo had all chosen to await another day. Gore, moreover, did not feel that the Republican battle between George Bush and Bob Dole would produce an inevitable winner. And given the "Super Tuesday" concentration of southern state primaries, he thought it was possible to stake a claim to a large bloc of convention delegates.

But his hopes suffered a jolt when Hay came back with fundraising projections that failed to come close to the money Gore thought he would need to compete on Super Tuesday. So Gore took his staff off high alert. He telephoned his friend Mike Piggot of the *Nashville Banner* and told him he had decided against making the race. Piggot duly reported the information.

Then lightning struck in the person of Nate Landow, a Maryland land developer and veteran filler of Democratic war chests, whose personal wealth was publicly estimated to exceed $100 million. Together with men of equivalent means, Landow had formed a political action committee called IMPACT '88 which could easily generate the money needed to jump-start a presidential campaign. The members of IMPACT '88 had all been involved in the 1984 Mondale disaster and most, like Gore, were convinced the Democratic Party had to move toward the center or become a quadrennial laughingstock. Many in the group had already aligned themselves with candidates, but more than a dozen, including Landow, had not.

A strong-willed, sometimes overbearing man with alleged connections to gambling interests in his home state, Landow called Gore and offered financial support if he decided to run. Gore did not commit himself then. But a week later, Gore invited Landow to a meeting at the Capitol Hill apartment of his parents. There Landow assured him that he was ready to commit $250,000 to Gore's campaign and could line up at least a dozen other supporters. "I think the assurance of $3 to $3 1/2 million in the bank gave him a certain comfort level," Landow recalls.

Gore also received encouragement from longtime Democratic pollster Peter Hart, who told him the country would be receptive to a centrist Democrat. For more personal advice, Gore called Walter Mondale and Jimmy Carter to ask about the toll campaigning had taken on their personal lives. He was swept by a feeling of sadness as he contemplated long periods away from his son and three daughters. Later in the campaign, David Frost asked him when he had last cried. Gore responded, "I remember early in the morning, when I was very close to reaching the decision that I was in fact going to run, going to each of their beds as they were still sleeping, and thinking of each of them and the time that would be taken from them. That was the last time."

On April 10 Gore held a press conference in the historic Senate Caucus Room and announced his intention to form an exploratory committee "in preparation for my formal entry into the race later this spring." He said he would campaign "in every region of the country," in effect, a declaration that he was more than a Super Tuesday southerner. When a reporter—forgetting that Gore had celebrated his thirty-ninth birthday the previous week—asked whether at thirty-eight, his youth would be a problem, Gore replied, "If I were only thirty-eight years old I wouldn't even consider this." He added, "In the aftermath of eight years under President Reagan, the oldest president in our history—Americans may well decide as they did in 1960 that it is time for our country to turn to youth, vigor, intellectual capacity, and a determination to face the problems of the future with vigor and energy."

Gore's youth raised questions of whether this was a trial run or a run for the vice presidential nomination. Gore responded to the vice presidential issue bluntly. "I have no interest in it. I might well turn it down. I probably would. I have no interest in it. Vice President Bush will demonstrate again this year it is a political dead end."

Gore formally declared his presidential run from the steps of the Smith County Court House, but few members of the Tennessee congressional delegation were on hand. Not untypically, Gore had waited until the last minute to inform them, leaving many with unbreakable commitments. But his entire family was present. Albert Gore, Sr., had been ecstatic when his son broke the news. "I picked up the phone," he recounted, "and Al said, 'Dad, the word is go.' I yelled like a banshee Indian, I was so happy." At seventy-nine, he was still in good health and his mind was sharp. "I am running one flat-footed mile each morning," he told a Tennessee reporter. "I believe I have one more fight left in me."

But Al, Jr., had used the eleven weeks between his announcements poorly. The staff he assembled was no better than okay. His message was unformed. And his campaign strategy consisted only of hitting the Super Tuesday states hard.

"We were sophomores trying to play in a post-graduate game," recalls Roy Neel, the former *Nashville Banner* sports writer who would later become Gore's chief of staff, and Clinton's deputy chief of staff in the Clinton White House.

Gore's financial resources were limited, particularly early on, and his IMPACT '88 support fell far short of the help Dukakis got from Greek-American donors. Most of the more experienced political operatives were already claimed, and in some states, there were none to be had. Even across the South, Gore found that Representative Dick Gephardt—yet to surrender his credentials as a moderate—had muscled him out, already having claimed the best political organizers.

For his campaign manager, Gore found Fred Martin, a dark-haired, slightly built "B List" veteran of the Mondale campaign, then working in the Washington office of New York Governor Mario Cuomo. Gore, in Martin's view, proved to be a micro-manager of every aspect of the campaign, incapable of delegating any authority. Martin would come to see him as "a control freak" and recalls that when Gore was on the road, he would phone six to eight times each day. "It was soup to nuts. He was into every large issue, and every petty detail from Tipper's schedule, to car pools, scheduling, hiring, and thank you notes. He spent an enormous amount of time handling crap."

Martin maintains that the most fundamental public misconception about Gore is that he is superorganized and disciplined. "He is totally without discipline. He will put off the task of writing a speech and then pull an all-nighter like a college kid. The Carthage announcement with [speechwriter] Bruce Reed was a total nightmare. They were up until 6 AM working on it."

The speech itself was a bomb. Delivered from the steps of the Smith County Court House, this time with the audience well sprinkled with elected Tennessee officials, Gore scatter-shot his way through every cliché in the book. At first, he seemed to feel that Americans were still preoccupied with the by-then stale Iran-Contra scandal. "I seek this office to restore the rule of law and respect for common sense to the White House. Americans in every region and in both political parties have been shaken by the betrayal of public trust, the theft of public money, the shredding of public documents, and the dishonesty of public officials." In a Gore administration, he promised, "Any government official who steals from the American people or who lies to the United States Congress will be fired immediately."

Gore talked about arms control and the depleting ozone layer. He promised to achieve a 100 percent literacy rate by the year 2000, to strive for "perfectionism" rather than "protectionism," to join cities in battling crime and drugs, to fund "an affordable health care system," to "make new investments to achieve a cure for AIDS," to "confront threats to the environment," to "negotiate with the Soviet Union to end the threat of nuclear arms," and to "heal the divisions among Americans."

The speech said everything and, therefore, nothing. It defined nothing about Gore and his mission. One supporter complained that too much of what Gore had to say involved nuclear arms control and the environment, very difficult issues to sell during a presidential campaign. George Will labeled them "not even peripheral." Michael Kinsley wrote, "Gore's style of moderation is to go instead for issues that are 'difficult' in the sense of being obscure or complicated, but not contentious. Even Gore's greatest genuine political contribution—his promotion of the 'Midgetman' mobile single-warhead missile—has the flavor of high-minded nonideological cogitation." But Governor Ned McWherter, the self-described "redneck" who would recruit nearly all the southern endorsements that came Gore's way, saw the bright side. "You know the guy eating bean sprouts in California probably shook his head in agreement when Al talked about ozone," he said.

Gore's first major decision involved the scale of effort, if any, to make in the first two contests, the Iowa caucus and the New Hampshire primary. Both were critical to establish credibility in the big contests ahead, but he was running far behind in each. To start out with back-to-back wipe-outs could doom him in the Super Tuesday events.

"We had conflicting advice from different advisors, and a not totally well-grounded candidate hearing all these different versions of what he should do," Gore aide Roy Neel recalls. "It is almost impossible to determine how any of the critical decisions were made because there was no structure to it at the time."

Gore concluded that Iowa was lost. Gephardt, a Democratic Leadership Council moderate like himself, had moved left—partly to distinguish himself clearly from Gore and partly to appeal to the liberals who packed Iowa's Democratic party. While that might win Gephardt Iowa, Gore saw it has hurting Gephardt in other states.

"We saw Gephardt as having been pushed by his staff to flip-flop on a number of issues for short-term political gains, and it really wasn't doing him that much good," recalls Neel. "Al never forgot that. He thinks the worst thing you can do is flip-flop back and forth for opportunistic reasons. And he carried that view right into the White House. On the economic package, national security, and a lot of other issues, he would always urge the president to stick to his guns."

Gore decided to risk a strategic retreat from Iowa, with a statement that was typically grandiloquent. "There is something wrong," he declared, "with a nominating process that gives one state the loudest voice and then produces candidates who cannot even carry that state."* Later he would say that the nominating process "has pushed all our candidates toward a single, homogeneous view that is wildly exciting to a minority of Americans." On the stump, his most consistent message was that the Democratic Party could not win the presidency without winning the South and that he alone among those in the race could offer that hope. The comic strip *Doonesbury* responded by depicting "Prince Albert" in a Jack Daniels baseball cap saying, "Y'all wanna hear my coon dog call?"

With the withdrawal from Iowa, Gore began distinguishing his own positions from those of his "homogeneous" opponents. He maintained that he had supported the invasion of Grenada where the others were on record against it. He had backed the MX missile and the Midgetman, programs that had made possible the Reagan administration's "Zero Option" deal banning intermediate-range nuclear weapons. And he was opposed to a general nuclear freeze, arguing it would undermine nuclear stability. "If the Midgetman can lead to a more stable situation, then we ought to test it." Gore had also supported humanitarian assistance to Nicaragua's Contras, and endorsed air strikes against Libya.

Democrats, Gore claimed, had given the nation the impression they were against "every single weapons system that has ever been proposed." He portrayed himself as a more thoughtful internationalist. "When the Ayatollah Khomeni said he was going to slow down our access to 70 percent of the oil available to the free world," Gore said, "nobody else was willing to say that the navy had a right to keep the sea lanes open. Everyone else opposed that. I was the only one to support it."

But noting that Gore's record over the years was not all that different from the Democrats he was criticizing, Gephardt said, "Maybe the next debate should be between the old and the new Al Gore."

---

* Michael Dukakis would carry Iowa in the November election.

Still, the Democrats remained a dovish group. Gary Hart suggested during one debate that any money spent in Nicaragua be for the sole purpose of relocating enemies of the Sandinista regime. Jesse Jackson felt such aid should be administered by the Red Cross "instead of the Defense Department." Michael Dukakis suggested threatening to withdraw American troops from South Korea to Japan unless South Korea liberalized its regime, a proposal Gore called "wildly unrealistic."

At another debate Jesse Jackson asked for a show of hands "if you know someone who personally owns an MX missile." When no hand was raised, Jackson concluded, "We make more of what the world wants less of."

Gephardt wouldn't budge in his opposition to most of the big weapons programs. "Are we safer now than we were a trillion dollars ago?" he asked. Babbitt called Contra aid "nothing more than a slow motion soldier-of-fortune mentality."

At a Democratic Leadership Committee debate in Washington, Gore said the other Democrats on the platform had given the party a reputation for "retreat, complacency, and doubt."

"Let's not talk about each other the way Jeane Kirkpatrick and Ronald Reagan talk about Democrats," scolded Gephardt.

"I don't think it helps to be knifing each other," complained Senator Paul Simon.

"If you can't stand the heat, get out of the kitchen," Gore replied.

"There's no doubt Al threw some bombs early," Neel recalls. "You have to do that in order to get noticed. The alternative is to run the sort of 'nice guy' campaign Bruce Babbitt tried that year and wind up with no delegates but with everybody liking you."

Particularly grating to the others was the fact that Gore himself had supported a nuclear freeze in the past and had voted for sharp reductions in the Reagan defense budgets. He was against "Star Wars" and was tepid, at best, on the Contras. At a debate in

Dallas, Gephardt snapped, "Lately, you've been sounding more like Al Haig than Al Gore."

Gore said, "That line sounds more like Richard Nixon than Richard Gephardt."

Perhaps no one took Gore's blasts at the faltering Gephardt harder than Gephardt's campaign manager Bill Carrick. With his candidate obviously headed nowhere, Carrick's frustration showed when he was asked whether he looked forward to squaring off against the Gore team on Super Tuesday. "I can't wait," he said. "It's blood lust. Let me at him. I hate all of them. I think that they are the phoniest two-bit bastards that ever came down the pike, starting with Al Gore." Carrick later apologized. Eight years later he was allowed to run the Clinton-Gore reelection campaign in California.

*   *   *

In an interview with Gore at Harvard, Marvin Kalb probed for evidence of political courage. He asked whether Gore had been telling the American people anything "that has gotten them mad" or "changed their minds" on an issue. Gore replied, "Coming from a state with 100,000 tobacco farmers, it was not easy to tell them that 350,000 people die unnecessarily because of smoking each year, and then leading the fight for the toughest possible health warnings and measures where smoking is concerned."

At the Iowa debate Gore was asked for his opinion on the tobacco allotment program, a federally mandated and administered plan that restricts the acreage on which tobacco can be grown, thereby raising the product's price and making the plant a lucrative cash crop for tens of thousands of small farmers who either grow it themselves or sell their allotments to others.

Gore endorsed the program without reservation, as he had many times in previous years. "I strongly support the tobacco program as it is," he said. "As long as it's legal and is going to be grown and sold and that's the case now and is going to be the case, then of course we have the right to structure the marketplace and say the money that is earned growing tobacco should go to the small family farmers rather than to a few large companies."

Once down in North Carolina, Gore found many farmers as well as others in the tobacco establishment skeptical of him. He decided to address the tobacco issue again at Winston-Salem's toney Bermuda Run Country Club. This time, without retreating from his commitment to stronger warnings, he emphasized his emotional commitment to "small farmers, tens of thousands of whom find it possible to remain on the farm because they have that extra few thousand dollars each year."

"I tell you," Gore continued, "I've plowed the ground, put in the seed beds, I've planted it, hoed it, wormed it, suckered it, cut it, spiked it, put it in the barns, stripped it, and sold it. I know what it's about, how important that way of life is."

In both North Carolina and Tennessee, Gore found that he could say anything he wanted against smoking and could flail away at the tobacco companies to his heart's content with no political fall-out so long as he continued to protect and defend those who actually grew the plant. Years later, as a White House hawk in the battle against Big Tobacco, Gore told Clinton advisor Dick Morris, "I can only speak for Tennessee, but when I voted to require warnings on cigarette packs, everyone said it would be my political death, but I went out and explained, 'This isn't good for you. It especially isn't good for kids, and I think we should warn everyone about the health hazards.' I remember I gave that speech right in the middle of a small town in tobacco country, and they were all nodding their heads as I spoke."

At the 1996 Democratic Convention, Gore gave an emotional description of his sister's final hours before her death from lung cancer. The press, however, was quick to dig up Gore's comment on the virture of tobacco farming. Clearly there is some hypocrisy in a man who views those who sell tobacco as "killers" but those who grow it as worthy of subsidy and protection. But, in fact, there has been no substantive change in Gore's position from 1988 to 1996, or, for that matter, to 1999. To discourage young Americans from smoking, he has endorsed a variety of federal steps: strong warning labels, radical tax increases to drive up the price per pack, and providing the Food and Drug Administration with authority to regulate the nicotine content of both the plant and the product. At the same time, Gore knows the allotment regime effectively guaranties good prices for the small farmer and he purports to see no relationship between robust economic health for those who grow tobacco and cancer for those who smoke it.

*   *   *

As national attention began to focus on the Iowa caucuses, Gore made his second major tactical decision of the campaign—to suspend nearly all efforts in New Hampshire.

"In my view, that was the biggest mistake we made," says Neel. "We were behind there, but we had enough time to campaign in the state and pass a few of the stragglers. No one was going to beat Dukakis there. But we might have come in as high as third." It was, as was the decision to withdraw from Iowa, Gore's call. His advisors, both formal and informal, were divided in their counsel.

Gore finished last in Iowa, where Gephardt prevailed, and fifth in New Hampshire, won by Dukakis. Jesse Jackson was running stronger than expected. Hart was out. Biden quit. Simon was hanging on for Illinois. And Gore was banking everything on Super Tuesday, with its twenty state contests. But even some of his supporters were getting queasy. For example, Jerry Berlin, one of his moneymen in Florida, said that while everyone in IMPACT '88 could raise $250,000, "Gore should not expect the money to be on his desk in the morning." Rather, his backers "have to be motivated." Gore "must prove to be a successful candidate for the funds to begin to flow." There was the sense Gore had been doing a poor job at conveying who he was and why he wanted to be president. *Business Week* cruelly complained that Gore's "cloying, ultra-pasteurized persona seems more attuned to the Lawrence Welk generation of Democrats than to blasé Yuppies."

Few in the working press were very fond of Gore. Many of those assigned to his campaign saw him as "the school prefect, a self-important goody-goody who looked as if he'd been born in a coat and tie." It was during the campaign that what became a clichéd gag about Gore gained currency: How can you tell Al Gore from the Secret Service agents guarding him? He's the stiff one.

In counterpoint, Gore's Harvard mentor Martin Peretz at *The New Republic* endorsed his former student as the man with the clarity of vision and complexity of mind to set aright a country which, after eight years of Ronald Reagan, was "burdened by debt and driven according to a carefully calibrated calculus of regional conflict, class antagonism, and racial enmity." To Gephardt's "crude populism and unwarranted grievance," the magazine said, the Missouri congressman had "grafted on a xenophobia so ugly and so deluding that it reminds us of the disastrous 'America First' movement during the late 1930s." As for Dukakis, his sin was a "rigidity" that "derives from no great passion for ideas, no deep convictions about issues," but rather "an overweening estimate of himself."

*   *   *

Gore's first success was in managing to "steal" the Wyoming caucus, giving him at least a detectable pulse going into Super Tuesday. He could barely wait for the southern-dominated contest, telling one journalist, "Wham, we're talking about a third of the delegates right here."

"In hindsight, this campaign never really had a chance," Neel concedes. "We were not going to win in 1988. But Al Gore thought we were. At least, until the very end, he could see things break in a way that could wind up getting him the nomination."

As he campaigned across the South, Gore was aiming to attract the same people his father had needed in 1970: traditional, white, working-class Democrats who felt the party had gone too far left. Late in Albert, Sr.'s, day they had been known as "Wallace Democrats"; in Al, Jr's, "Reagan Democrats." To these folk Gore's pitch was regional and down to earth. He was one of them. He had been raised in their country, done the sort of work they did, and knew their problems. "I'm running to bring the White House back to the grass roots, to put it on the side of working men and women," he declared.

Virtually abandoned was all talk of the ozone layer or global warming, Gore's developing environmental *cause célèbre*. In one earlier debate, Gore had chosen to lecture on the subject, beginning, "This problem of the greenhouse effect is going to be one of the most severe environmental challenges we have ever faced in the entire history of humankind."

Jesse Jackson replied that "Senator Gore has just showed you why he should be our national chemist."

Gore wanted to provide his opponents with no more opportunities for that kind of stab. When his own pollsters persuaded him the issue was failing to register, he dropped it from his standard stump pitch. And while he would devote a later speech to a proposal banning the use of ozone-depleting chlorofluorocarbons, for the balance of the campaign environmental issues were accorded a lesser role.

And Gore did more than tone down his environmental views—he sold out the interests of environmentalists and his own state for a mess of North Carolina political pottage.

The issue involved a mill owned by International Champion Corporation in the Great Smokey Mountain city of Canton, North Carolina, which manufactured juice cartons, fast-food cups, and other white paper products. Since it had begun operations in Canton in 1908, Champion had been polluting the Pigeon River with some forty to forty-five million gallons of bathwater-hot toxic waste every day. The river developed a dark brown hue, the result of chemicals known as tanins and lignins that were released after 4,800 tons of wood chips were hauled daily into the mill and soaked with twenty-nine million gallons of water. The pulp was then bleached with chlorine before being made into the final paper products.

Above Canton, the Pigeon River was a crystal clear haven for rafters and trout fishermen as it wound its way among the green loblolly pines, sweet gums, beeches, and box elders. Below Canton it was, in the words of *Time* magazine, "transmogrified into a sludgy mess that looks like oily coffee and smells as bad as rotten eggs."

"Toxic chemicals have left the river filled with sludgeworms and deformed, mutant bottom feeders like suckers, stonerollers, and carp," reported *U.S. News* in 1988. "Fish in the area have been found to have nearly four times the level of dioxin—the active agent in agent orange—considered safe. The North Carolina Health Department years ago issued a warning against eating fish from the Pigeon River below Canton." On a cheerier note, local myth gave the chemical waters of the Pigeon River some awesome healing powers. "You throwed your dog in it and it cured the mange," declared one Canton resident. "Poison ivy and athlete's foot too," added another.

But it was the economic rather than the medicinal value of the Champion operation that commended itself to North Carolina officials. Champion in the late 1980s was employing about two thousand people from Canton and the surrounding Hayward County area, paying high wages in an otherwise poor community. Because of its economic importance and threats by the company to shut down if forced to meet stringent environmental standards, North Carolina traditionally granted the company a variance from the Clean Water Act of 1971. Under the act, Champion's effluent would have been measured in color units, with a reading of fifty required one-quarter mile downstream to satisfy clean water standards.

Champion's measurements were often in the hundreds, although in talks with the state and the Environmental Protection Agency (EPA), it had indicated it could do much better.

About thirty-seven miles downstream from Canton, the Pigeon River enters Tennessee. There, where local folks garnered all of the negative effects of the polluted water but few of the economic benefits of the plant, the variance had provoked bitter opposition. This was particularly true around Hartford, the first Tennessee town touched by the river. Not only was the Pigeon worthless for potentially lucrative recreational purposes, but *U.S. News* reported that residents had nicknamed the place "Widowville," because of the high incidence of premature deaths, particularly from cancer. While statistical support for any linkage was sketchy, and causality was never established, many locals regarded pollution by Champion as the culprit, and by 1987, residents had formed organizations like the Pigeon River Action Group and the Dead Pigeon River Council to demand change.

Convincing North Carolina to revoke its clearance seemed a nonstarter. Their real target was the EPA, which had the final say. But if the people of East Tennessee could rally environmentalists by the hundreds, Hayward County, North Carolina, could rally thousands of Champion supporters who claimed their livelihoods were at stake and took seriously the company's insinuations that excessive regulatory zeal could force it out of the area.

Enter candidate Gore. By late 1987 Gore realized that to wage an effective campaign in North Carolina he needed two things: the support of local political leaders, and money. Specifically, Gore desperately wanted the endorsement of Congressman James Clark, whose district included Hayward County, and the financial support of Wallace Hyde, a North Carolina stalwart of Landow's IMPACT '88 group. Late in 1987 Gore breakfasted in Johnson City with Representative Clark's son (who represented Champion), Hyde, and other political leaders. He then met at least twice with Champion officials. Shortly thereafter, Gore's congressional office put out a press release heralding Champion's willingness to curtail its pollution to eighty-five color units at the Tennessee state line. Gore termed the offer "highly significant," adding: "Hopefully, Champion's recent offer represents a breakthrough that will result in the final resolution of this difficult situation." Gore wrote the EPA conveying the offer.

Gore's close friend and ally, Governor McWherter, quietly assented to the deal, but environmentalists were furious. For one thing, the thirty-seven-mile "mixing zone" that would be accorded Champion was thought to be the most generous in the nation and would mean continued toxic waste for the downstream areas of North Carolina.

Second, the eighty-five units level was still above EPA standards. Indeed, EPA official John Marler announced that the terms contained in the Gore letter were not new and that eighty-five units had always been the starting point in EPA-Champion discussions. In other words, Gore's self-proclaimed "breakthrough" amounted to little more than political showboating, involving an offer already on the table. Further progress in the EPA-Champion negotiations would now be blocked for years. Gore's intervention emboldened the company to do no more, while the EPA was reluctant to challenge the famously pro-environmental Gore.

So Gore got his political payoff. Clarke endorsed him, his administrative assistant confiding, "If people say [Gore] flip-flopped, that's fine. We want him to flip-flop in our direction." One of Gore's local supporters conceded his candidate was tarnished "by the way he's been used as a political tool by Champion International and Jamie Clark."

In the weeks following his intervention, Gore would have no reason to think his political calculation had been wrong. On Super Tuesday night, his victories included both North Carolina and Tennessee and he marshaled his resources for the push that he hoped would win him the nomination.

CHAPTER ELEVEN

FAILURE

GORE'S CONFEDERATE battle flag was rising. As the returns poured in to his hectic, paper-strewn "war room" at Nashville's Opryland Hotel, he saw the possibility of victory across the length and breadth of the South. Exit polls gave him a shot at victory in as many as a dozen states.

The actual returns, while not that electric, were still good: outright wins in North Carolina, Tennessee, Kentucky, Arkansas, and Oklahoma. He also had Nevada and was running a strong second in five other states. Gore quickly gave bullish assessments of the night's work to network interviewers and scampered downstairs to the ballroom where a Dixieland band was playing "Rocky Top, Tennessee," and where Albert Gore, Sr., was telling reporters, "Sometimes I feel like jumping up and down and shouting hallelujah." Even before he reached the podium, political friends like Senator James Sasser and Representative James Cooper slapped his back, pumped his hand, and told him that he now had a real chance to capture the nomination.

Gore spoke to his supporters as though he had just won the nomination by acclamation. "There's no doubt about one thing—

this is a Super Tuesday. Today you and I launched a great cause. We're going to put the White House back on the side of the working men and women for a change." He told reporters his campaign would place ten thousand fundraising calls during the next forty-eight hours to make sure it had the wherewithal to build on the evening's momentum.

But on sober reflection, Gore's showing was no better than the third most important story of the evening. On the GOP side, George Bush had taken everything in sight, locking up the Republican nomination, and raising the question of whether the Republicans would sweep the conservative South no matter who the Democrats put up. Then there was Dukakis winning the vital southern bookends of Texas and Florida, the biggest southern states of all. And the large black vote in the South had gone overwhelmingly to Jesse Jackson. The bottom line was that southern Democrats had not spoken with one voice. They had spoken with three, maybe even four.

Following Super Tuesday Gore's initial plan was to focus on upsetting Dukakis in the mega-states of New York and California, skipping Michigan, Illinois, and Colorado. As tune-ups for New York, Gore would aim to win Wisconsin and Connecticut. In fact, Gore's campaign manager, Fred Martin, quietly made a deal with the Simon campaign to stay out of Illinois, in exchange for Simon skipping Wisconsin.

Albert Gore, Sr., hated the plan because he thought his son was a good enough candidate to fight and win anywhere. "You have the momentum now," he bellowed. "You can't claim to be a national candidate unless you fight it out in every state. If you demonstrate the will, you can do it."

"Including Illinois?" asked Al Gore, Jr.

"Especially Illinois."

Fred Martin was aghast. Illinois media would cost a fortune—and Gore's campaign didn't have it. Illinois also had two favorite sons in contention—Paul Simon and Jesse Jackson—with Dukakis well positioned to finish third. What's more, Simon would feel he had been double-crossed and would probably strike back by coming into Wisconsin.

Martin began making these points, but Gore cut him short.

"We're going to Illinois," he said.

"The obedient son," murmured Martin under his breath. Martin regarded it as "the worst big decision we made during the campaign."

Gore now needed money faster than his campaign could generate it. He approached banks and began taking out personal loans. As collateral he used projected donations and federal matching funds. The campaign tried to keep this secret, but a week or two after Gore's people denied the story to Mike Piggot of the *Nashville Banner*, Gore disclosed the information publicly, winning plaudits for his candor.

Gore's mistake in choosing to do battle in Illinois was compounded by the curious effort by old family friend Armand Hammer to intervene in the contest. After landing for a campaign stop at a small Illinois airport, Senator Simon was told Hammer had been trying to reach him. Returning the call, Simon was stunned to hear Hammer's voice at the other end of the line baldly offering the Illinois Senator the cabinet position of his choice in a Gore Administration should he choose to drop out of the race and endorse his junior colleague from Tennessee.

"Al had nothing to do with the call," says Neel. "He was always extremely sensitive about his father's relationship with Hammer."

But Al Gore Jr. had his own relationship with Hammer. Neil Lyndon, who ghost-wrote Hammer's memoirs and served as a consultant to Hammer during the mid-1980s, has written that "Hammer, his wife, his corporations and junior members of his family all made contributions to Gore's campaigns up to the maximum amounts allowable by law." Writing in London's Sunday Telegraph in 1998, Lyndon recalled that Hammer and Gore frequently met for lunch or dinner during Hammer's visits to Washington "in the company of Occidental's lobbyists and fixers," and that the Gores regularly attended Hammer's Glitzy Washington bashes. "Separately and together, the Gores sometimes used Hammer's luxurious private Boeing 727 for their own journeys and jaunts," Tipper taking advantage of one such flight to solicit money from Hammer for her battle against rock porn. Hammer was Gore's guest at the 1981 Reagan inauguration and used the Tennessee senator to obtain a favored place at the 1989 inauguration of George Bush.

Whatever prompted Hammer to intervene with Paul Simon on Gore's behalf, Simon angrily rejected the offer and won Illinois, edging Jesse Jackson, who the same day stunned everyone with his smashing victory in Michigan. Gore barely registered in either state.

After doing poorly in Colorado, Gore made half an effort in Wisconsin and managed to run a distant third. He did even worse in Connecticut.

Gore limped into New York, the third man in what was now down to a three-man field with Jackson still on Dukakis's tail. Without a strong showing here, Gore would no longer have a campaign. What followed was a spectacle at once so abrasive and pathetic as to make many question whether Gore would ever again be taken seriously as a national candidate.

Gore failed to win Governor Mario Cuomo's endorsement, but he did win that of New York City Mayor Ed Koch. Koch, however, brought nothing but controversy to Gore's campaign, as when he said Jews would be "crazy" to vote for Jackson.

"Everything in New York was a mistake," recalls Neel. "Dukakis was groveling for Koch's support but we were unlucky enough to get it."

Gore had made another mistake in hiring David Garth to mastermind his New York media campaign. Garth, who had helped run the media campaign of Yitzhak Shamir—the hardline Likud candidate who had just been elected Israel's prime minister—was a superhawk supporter of Israel. At Garth's insistence, Gore, in an act that can most charitably be described as reflecting political immaturity, aligned himself with Shamir's refusal to begin negotiations with the

Palestinians on "land for peace." The "land for peace" proposal was presented on the air by President Ronald Reagan and Secretary of State George Shultz. Thirty members of the Senate—all with strong records of support for Israel—had written Shamir, urging him to begin talks. Young Gore wrote his colleagues taking exception to their advice and paid a call on Shamir to emphasize his support. The move backfired, looking less like an act of political courage than of political pandering.

Gore was also responsible for discovering the "Willie Horton" issue, and as such, his fingerprints are on one of the smoking guns used by George Bush to dispatch the campaign of Michael Dukakis. The event was barely noticed at the time. During the New York campaign's final debate involving all three candidates, Gore noted that Massachusetts had a weekend prison furlough program and reported that while Dukakis was governor, two convicted murderers had committed additional murders while free on weekend passes. Then he asked Dukakis, "If you were elected president, would you advocate a similar program for federal penitentiaries?"

"Al, the difference between you and me is that I have to run a criminal justice system. You never have," Dukakis replied, evading the issue. Gore insisted on a response, but Dukakis—with the dull arrogance that became emblematic of his style—again temporized, and the debate moved to other questions. A Republican media consultant named Floyd Brown watched the exchange, and did the digging that resulted in the future newspaper and television ads about the paroled rapist-murderer Willie Horton, which Bush's campaign manager Lee Atwater used against Dukakis. Because Horton was black, critics denounced the ads as racist. But by then, Gore's role in raising the issue was forgotten.

Even at this late stage of the campaign Gore had yet to define himself. As Sidney Blumenthal wrote in the *Washington Post*, "The premise of Gore's campaign, above all, has been his unironic conviction that he will be president. His critics say he has wanted to be everything, but he has refused to fix himself as anything in particular for long. Gore has run as an antipopulist and a populist—also, at various times, as a conservative, a moderate, and a liberal."

By this time, several observers felt that Gore was merely harassing Dukakis, obstructing, in the words of columnists Jack Germond and Jules Witcover, "the only candidate who can save the party from either nominating Jesse Jackson or setting off the political chaos that would result if they passed over him." In the end, Gore won only 10 percent of the vote in New York, way behind Dukakis's 51 percent and Jackson's 37 percent.

Gore returned to Tennessee and announced he was "suspending" his campaign rather than formally ending it, thus permitting his delegates to attend the convention and participate in its deliberations. "I was doing great until I turned forty," he quipped.

"We set out to move the Democratic Party toward the center of American political thought," he continued. "We also spoke out for a new Democratic foreign policy based on standing up for American principles in the world and standing by America's friends.

"Our cause can be posed as a question: 'Will Democrats speak again as we once did for a majority of our countrymen and women, or are we destined to wander in dissent?'"

Several weeks after his withdrawal, Gore shared his assessment of why he failed to win with a reporter from the Scripps Howard News Service. "Money was a big factor," he explained. "This race this time around almost required you to raise $20 million to $30 million.... " Gore had managed to raise $10 million, which was, he acknowledged, no small accomplishment.

Most of those who worked for Gore felt no sense of final failure as his campaign ended. They were convinced he had the ambition and tenacity to fight again for the nomination four or eight years down the road. Most also saw Gore as a generally good man to work for. He was loyal to his staff and his friends. He seemed to care about the people around him. And his love for his family was genuine and deep. "You can have an open yet confidential and trusting relationship with him," Martin recalls. "But he is very temperamental. He can be warm and intimate one day, distant, cold, and critical the next. He will sometimes nitpick himself and the people round him. It can get tiresome."

And he is introspective. He can be, and was, analytical about failure, but deep down there was an emotional sense of having failed to fulfill an important obligation, of having not measured up to expectations, of having left that last big chore on father's list undone. He had lost a race for the presidency of the United States and turned forty at the same moment. Who knows? Maybe Bush or Dukakis would serve two full terms. Maybe 2000 would be his next real opportunity. He had to take stock of himself and where he was heading now.

But before that process began, Gore had a fairly narrow brush with the vice presidential nomination. Visiting home after suspending his quest for the office, Gore again disdained vice presidential suggestions, saying, "I'm not seeking it, and I have no interest in it." To whatever extent that statement was true when uttered, it did not at all reflect Gore's state of mind when the Dukakis camp let it be known that he was on a "short list" of vice presidential contenders that also included Gephardt, Representative Lee Hamilton of Indiana, and Senator Lloyd Bentsen of Texas.

Gore met twice with Dukakis, sessions that were devoted pre-eminently to strategy, key states to visit, issues to hit, weaknesses in the Reagan-Bush record to be exploited. Gore confided to friends he didn't think he was being auditioned as a possible running-mate; Dukakis, he thought, had already settled on someone else.

But both Gore and Tipper were interviewed by Paul Brontas, head of the Dukakis vice presidential search committee. They denied extramarital affairs. Gore assured Brontas that his "I smoked pot" disclosure earlier in the campaign was both accurate and complete and that he had not touched the substance since mid-1970. Asked whether she had ever seen her husband depressed, Tipper replied, "Yes, once... the night of the New York primary."

As for Nate Landow and his IMPACT '88 friends, there were

no regrets. "We felt good about what we did," he says. "We all developed a personal feeling for the quality of the man and his intelligence. He impressed us with his ability, his strength, his presence. We lost. But nobody was unhappy or disillusioned about their support of him once he got in the race."

The enthusiasm of Landow and other IMPACT '88 players was soon put to the test as Gore asked their help in retiring some $1.6 million in campaign debts. The group performed nobly. He found other sources too. Gore may have been a so-so political risk, but he was an excellent credit risk.

*   *   *

Early on the afternoon of Monday, April 3, 1989, Senator Al Gore, Jr., Tipper, and six-year-old Al Gore III settled into their box seats to watch Opening Day festivities at Baltimore's Memorial Stadium. The Orioles were matched against the Boston Red Sox. Gore and Tipper had become Red Sox fans during their years in Boston, occasionally making it over to Fenway Park to watch Carl Yastrzemski, Tony Conigliaro, Rico Petrocelli, and George Scott play. Now Yaz was gone and Mike Greenwell was in left field, while names like Burks, Rice, and Boggs had replaced the others. Roger Clemens was the pitcher starting for the Bosox against someone named Dave Schmidt. Baltimore had lost twenty-one consecutive games to start the 1988 season. They seemed a good bet to lose this first game too.

Had Gore's eyes wandered over toward the presidential box, he would have seen that President George Bush (on hand to toss out the first pitch) and his senior national security advisors—Jim Baker, Dick Cheney, and Brent Scowcroft—had been joined by Egypt's President Hosni Mubarak. Gore had limited respect for Bush and thought him fortunate to have escaped serious legal entanglement in the Iran-Contra scandal. But Bush had beaten Dukakis by stamping him as the orthodox liberal he was, exactly what he—Gore—had warned would happen during his own campaign.

Bush took to the pitcher's mound, his weak throw rescued by Oriole catcher Mickey Tettleton who rushed forward to grab it. The game itself was a thriller, going into extra innings. In the bottom of the eleventh, with one out and Tettleton on third, the weak-hitting Craig Worthington slapped a ball over the infield. Tettleton scored the winning run.

Walking among the excited fans after the game, Gore held his son by the hand as they navigated the parking lot. But the high-spirited six-year-old broke free, scooting into the path of a 1977 Chevy. With a terrifying crack, the boy's body was hurled thirty feet through the air. When he landed, he was scraped along the ground for another twenty feet before he rolled into a gutter. "I ran to his side and held him and called his name," Gore recalled, "but he was motionless, limp and still, without breath or pulse. His eyes were open with the nothingness stare of death, and we prayed, the two of us, there in the gutter, with only my voice. Slowly, painfully, he fought through his shock and fear and latched onto the words as a beacon to find his way back to the street, where others now gathered, including two off-duty nurses who, thank God, knew enough about the medical realities to keep him alive in spite of his massive injuries inside and out."

Gore had begun applying CPR before the nurses, Victoria Costin-Siegel and Esther O'Campo, came forward and took over. Then the ambulance arrived. The paramedics worked to stabilize the boy's condition, and he was rushed to John Hopkins Medical Center.

Young Albert, pale, the blood drained from his lips, but still conscious, was wheeled in through the wide doors of the hospital, his parents walking grimly beside his stretcher.

Dr. David Dudgeon, one of the hospital's leading orthopedic surgeons, was on duty for the case. Albert was immediately taken to surgery.

Albert's condition, Dr. Dudgeon reported, was critical but stable. He had second-degree burns on his arms and legs, crushed ribs, a bruised lung, a broken collar bone, a bruised kidney, and a ruptured spleen, which Dudgeon would try to save. He had also suffered a "closed head" concussion, which meant there was no internal bleeding.

The following day the Gores released a statement thanking those who had sent their good wishes to the family. "Albert faces a long, tough road before he's back to his old self," they said, "but he has a strong spirit and we have faith in God's healing grace." Gore placed his regular Senate schedule on hold, though he did return to the floor to vote in favor of increasing the minimum wage. The Gores' took a hotel room across the street in order that one or the other could be at the child's bedside twenty-four hours a day.

Four days later, a terrifying setback: the boy grew weak and pale. He was bleeding internally. His life was again in danger. Dr. Dudgeon determined the problem was the spleen and performed a splenorraphy, surgically removing more than half the organ, and repairing the remainder. But there were other complications to come. Albert's kidney was more than bruised—it was severely injured. His broken collarbone included nerve damage, requiring microsurgery and painful physical therapy. And a pin had to be inserted in his left leg, still in traction. Nonetheless, Dr. Dudgeon upgraded the boy's condition to "satisfactory" just over two weeks after the accident. On April 23, Albert was sent home. Later, skin grafts would be performed to repair the burned areas on his body.

Twice during young Albert's hospital stay Gore phoned his friend Nate Landow, saying he needed a break from the ordeal and wanted to have dinner in "Little Italy." They went to Sabbatinos. Landow recalls Gore's clinical assessment of Albert's treatment at the Children's Center and his optimism that his son would recover fully. "As you might expect, Al had also become as knowledgeable about the medical procedures involved as any non-doctor you will ever meet."

And Gore had made a big decision. He would devote more time to Tipper and the children. The presidency could wait. He would not be a candidate in 1992.

CHAPTER TWELVE

"EARTH IN THE BALANCE"

GORE HAS DESCRIBED his son's accident as the "catalyst" for his decision to begin work on *Earth in the Balance*, and some mythologists have pictured the hospital-bound senator working in a nurses' station on the pediatric floor, filling legal pad after legal pad with gifted prose while his son mended down the hall. While Gore did some minor scribbling in the room, his own "acknowledgments" make clear the writing process was considerably more complex, involving a staff-directed search for the right publisher and editor; an enormous amount of research and editorial guidance performed by everyone from an assistant named Yehudah Mirsky to the late Carl Sagan; elaborate chapter and subject area critiques volunteered by academicians and other friends and acquaintances; and some polishing on drafts that at times reached six hundred pages, apparently performed by anyone in Washington with a pencil and a few hours to spare. Gore wrote much of the book at his parents' Capitol Hill apartment.

Despite all the cooks, the stew is quintessential Gore, reflecting his philosophy, values, attitudes, biases, emotions, peeves, thought processes, and agenda. With the exception of those chapters where Gore ventures far beyond his depth to offer psychiatric and philosophic explanations for man's alleged abuse of the environment, the quality of writing does not fall too far behind Whittaker Chambers' brilliant *Witness*. As a work of psychological self-revelation, it is better than Richard Nixon's *Six Crises*; as a policy blueprint by someone on the cusp of supreme political power in this country it is *sui generis*.

Gore's own obsession with metaphors pulled from the era of Nazi Germany has led an unkind wag here and there to refer to the book as *Mein Planet*. Commentator Tony Snow, the former Bush speechwriter, has discerned a remarkable parallelism between the societal views of Gore and the crazed intellectual meanderings of Unabomber Ted Kaczynski. Closer to the mark, however, is the profound fiction of Fyodor Dostoyevsky. For it is the soul neither of the political totalitarian nor the social misogynist that is revealed in the pages of *Earth in the Balance*. It is the Grand Inquisitor.

Gore declares at once that his enterprise is partly cathartic. His son's brush with death has made him "look inside myself and confront some difficult and painful questions about what I am really seeking in my own life, and why." He sees the environmental crisis as a metaphor for his own unrest, "an inner crisis that is, for lack of a better word, spiritual." He sees hypocrisy in his life: the use of air conditioning in his car while heading for a speech on the danger chloroflorocarbons pose to the ozone layer, "my own tendency to put a finger to the political winds and proceed cautiously." He vows that he will now abandon this calculating approach. No longer will he practice "the failures of candor, evasions of responsibility and timidity of vision that characterize too many of us in government."

Gore begins the body of his book with a description of a visit to the Aral Sea in the former Soviet Union, now drying up because, to irrigate cotton-growing land, the government diverted the rivers that fed it. Ships rot in what is now desert. Local canneries use fish imported from Siberia.

This is one of many environmental catastrophes Gore enumerates: radioactive waste has killed millions of starfish in the White Sea. Dolphins have died in the Riviera and Gulf of Mexico and seals in the North Sea because pollution has placed them under too much "environmental stress" to resist viruses. Gore says the "hole in the sky" observed above the Trans-Antarctic mountains was produced by chlorine from chloroflorocarbons attacking the ozone layer. Rain forests cumulatively equal in size to the state of Tennessee are destroyed each year. There is evidence that global warming—a heating of the climate caused by the release of carbon dioxide and other "greenhouse" gases by the burning of fossil fuels—has already thinned the north polar icecap by 2 percent within the past decade. Other symptoms of global warming include the increasing number of days over 100 degrees Fahrenheit at various locations and "the new speed with which the sun burns our skins." Further, "this increase in heat seriously threatens the global climate equilibrium that determines the pattern of winds, rainfall, surface temperatures, ocean currents, and sea level. These in turn determine the distribution of vegetative and animal life on land and sea and have a great effect on the location and pattern of human societies."

Gore next dips into "chaos theory" to show with terms like "equilibrium," "disequilibrium," and "new equilibrium," how the process reinforces itself. Exemplifying this close cousin to Marxism—thesis, antithesis, synthesis—Gore urges that killing rain forests lowers the moisture content of the air, which means less rain, which means more dead trees. Carbon dioxide raises temperatures on the tundra, which melts permafrost, which releases methane, which is a far more potent greenhouse gas, which accelerates the warming process.

Gore maintains that "human civilization is now the dominant cause of change in the global environment." One reason is exploding population growth. It took from the beginning of time until 1945 for the world's population to reach two billion. Now it is over five billion and early in the next century it will reach nine billion. This has been coupled with the fruits of the industrial revolution, giving man an unprecedented ability to pollute the earth, and a dominant ethic that seeks to maximize short-term rewards rather than recognizing an obligation to save the earth for future generations.

In a chapter that foreshadows his political technique in mobilizing opinion behind his definition of the "crisis," Gore warns against waiting for proof before taking action. *"A choice to 'do nothing' in response to the mounting evidence is actually a choice to continue and even accelerate the reckless environmental destruction that is creating the catastrophe at hand."* Clearly Gore is targeting dissenters in the scientific community who warn that not enough is known about global warming to warrant massive changes in energy usage. That these dissenters include the likes of Richard S. Lindzen of MIT, and some of the most distinguished climatologists, is of little moment. Indeed, even if the evidence isn't all in, there is no excuse for delay. "Research in lieu of action is unconscionable."

Gore argues that a prime reason why nothing has been done is that the views of a minority of dissenters have been accorded far too much weight, particularly by the media that prefer "to emphasize controversy and disagreement. In this case, when 98 percent of the scientists share one view and 2 percent disagree, both viewpoints are sometimes presented in a format in which each appears equally credible." Somehow, to support that charge Gore manages to cite the church's persecution of Galileo. But Gore, of course, has his history garbled. Galileo was the minority skeptic. It was the 98 percent who were wrong.

Gore continues, asserting that global warming will likely produce rising seas and catastrophic flooding for the one-third of humanity that lives within sixty miles of a coastline. Thus, "we must act boldly, decisively, comprehensively and quickly, even before we know every last detail about the crisis," because "the climate changes that we are now bringing about by modifying the global atmosphere are likely to dwarf completely the ones that caused the great subsistence crisis of 1816–19, for example, or that set the stage for the Black Death."

Gore sees other problems, including the destruction of rain forests in South America and elsewhere, the accumulation of solid waste, and, of course, the vanishing ozone layer. He has heard of great schools of blind fish being identified in Patagonia. Surely this is related to excess doses of radiation they receive in their ozone-depleted environment.

But global warming is Gore's obsession. Global warming "threatens an environmental holocaust without precedent," he says. "Yet today the evidence of an ecological *Kristallnacht* is as clear as the sound of glass shattering in Berlin." Gore repeats the analogy many times. Indeed he declares the struggle against environmental abuse to be a "continuation" of the struggle against Nazi and Communist totalitarianism, "a crucial new phase in the battle for freedom and human dignity."

In part, he claims the problem is that "our economic system is partially blind." It sees the value of things like manufactured goods, food, and housing, but not "fresh water, clean air, the beauty of mountains, the rich diversity of life in the forest." It assumes that natural resources are limitless "free goods." Excluding the calculation of "bad things," like waste and pollution, "is similar in some ways to the moral blindness in racism and anti-Semitism."

Gore then devotes an entire chapter to "dysfunctional civilization." He cites with little critical comment the view of the fanatical "deep ecologists" who see humanity as the "pathogens" infecting Earth with an AIDS-type virus, global warming being the Earth's "fever."

Beyond that, Western civilization has produced a population of "addicts" whose addiction reflects "a continuing need for distraction from psychic pain." Gore says, "I believe that our civilization is, in effect, addicted to the consumption of the earth itself. This addictive relationship distracts us from the pain of what we have lost: a direct experience of our connection to the vividness, vibrancy and aliveness of the rest of the natural world."

The loss of rain forests, the ozone hole, the accelerated extinction rate for natural species, and global warming "suggest a violent collision between human civilization and the natural world." And those who refuse to endorse Gore's view of these events are "enablers," allowing the addictive pattern to continue.

Gore continues to play shrink, likening man's quest for psychic relief to psychoanalyst Alice Miller's well-known description of the "gifted child," who, deprived of unconditional parental love, seeks it in other pursuits—a condition many have seen in Gore himself. Yet another metaphor occurs to the author, the "dysfunctional family." Here Gore sees the personal relationship with God supplanted by an authoritarian father whose rules cannot be questioned. "It is not uncommon for one member of a dysfunctional family to exhibit symptoms of a serious psychological disorder that will be found, upon scrutiny, to be the outward manifestation of a pattern of dysfunctionality that includes the entire family."

Just when the reader thinks Gore has taken pseudo intellectual gibberish to heights of self-parody rarely achieved, Al the shrink becomes Al the *kvetch*. "[W]e have constructed in our civilization a false world of plastic flowers and AstroTurf, air conditioning and fluorescent lights, windows that don't open and background music that never stops, days when we don't know whether it's rained or not, nights when the sky never stops glowing."

Then it's back to the preferred Grand Inquisitor role. The root problem is that civilization has followed secular philosophers rather than the word of God. God's command to Noah was really, "Thou shalt preserve biodiversity." Religions make man an integral part of God's universe. The problem is with philosophers like Descartes, who urge "that human beings should be separate from the earth, just as the mind should be separate from the body, and that nature is to be subdued, just as feelings are to be suppressed." (One would think that Descartes, credited as the father of modern science, ought not so lightly to be libelled.)

Gore takes the reader on what might be called a "tour de farce" of several of the world's religions, seeking to establish that the spiritual link between man and nature, now under assault by modern American consumerism, is a fundamental part of man's heritage. He attributes a lyrical passage to the American Indian, Chief Seattle, expressing reverence for the sky, the land, "the freshness of the air and the sparkle of the water," but omitting the rather salient point that scholars long ago concluded that Chief Seattle never uttered any such words.

Gore made use of his association with Asian American fundraiser Maria Hsia to obtain some research material on the relevant cosmology of Buddhism. He reports that in the *Lotus Sutra*, "Buddha is presented metaphorically as a 'rain cloud' covering, permeating, fertilizing, and enriching 'all parched living beings, to free them from their misery to attain the joy of peace, joy of the present world and joy of Nirvana....'"

He also quotes Hindu doctrine to the effect that "the Earth is our mother, and we are all her children," which is followed by what one critic called "a tedious, blathering screed in praise of the doctrine of Earth Goddess Worship."

Gore is chippy about modern science. "But for the separation of science and religion, we might not be pumping so much gaseous chemical waste into the atmosphere and threatening the destruction of the earth's climate balance." (Critics suggest that but for the separation of science and religion, we would still be teaching that the sun revolves around the earth.)

Plato is another Gore villain because he is said by the author to have believed intellect somehow stood above the world, while the good Aristotle declared the earth, through man's senses, to be the source of all thought. Gore again trashes Descartes for distancing intellect from nature with "I think, therefore I am." And Sir Francis Bacon is judged no less guilty because he divorced science from religion. Bacon, Gore says, held that facts derived from science had no moral significance; on the other hand, only "moral knowledge," the distinction between good and evil, was the appropriate realm of the church. (At least one Bacon scholar has criticized Gore for grossly distorting the views of Sir Francis, who believed that man must seek to understand nature in order to control it for his ultimate betterment.)

Of course, Gore—as the Almighty's agent—is not beyond infusing his own modern judgments of good and evil into his presentation. Good are those members of the environmental "resistance," who have "taken the fight for the environment from the scientific journals and symposia to their own backyards and from there to corporate board rooms and the halls of Congress." Evil are those industry lobbyists representing the manufacturers and users of fossil fuels and other environmentally damaging products, "self-interested cynics... seeking to cloud the issue of the environment with disinformation."

Then the Holocaust again. He recalls that in describing Adolf Eichmann, Hannah Arendt employed the term "banality of evil" to depict the thousands of tiny bureaucratic acts that, divorced from any considerations of the overarching moral horror, helped organize and execute the Holocaust. Gore condemns those who methodically go about their ways of work and life, doing things that add up to destruction of the environment. Presumably Gore's indictment now embraces everyone from the oil field roughneck, to the service station attendant, to the soccer mom piling kids into her gas-guzzling minivan, for their roles in the environmental holocaust he has described.

Gore urges that with the Cold War over, the United States should think of environmental protection as the supreme strategic issue and make it "the central organizing principle for civilization."

Steps must be taken to stabilize the world's population. The government should subsidize "environmentally appropriate" technologies and penalize those that despoil the environment. The internal combustion engine should be phased out within twenty-five years. Governments must develop new ways of measuring their national products to account for environmental degradation of one form or another. International treaties must be developed to require states to protect the earth and its climate. A global Marshall Plan must be developed transferring environmentally appropriate technologies to the third world, helping them to achieve stable population growth and sustainable economic progress. And the world's population must be educated to the important task at hand.

Gore also proposes a dozen or so micro measures, ranging from the government using its purchasing power to encourage the development of environmentally safe products, to the creation of a new FDA-type agency that would review new technologies, guaranteeing large profits for new "safe" ones. This or a related agency might clamp new export controls on environmentally unfriendly technologies.

Gore has acknowledged that writing the book was a form of catharsis, helping him come to grips with the changes and disappointments in his own life. Invoking yet another metaphor, he compared his life to a sandpile. "A sandpile will grow until it reaches the critical state. If the slope is greater than the critical value—the supercritical state—then the avalanches will be much larger than those generated by the critical state. A supercritical pile will collapse until it attains the critical state."

His son's near death, the losing primary campaign, and other events had pushed his life to the supercritical state. "But change came cascading down the slopes of my life, and I settled back into what had felt like maturity before but was now fuller and deeper. I now look forward to the future with both a clearer sense of myself and of the work I hope to do in the world."

Earth in the Balance was certainly the most influential book written by a working American politician, at least since Barry Goldwater's ghost-written, low-brow manifesto, *The Conscience of a Conservative*. *Earth* sold half a million hardback copies, made Gore the most prominent environmentalist on earth, and helped win him a place on the 1992 Democratic ticket, putting him in a position to nudge the world in a direction that led in 1997 to the Kyoto Treaty on global warming. By any reasonable standard that is a lot of mileage for a book pathetically one-dimensional in its view of Western civilization, shabby in its ignorance of economics, simplistic in its approach to problem solving, and grandly certain of a crisis that has not been proved to exist—despite a massive scientific effort funded by the U.S. government to the tune of more than $2 billion a year.

One place to start a critique is with Gore's complaint about the rapid growth in world population. Exactly why did it grow from 2 billion in 1945 to 5.5 billion in 1992 when *Earth in the Balance* was published? Could the answer be the very "dysfunctional civilization" Gore spends most of his book despising? Is this the same civilization that has added decades to human longevity by conquering epidemics, drastically lowering infant mortality, and multiplying food production? And had Gore even glanced at the performance of North America and Western Europe in the years since 1945, he would have seen purer air, cleaner water, and far more trees, despite civilization's "dysfunctional" state.

On the other hand, his visit to the Aral Sea should have alerted him to the record of a powerful centralized government bureaucracy appropriating to itself the role of supreme environmental arbiter. Indeed, one of the Communist apparatchiks' favorite arguments to peasants against the existence of God was that no Supreme Being could be so perverse an idiot as to make the Russian rivers flow north into the Bering Sea rather than south into the nation's more parched regions, a situation they proposed to correct, with the kind of results

Gore witnessed. Even as *Earth in the Balance* was being written, a reunited Germany was in the process of dismantling the smoke-belching, coal-burning, steel-making behemoths that were monuments to centralized planning in the Communist-run German Democratic Republic. And while on the subject of centralized government planning, Gore might have looked more closely at the destruction of rain forests in places like Brazil and Indonesia where government policy, and subsidy, is compounding if not creating the problem.

Gore's assault on the separation of science and religion is so utterly brainless that the reader is almost forced to believe the senator was trying to articulate something other than the plain meaning of his words. His hero, Galileo, was persecuted by those who believed science and religion were one. Does Gore really seek to cast his lot with the flat earth crowd? The folks who would imprison, even kill a man who concluded the earth revolved around the sun? His fellow Tennesseans who prosecuted the teacher Scopes for instructing his class on Darwin? Surely, one hopes, Gore had a far milder message in mind, a message about a God who instills reverence, love, respect, decency, integrity, charity, and humility into his subjects, but does not dictate permissible and impermissible investigation.

Gore's diatribe against everything from air conditioners to AstroTurf smacks more of a nostalgic anti-modernism than reasoned analysis. Yet the world of horses and buggies was no environmental nirvana. As John Hood observed in the Fall 1995 *Policy Review*, a single horse produces about forty-five pounds of manure each day. Before the automobile, massive amounts of manure collected on city streets presenting equally massive problems of air and water pollution. Cities had a big job disposing of this waste, not to mention the 15,000 carcasses of horses that died each year in turn-of-the-century New York.

Hood also recalled one British writer's description of London in the mid-1880s: "It is a vast stagnant swamp, which no man dare enter, since death would be his inevitable fate. There exhales from the oozy mass so fatal a vapor that no animal can endure it. The black water bears a greenish-brown floating scum, which forever bubbles up from the putrid scum of the bottom."

Hood further reminded Gore that much of the improvement in agricultural productivity is due to the chemicals environmental activists like himself tend to condemn out of hand. "Even today herbicides and pesticides make fruits and vegetables cheaper and more attractive. One study by Texas A&M University researchers found that without pesticides potato yields would drop 50 percent, orange yields by 55 percent, and corn yields by 78 percent. Prices for these commodities would rise tremendously without pesticides."

Another critic of Gore's work, philosophy professor James G. Lenox, wrote: "Life lived in submission to the natural forces of climate and disease, lived without labor-saving technology, without the fruits of sophisticated agricultural techniques, and without modern medicine is, to borrow a phrase from... Thomas Hobbes, 'solitary, poor, nasty, brutish, and short.' To be 'alienated' from nature in *that* sense is, if human life is the standard of value, a supremely good thing."

Surveying Gore policy recommendations in the *Yale Law Journal*, economist Robert W. Hahn called them "an incredible laundry list which could easily result in central planners selecting environmentally and politically correct products and technologies. It is nothing less than environmental socialism." While Gore recommends photovoltaic cells, wind-generated energy, and the like, he fails to test these ideas against the reality of cost-effectiveness and the economic law of supply and demand. Indeed, an understanding of a market economy seems completely beyond his appreciation.

But if Gore's treatise was ignorant of economics, his scare scenario on global warming also came under attack from qualified and credible scientists. While no one doubted that levels of carbon dioxide and other greenhouse gasses have increased, there is a great deal of uncertainty about the extent of global warming this produces.

Records maintained by the United Nations Intergovernmental Panel on Climate Change show that over the last hundred years (1890–1990) world temperatures have risen by only .45 degrees Centigrade—far *less*, by at least half, than what most global warming models would indicate. And some of that temperature increase might be attributable to other factors. For example, several scientists claim that because cities are warmer than rural areas, urbanization produces "heat islands" that lead to higher readings. Moreover, much of this century's warming occurred *before* 1940. Between 1940 and 1965 global temperatures actually went *down*. Indeed, by the 1970s some scientists were warning about another ice age, and one leading British science writer, Nigel Calder, predicted in his book, *The Weather Machine*, that at least two billion people would die as a result of global freezing, with such nations as Ireland, Great Britain, the Scandinavian countries, and Switzerland becoming uninhabitable.

The mid-1970s initiated another warming trend, but given previous temperature fluctuations, the sort of alarm sounded by Gore seems wildly excessive.

There was also profound disagreement as to the effect of a modest temperature rise. Rather than the shattering windowpanes of *Kristallnacht*—Gore's metaphor for environmental catastrophe—many global-warming skeptics could hear the future clinking of champagne glasses as citizens toasted bumper crops of wheat, splendid new trees, plants that had never before grown quite so far north, and winter nights that were slightly warmer and more often frost-free than those they recalled from years gone by. Trees and plants might benefit not only from warmer weather and increased rainfall producing a longer growing season, but also from an environment richer in carbon dioxide. According to the U.S. Department of Agriculture, ten of the eleven years prior to 1997 have set new records for the combined global average yield of corn, wheat, and soybeans combined.

Neither in *Earth in the Balance* nor any time since have Gore or those scientists echoing his cause made a case that could stand the test of peer review linking global warming—actual or projected—to a material worsening of hurricanes, droughts, floods, or other adverse weather conditions. There would certainly be winners and losers, places where the growing season got longer, others where desert areas increased due to drought. But the droughts would be fewer. To whatever extent it happens, global warming is expected to take the form of slightly milder winter temperatures at night in the northern latitudes accompanied by more evening clouds and slightly higher levels of precipitation. But even here there is doubt. For example, temperature records of the last fifty-five years have discerned no significant warming at either pole.

From all indications, Gore had yelled "Wolf!" when there may well have been nothing worse than a tame old dog in the field. But unlike the lad in Aesop's fable, the senator from Tennessee had enlisted a veritable army of shepherds willing to scream that they too could discern the beast. At one university gathering, for example, Claudine Schneider, then a congresswoman from Rhode Island, blurted out, "Scientists may disagree, but we can hear Mother Earth and she is crying." Perhaps, but public policy requires a firmer foundation than that.

Still, Gore was in a good position to generate such support. As chairman of the Senate Subcommittee on Science, Space and Technology, he had control over the funding for NASA as well as any number of research budgets. He was articulate on the issue. And, of course, he could stack committee hearings with the witnesses he found most persuasive.

Gore held his first round of hearings on global warming in 1981, when environmental activists were still defrosting from the Ice Age scare. Gore was ahead of his time, and few environmental activists were eager to campaign against fossil fuels when the logical alternative was nuclear power. But the hot summer of 1988 fired the issue anew. In testimony before Gore's subcommittee, James Hansen, director of the Goddard Institute for Space Studies, said he was "99 percent certain" that global temperatures had increased.

In 1990 the Intergovernmental Panel on Climate Change (IPCC) issued its first Working Group assessment of the issue, predicting substantial warming and a rise in sea levels by the end of the next century. The prediction was hedged because it was based on large-scale computer modeling rather than projections derived from the past century's experience. One poll of the participants found many did not share the pessimistic projections.

Still, more than any other event, the IPCC report, cautiously worded and filled with caveats, was seized upon by Gore and his minions to "prove" scientific consensus that global warming had occurred, would increase, and that the consequences would be bad if not disastrous. But a Gallop poll showed that 53 percent of the scientists sampled believed that no global warming had occurred to date while another 30 percent weren't sure. Another poll commissioned by the activist organization Greenpeace reached similar conclusions, and a panel commissioned by the National Research Council concluded that the facts did not yet justify costly actions. A subcommittee of the National Research Council panel predicted the United States would have little difficulty adapting to any climate change that did result from enhanced carbon dioxide levels.

Nevertheless, global warming was, as MIT meteorologist Richard Lindzen noted, the perfect cause for activists advocating: "energy efficiency, reduced dependence on Middle-eastern oil, dissatisfaction with industrial society (neopastoralism), international competition, government desires for increased revenues (carbon taxes), and bureaucratic desires for increased power." Gore continued to use subcommittee hearings and "round tables" to assert that dissenters from his global warming views were eccentrics, energy industry whores, or both. Even prior to publication of his book, his own writing had described the problem in near apocalyptic terms. In a *New York Times* op-ed piece for Earth Day 1990, he described global climate change as "the single most serious manifestation of a larger problem: the collision course between industrial civilization and the ecological system that supports life as we know it." The problem was "drastically changing climatic patterns that affect the distribution of rainfall, the intensity of storms and droughts, and the direction of prevailing winds and ocean currents which in turn drastically affect our weather and climate." Dissenters were issued the sternest of warnings: "As you make your choice, bear in mind that you're choosing not only for your own generation but for your children and grandchildren as well. And remember too that our abuse of the environment could lead to the eradication of more than half of all species within the lifetimes of our children."

Never had a more dire prognostication rested on flimsier evidence. But Gore's op-ed piece was noteworthy for something that has been a consistent feature of his work in the area: the utter refusal to consider the cost of action needed to ameliorate the stated danger and to balance that against both the cost of the danger and the likelihood of its occurrence. In the *New York Times* Gore blandly assured skeptics that some elements of a solution would actually save money—for example, ending subsidies for logging operations on federal lands, as though that exceedingly modest measure would correct "the collision course between industrial civilization and the ecological system that supports life as we know it."

At the time Gore was beginning to publish his views, economist William Nordhaus of Yale was arguing that "those who argue for strong measures to slow greenhouse warming have reached their conclusion without any discernible analysis of the costs and benefits...." By the time Gore as vice president was trying to force his policies upon the world, his utter failure to consider the costs versus the benefits of his proposed action undermined support for his approach even among economists at the Clinton White House.

At the senator's hearings, dissenters always found themselves outnumbered, and Gore's questions to them were often hostile. In background sessions, the press was urged to treat dissenting academics as practitioners of "junk science." Classic was the case of Sherwood B. Idso, the much-published scientist with the U.S. Water Conservation Laboratory in Phoenix, who had been conducting the world's longest continuous carbon enrichment study. Idso described how he had planted eight sour orange trees, enriching four with an additional 300 parts per million carbon dioxide while otherwise maintaining identical conditions between them and four control group trees. After eighteen months, the trees exposed to additional carbon dioxide were 2.8 times as large and bore ten times the amount of fruit as the control group trees. Idso concluded that if the nation slightly expanded its forests and continued to make its use of fossil fuel more efficient, "nature itself will protect us from the possibility of significant global warming, while at the same time receiving considerable benefits of its own."

Gore mobilized his Praetorian Guard of carefully selected scientists and struck a blow himself by asserting that a film Idso had made on the beneficial effects of carbon dioxide on trees and plants had received its funding from the coal industry.

Gore: "Just for the record, your film, which has been widely circulated by the coal industry and by OPEC, was financed by the coal industry. Is that correct?"

Idso: "It was."

Gore: "And it was made by a company which you established on the side? Is that correct?"

Idso: "It was—it was helped to be made by a company which I established on the side but which I haven't been associated with for about a year now."

Gore: "I see. Who's the head of that company, for the record?"

Idso: "My wife."

Among many of Idso's fellow scientists, the session at which he provided testimony became known as "The Inquisition," with Gore the chief inquisitor. But while Gore attacked Idso's motives, Idso's actual findings—that increased levels of carbon contribute to more luxurious plant growth—were never seriously challenged. According to the University of Arizona's Robert Balling, "What Senator Gore could not disprove, he sought to discredit."

Gore had far more difficulty discrediting the views of another dissenter from his apocalyptic view of global warming, Dr. Roger Revelle, his professor at Harvard and lead-off witness to Gore's first-ever hearings on global warming in 1981. Revelle had done more than anyone else to call attention to rising levels of carbon dioxide in the air, but he considered its impact on global climate difficult to predict with confidence and argued that since both the problem and solution required carefully nuanced understanding of the stakes, years of further study should precede costly societal adjustments.

Revelle did not lose his composure during the hot, dry summer of 1988, by which time he had spent several years as professor at the Scripps Institute of Oceanography in La Jolla, California. In an exchange of correspondence with Representative Jim Bates regarding whether the lengthy heat wave represented man-induced climate change, Revelle wrote: "Most scientists familiar with the subject are not yet willing to bet that the climate this year is the result of 'greenhouse warming.' As you very well know, climate is highly variable from year to year, and the causes of these variations are not at all well understood. My own personal belief is that we should wait for another ten or twenty years to really be convinced that the greenhouse effect is going to be important for human beings, in both positive and negative ways. From this belief I conclude that we should take whatever actions would be desirable whether or not the greenhouse effect materializes. A transition to nuclear power and development of publicly acceptable means for water and energy conservation are actions of this type."

It is not that Revelle discounted the likelihood of some warming. But unlike Gore, he saw no cataclysm in the offing. While he knew that warming could pose some challenges, Revelle also saw some potential benefits. With far more political sophistication and intellectual restraint than his former student, he recognized that draconian measures to solve the problem via some grand international design simply would not work. For example, coal may be the biggest carbon-generating culprit. But neither Russia nor China—who own 50 and 15 percent of the world's reserves, respectively—would likely display much enthusiasm for restricting coal. Nor, for that matter, would the United States, with 25 percent of the world's reserves. Indeed, with the prospect of warming making at least part of the Siberian tundra suitable for trees and agriculture, the Russians might be in favor of global warming.

In a July 1988 letter to Senator Tim Wirth, Revelle also noted that solving the problem "will probably require a great deal more use of nuclear energy as a substitute for fossil fuel." He added that simply expanding the world's boreal forests as the climate warms "could reduce carbon dioxide emission very drastically, to a quite safe level."

Yet another project urged by Revelle: "Sequestration of organic carbon in the deep sea by stimulating spring phytoplankton production in high latitude oceans." Years after his death, scientists continue to urge consideration of this method of expanding the "carbon sinks," essentially creating organisms to absorb large amounts of the compound.

In 1991 Revelle, joined by University of Virginia scholar, S. Fred Singer and Chauncey Starr, founding director of the Electric

Power Research Institute and winner of the 1991 National Medal of Technology, published an article in the inaugural issue of *Cosmos*: "What to Do About Greenhouse Warming: Look Before You Leap." The article, which was distributed by the Cosmos Club to its three thousand members, noted that despite agreement on the increase of carbon dioxide in the environment, "There is major uncertainty and disagreement about whether this increase has caused a change in the climate during the last century. There is also disagreement in the scientific community about predicted future changes as a result of further increases in greenhouse gasses."

Revelle and his colleagues discussed the strong possibility that modest global warming and increased carbon dioxide would offer certain benefits to humanity such as extended forestation in northern regions, and argued that many scare scenarios had little scientific documentation. "It is the extreme climate events that cause the great ecological and economic problems: crippling winters, persistent droughts, extreme heat spells, killer hurricanes and the like. But there is no indication from modeling or from actual experience that such extreme events *would* become more frequent if greenhouse warming becomes appreciable." The three scientists warned: "Drastic, precipitous—and, especially, unilateral—steps to delay the putative greenhouse impacts can cost jobs and prosperity and increase the human costs of global poverty without being effective."

Revelle, who had a history of heart problems, died in July 1991 in his early eighties. His views, as expressed in the *Cosmos* article, generated no public discussion until they became the centerpiece of an article by *Newsweek*'s Gregg Easterbrook in *The New Republic* of July 6, 1992, and of later columns by George Will and other commentators, including Richard Lesher, president of the U.S. Chamber of Commerce. In addition, the initial article was accepted by Dr. Richard Geyer of Texas A&M for republication in a collection he was editing entitled, *A Global Warming Forum: Scientific, Economic, and Legal Overview*, published by CRC Press.

Gore could not possibly attack the memory of a man he had heralded as his personal guru on the subject. So he and his staff set out to discredit Revelle's co-authors, claiming they had misrepresented his views while coercing him into being identified as their co-author.

Shortly after the Easterbrook article appeared, Dr. Justin Lancaster, a former Harvard research associate who was close to Revelle, received a personal telephone call from Gore inquiring about Revelle's mental capacity in the months before he died and whether the *Cosmos* article accurately reflected his views. Gore suggested that Lancaster, perhaps joined by other scientists, write a response to the Easterbrook article. Gore also worried about republication of the article in book form.

On July 20, 1992, Lancaster, at Gore's prodding, phoned Singer and unsuccessfully attempted to browbeat him into removing Revelle's name from the CRC republication of the *Cosmos* article. During the exchange, Singer insisted that Revelle had been intimately involved with the article's preparation over the better part of a year and had been responsible for several changes in the text, signing onto the final version in a meeting at his California office.

Despite this conversation, Lancaster drafted a letter to *The New Republic* denying Revelle's co-authorship of the article, raising questions as to whether it represented his views, and saying he had not been interested in authorship, but "later assented only reluctantly, yielding to personal pressure from the authors."

In striking contrast to these allegations, in a July 20 draft of a cover letter addressed to Senator Gore, Lancaster stated, "Roger was mentally very sharp to the end. Also he was not casual about his integrity.... It is probably fair to say that Roger thought about and probably agreed with the overall thrust of the article...."

In a deposition taken as part of a later libel suit filed by Singer, Lancaster claimed he never sent the letter to Gore, but did send it, along with a draft of his *New Republic* letter, to Anthony Socci, a

Gore staffer on the Senate Commerce Committee. Kathleen McGinty, a member of Gore's personal staff, also received *The New Republic* draft. She recommended that Lancaster not deny that Revelle co-authored the piece, since he quite clearly allowed his name to go on it. A toned down version of the letter eventually appeared in *The New Republic*.

Egged on by Socci, Lancaster wrote a letter to Singer attributing to him the statement that Revelle had not approved republication of the article. On August 7, 1992, Singer responded to the Lancaster letter, saying that any suggestion Revelle did not want his name on further publications was "completely incorrect." Said Singer, "I did not make such a statement, Roger never made such a statement; nor did such a matter ever come up in our discussions."

But Lancaster wasn't finished. On August 17, 1992, he wrote Geyer, the Texas A&M editor, charging that "Roger was not eager to be a co-author on the Singer paper" that Singer had pressured him into lending his name to the enterprise, and that Revelle was "uncomfortable" with the piece.

In an October 20 letter to Ms. Helen Linna and Ms. Barbara Caras of Boca Raton, Florida, both of whom were associated with CRC Press, Lancaster insisted, "The article erroneously, and perhaps unethically, bears the name of Roger Revelle as co-author."

Later that month, he again wrote Ms. Linna stating Revelle was not an author of the *Cosmos* article which was "misleading and unscholarly," and that subsequent to Revelle's death, "Singer ambitiously distributed the article and has sought republication in a singular attempt to undermine the pro-Revelle stance of Senator Al Gore, Revelle's former student."

The notion that the *Cosmos* article—which never mentioned Gore's name—was directed against Gore was absurd. In 1990, when the three co-authors decided to undertake the project, Gore's book, *Earth in the Balance*, had yet to be published, and his selection as the Democratic vice presidential candidate was two years away. The

Easterbrook *New Republic* piece, published more than a year after the *Cosmos* article, did contrast Revelle's views with those of his former student. But even those who see conspirators behind every grassy knoll would have trouble making the "Singer-Easterbrook-Peretz" axis work.

Then Socci weighed in. In a four-page letter to Robert Grant, president of CRC Press, dated October 27, 1992, Gore's staff assistant stated: "To put it bluntly, in my opinion Fred Singer, and to some extent, Chauncey Starr, had clearly set out to discredit Senator Gore, as well as Senator Gore's concerns regarding emissions and the threat of global warming, having prevailed upon, and unconscionably misused the late Roger Revelle in the process, at a time when Revelle was extremely ill and fragile, hardly a license for inclusion in this volume." Despite his full-time status as Gore's man with the Senate Commerce Committee, Socci identified his affiliation as "Dept. of Paleobiology, Smithsonian Institution," an honorary association.

Singer had also been invited to speak at a Roger Revelle Memorial Symposium held in Cambridge on October 23 and 24. He told the chairman he intended to circulate for discussion Revelle's *Cosmos* article. In a later libel suit against Lancaster, Singer alleged that Lancaster pressured those running the program to withdraw his invitation to participate and halt plans to disseminate the article. Lancaster prepared a paper of his own entitled, "Uncertainty About the Uptake of Excess Atmospheric CO2: Value to Decision Makers." In it, Lancaster alleged:

> Revelle did not write the *Cosmos* article and was reluctant to join it. Pressured rather unfairly at a very weak moment while recovering from heart surgery, Revelle finally gave in to the lead author, S. Fred Singer, who was a fellow Cosmos Club member. Singer has since distributed the article quite ambitiously; because it bears

Revelle's name it is being used for the purpose of undermining the environmental position of Revelle's former student, Al Gore.

On April 16, 1993, Singer sued Lancaster, claiming five counts of libel. His underlying claim was that Lancaster knew Revelle was a willing, knowledgeable co-author of the article, which was based in part on his own former writings.

On April 29, 1994, the lawsuit was settled prior to trial. Lancaster signed a statement saying, "I retract as being unwarranted any and all statements, oral or written, I have made which state or imply that Professor Revelle was not a true and voluntary co-author of the *Cosmos* article, or which in any other way impugn or malign the conduct or motives of Professor Singer with regard to the *Cosmos* article (including but not limited to its drafting, editing, publication, republication, and circulation)."

It would appear that if there was any conspiracy, it came not from scientists eager to discredit Al Gore, but from Al Gore's staff eager to discredit the politically inconvenient but honest findings of eminent scientists.

CHAPTER THIRTEEN

SETTING THE STAGE

AL GORE WAS A RELUCTANT warrior in the Persian Gulf crisis. Fresh from a reelection prance in Tennessee where, in an assertion of political health, he had spent $2.6 million while a sacrificial Republican lamb spent a mere $10,000, Gore had yet to emerge fully from the period of introspection following his son's accident. The boy was well on the road to recovery, but the senator continued to anguish over how his life should reflect the perspectives gathered during the ordeal. He was still working on his book about how civilization was abusing the environment, still holding hearings on global warming and other subjects of personal interest. At the same time, he confided to friends and a handful of journalists that his driving ambition for higher office had been blunted by a desire to spend more time with his loved ones. "All these things that had loomed so large," he would say, "not only in my daily life but in my whole set of priorities suddenly didn't amount to a hill of beans."

He was still touched by the "outpouring of empathy and compassion" from people whose paths he had crossed on Capitol Hill without ever getting to know—"people who ran the elevators at the Capitol and the subway car from the Senate Office Building to the

Capitol, police officers, janitors, secretaries, staff in the Senate."
These were people who "had, in many cases, gone through experiences worse than the one my family had gone through and were carrying these heavy burdens in their hearts, without giving any indication outwardly that I had picked up—partly because I wasn't paying attention."

Yet Gore could not escape the fact that he had established himself during the 1988 campaign as a leading moderate voice on national security issues as well as a contender for the 1992 nomination. His position on Iraq would be watched closely. His credentials in the area had been underlined in 1988 when he twice took the floor to condemn the failure of the Reagan administration to take a strong stand against Iraqi dictator Saddam Hussein's use of chemical weapons, once against Iran, and a second time against Halabja, a Kurdish village in the northern part of his own country. Gore had wanted Reagan to call for a special United Nations session to consider the matter. "I deeply believe that if this episode is allowed to stand," he said, "then governments contemplating the use of chemical weapons will conclude they may do so with impunity."

Whatever Gore's emotional state, Iraq's invasion of Kuwait would be an impossible issue to duck. President Bush was clearly moving toward war against Saddam Hussein. The president had painstakingly built an alliance of traditional European friends and Arab states worried about Iraq's aggressive designs. Further, he had won unanimous support from the United Nations Security Council for an economic and military embargo against Iraq and was now working to win authorization to expel Iraqi forces by "any means necessary" should Baghdad fail to withdraw from Kuwait by January 15, 1991. Bush maintained that he did not require congressional authorization to launch such an attack, but most on Capitol Hill believed he would seek such authority if he thought the resolution would pass both houses.

By November, Bush had made it clear he intended to build up

American troop strength in the area to 400,000—the number American military commanders said they needed to oust the Iraqis.

Gore sat on the Senate Armed Services Committee, which became the fulcrum of debate on the issue. Its chairman, Sam Nunn of Georgia, had built his power on a foundation of peer respect for his knowledge, competence, and integrity. Long regarded as a pro-military conservative, he had moved toward the center in recent years partly out of frustration with President Reagan's lavish military spending, and partly to broaden his appeal within the Democratic Party. Sam Nunn wanted very much to be president.

As Nunn saw it in late November, Bush was either heading for premature war in the Gulf or his actions made no sense at all. Nunn wanted to give the embargo more time to sap Iraq's military and economic strength. The CIA was saying that while the embargo was among the most effective in history, it could still take a year or more for Iraq really to feel the pinch. It was absurd to think U.S. forces could sit in the desert that long. The jerry-built coalition would come apart at the seams. Thus, the Bush administration was painting itself into a corner where the choices would be: fight now or fail. Bush had further raised the propaganda stakes by visiting American troops in Saudi Arabia and announcing that Iraq could not be allowed to become a potential nuclear threat.

Against this backdrop, Nunn began his hearings on U.S. military options in the Gulf. They could easily have been subtitled, "Hawks for Peace." One after another, some of the more prominent Cold War-era hard-liners warned the committee against the early resort to war in the Gulf. Admiral William Crowe, Colin Powell's predecessor as chairman of the Joint Chiefs of Staff, declared that initiating combat would fracture America's newly cooperative relationship with the Soviet Union. Moreover, the Arabs "would deeply resent a campaign which would necessarily kill large numbers of their Moslem brothers...." The best course would be for the United States to stick with the sanctions. "It would be a sad commentary if

Saddam Hussein, a two-bit tyrant who sits on seven million people and possesses a gross national product of $40 billion, proved to have more patience than the United States, the world's most affluent and patient nation," said Crowe.

Retired Air Force General David Jones, another former chairman of the Joint Chiefs, also opposed early military action. "My main concern with this latest scheduled reinforcement," he said, "isn't that we might choose to fight but rather that the deployment might cause us to fight, perhaps prematurely and perhaps unnecessarily."

And so went the parade of defense specialists carefully orchestrated by Nunn and his able chief-of-staff, Arnold Punaro. Former National Security Agency chief William Odom wondered whether the U.S. had sufficient stocks of smart munitions, and warned, "I don't think an air campaign can drive Iraqi forces from Kuwait."

James Webb, Reagan's former navy secretary, opposed military action as did Edward Luttwak, the self-styled Clausewitz who had parlayed the thinnest national security resume into the most expansive portfolio of presumed expertise. Luttwak criticized the Bush administration for "rushing into the Persian Gulf with boyish enthusiasm and no calculation of its interests in 1990 conditions."

Even Henry Kissinger, as bold outside of government as he had been cautious when inside, described the options available as "a series of 51-49 types of decisions." Kissinger did, however, come down on the side of military action because he believed that even if the embargo worked, the cagey Saddam would enter a series of dilatory negotiations rather than simply withdraw his forces.

There was good reason to believe that the dovish views of many government alumni reflected the views of senior colleagues bound by duty to support their commander-in-chief. Senator James Sasser, Gore's colleague and longtime Tennessee ally, had called Colin Powell aside at a social event and asked for his candid opinion of Iraq's army. "They're about as good as a pretty good NATO division," Powell had replied. That did it for Sasser. Kuwait wasn't worth the cost.

Gore apparently shared the reservations of his fellow liberal Democrats, who wanted to give the embargo more time. He worried that American troops were hunkering down for a costly, long-term commitment.

Gore endorsed the view of James Schlesinger, another hawk-turned-dove, who had held cabinet posts at the Pentagon, the CIA, and the Department of Energy. In an astonishing bit of poor analysis, Schlesinger told the committee the United States had three vital interests in the Middle East: the flow of oil, the security of Saudi Arabia, and the survival of Israel—none of which had been threatened by Iraq's invasion of Kuwait. "Iraqi withdrawal from Kuwait was not a vital interest on August 2," he said. "Bush has made it so." But, he added, "I do not think that it is necessary to achieve that objective for us to use force." Schlesinger predicted a military assault on Iraqi positions could result in "several tens of thousands" of U.S. casualties.

Gore joined Schlesinger's critique of the Bush administration. "Initiating a wide-scale offensive," Gore said, "could result in the deaths of thousands of American soldiers. That course of action also risks destroying the fragile international alliance that is united against Iraqi aggression and making the situation in the Gulf one of Iraq versus the United States."

"Instead of eliminating troop rotation and adding huge numbers of American forces, the president should be displaying American staying power for the long haul," he maintained. "It is American determination to make the economic sanctions work over a long period that is more likely to impress Saddam Hussein."

Gore also took a poke at President Bush's claim that he had the power to initiate war without congressional authorization. "I find it incredible that the president feels the need to obtain UN approval

for a U.S. offensive but won't commit himself to seeking congressional approval," he said.

Senator Nunn chalked Gore up as a likely ally, as did Senate
Majority Leader George Mitchell. The two Democrats co-spon-
sored a resolution demanding delay.

On November 29, the UN Security Council gave Bush the
green light to use force. In the House of Representatives, Bush had
wide support. In the Senate, the issue was closer. Two Republicans,
Mark Hatfield of Oregon and Charles Grassley of Iowa, might
defect. But Sam Nunn's coalition had surprisingly little support
among his fellow southerners with Alabama Senators Richard
Shelby and Howell Heflin, Florida Senator Bob Graham, and
Louisiana Senator John Breaux ready to support the White House.
Mr. Bush seemed safe.

With Secretary of State James Baker about to meet with Iraqi
Foreign Minister Tariq Aziz in Geneva in a last ditch effort to head
off hostilities, and votes of support assured in both houses, Bush, on
January 8, formally requested congressional action on a resolution
authorizing the use of force patterned on UN Security Council
Resolution 678.

The measure was considered during three days of somber
debate on the floors of both houses. Senator William Cohen of
Maine, who supported the resolution, spoke for many when he
called the vote "an hour of doubt, an hour of destiny." On the House
side, Charles Bennett and Sam Gibbons, who had voted for the 1964
Gulf of Tonkin Resolution that initiated the Vietnam War, said they
would each vote "nay." In the Senate, Sam Nunn's speech against
the resolution was interrupted by anti-war demonstrators chanting,
"No blood for oil."

Al Gore addressed his colleagues on the final day of debate. He
would later tell this reporter that he had agonized over the vote and
that it had been the most difficult one of his life. Nunn had done his

best to persuade his junior colleague of the merits of the position taken by a majority of his party. Nunn said a vote for delay was not a vote to foreclose the military option, but rather to give the embargo a chance to work. Senator Mitchell, on the other hand, said the issue was simply one of standing up for the principles of the Democratic Party. It was a time for party unity, not individual positioning.

On the floor, Gore recalled watching "when men and women from my home town in Carthage, Tennessee, joined the units of many other towns across this country, leaving their loved ones, saying goodbye to husbands and wives and children and parents preparing to become part of this army now massed in Saudi Arabia." At that point and even during the hearings, "I felt that I would support a move to continue the sanctions and hold open the option of force at a later time."

But, after the Baker-Aziz meeting in Geneva came to naught, "I found myself feeling that if I voted for the Mitchell-Nunn resolution I would do so hoping that it would not prevail." Even then he was tempted to vote for it, knowing the resolution favored by the president would pass. But, now, "I've come to the conclusion that I must cast my vote on the assumption that the view I express with that vote will become policy."

Most of the rest of the statement heaped criticism on President Bush for being slow to recognize the danger posed by Saddam, for incompetent diplomacy during the days immediately preceding Iraq's invasion of Kuwait, for failing to describe honestly the purpose of the build-up in the Gulf, and even for exaggerating the potential nuclear capabilities of Iraq.

But enactment of Mitchell-Nunn, effectively postponing military action until August, would require the withdrawal of up to half the troops now on the ground in Saudi Arabia. "I think the overriding effect of that withdrawal," Gore said, "would be to make it extremely unlikely that sanctions would then result in Saddam

Hussein's withdrawal from Kuwait or his overthrow in the near future."

"The risks of war are horrendous," concluded Gore. "The real costs of war are horrendous. Mr. President, what are the costs and risks if the alternative policy does not work? I think they are larger, greater, and more costly."

The final Senate vote was 52 to 47 for the Resolution. Ten Democrats broke ranks to support Mr. Bush. Among them, only Joseph Liebermann of Connecticut and two Nevada Democrats, Harry Reid and Richard Bryan, came from states outside the old Confederacy. And among the ten, only Al Gore, Jr., was considered a potential presidential contender in the coming cycle.

His vote, then, deserves to be recognized as an act of conscience and moral courage. The vote carried some potential benefits, but also great risks. If military action succeeded the credit would go to George Bush's leadership, not Al Gore's. If military action failed, the Democratic Party would likely discard him for higher office. Had he voted the other way, following the party line, he could have safely hidden behind the caution of expert opinion.

Nunn was noticeably cool in the weeks following the vote, and Mitchell would barely speak to him for months. But if the war went well, Gore's party would need him as a shield against political reprisal. And Gore's vote had shored up his standing among both southerners and supporters of Israel.

Outside Congress, potential presidential candidate Governor Mario Cuomo of New York was opposed to the use of military force, while in Little Rock, Arkansas, Governor Bill Clinton provided a response for the ages: "I would have voted with the majority, if it was a close vote, but I agreed with the arguments of the minority," said the governor. Put that in your pipe, but don't inhale it.

Even before the first American aircraft took off for Baghdad on the evening of January 16, some political analysts were already writing that Nunn had suffered the kind of fatal political lapse that spells death for presidential aspirants. Not only had he lost a critical vote on defense, but he had done so because his fellow southern Democrats had not trusted his judgment. As it turned out, they were right.

The war went well. American casualties were lighter than the "best case" scenarios. What even the most optimistic American analysts had not fully realized was that most of the Iraqi divisions were substantially understrength and that the "elite" Republican Guard units, rather than coming to the rescue of front-line forces, would turn and run for Basra or Baghdad. Their ultimate mission was the protection of Saddam Hussein and his Ba'athist regime. Defending the annexation of Kuwait was a task for conscripts.

As allied forces surged through Kuwait, the Iraqis fled north toward Basra along what would be called the "Highway of Death." Like George Bush, Colin Powell, Brent Scowcroft, and millions of other Americans who had seen the carnage on television, Al Gore believed enough was enough. There was no need to crush Iraqi forces further, or to chase after Republican Guard units, or to try to depose Saddam Hussein. Gore supported limiting the objectives of U.S. forces. As early as January 31, 1991, he had said on the floor of the Senate, "Let me be clear, then, about what we want. The removal of Iraqi forces from Kuwait is enough to warrant a suspension of combat operations."

For a brief period after the cease fire accord, a number of Republicans, most likely with active White House encouragement, tried to turn Democratic opposition to the war into a big political negative. Even before the results of the war were clear, Texas Senator Phil Gramm, a Republican and presidential aspirant, was seeking direct mail contributions to fight the "appeasement-before-country liberals." Mississippi Republican Thad Cochran emerged from one White House meeting to declare, "The fact of the matter is most of the Democrats voted to the left of the United Nations," while, after a similar session, House Minority Whip Newt Gingrich said, "You know, if Norm Schwarzkopf had to report to the Democratic Congress, we'd still be unloading the first five tanks and debating over which way they should point."

President Bush's popularity topped out at an unprecedented 87 percent. Sam Nunn's torch was so low, he would not even run for reelection to the Senate. Other potential presidential candidates— Congressman Dick Gephardt of Missouri, Senator Jay Rockefeller of West Virginia, Jesse Jackson, Dukakis's former running mate Lloyd Bentsen of Texas, and New York Governor Mario Cuomo— thought Bush was unassailable.

But the sense of political euphoria at the White House was short lived. Within weeks of the cease fire, Shiite and Kurdish uprisings against Saddam Hussein were crushed, with the plight of the Kurds in northern Iraq drawing elaborate media coverage.

The White House would provide emergency relief to the Shiites and Kurds, but nothing more. The break-up of Iraq and its absorption by Iran and Turkey was in the strategic interest of neither the United States nor its friends in the region.

By early September, Saddam began what would become a cat-and-mouse game with UN inspectors. Already they had found and dismantled a secret nuclear program, scores of Scud missiles, and an elaborate chemical weapons program. But as the inspectors continued to dig, Saddam responded with evasions, threats, and harassment. The defeated dictator began to thumb his nose at the UN and the United States.

Gore's stature as the tough Democrat now freed him to strike a few blows of his own. Asked by CNN's Larry King whether he thought President Bush had pulled American forces out too soon, Gore replied, "I do. I think General Schwarzkopf's advice was sound. I don't think we should have left Saddam's regime in place." Forgotten was Gore's own January 31 statement on the Senate floor: "The removal of Iraq forces from Kuwait is enough to warrant a suspension of combat operations."

To Larry King, Gore said, "We should have bent every pol-icy—and we should do it now—to overthrow that regime and make sure that Saddam Hussein is removed from power." And Gore had no shortage of silver bullets. "I'm not calling for a reinsertion of ground units into Iraq. I think we can remove this regime from power by a variety of other means. I think we ought to give assis-tance to those elements inside Iraq who are opposed to Saddam."

Of course, relying on groups with little organization, no national political base, few weapons, and no proven military capa-bilities to overthrow entrenched totalitarian governments is an ideal way to humiliate yourself as a major power, enshrine your adversary as a national hero, and get a lot of people killed. But since none of that ever comes to pass on "Larry King Live," "Nightline," or "This Week," Gore was safe out-hawking the Bush administration. Six years into their own administration, Clinton and Gore would have emptied their bag of patent remedies for getting rid of Saddam, but the Iraqi dictator would still hold power.

*   *   *

In August, 1991, Gore announced he would not run for presi-dent or vice president in 1992. "After my son's accident two years ago," he said, "and the amount of time I have been spending with him and my family, I didn't feel right personally taking myself away from them as much, as often as I know from past experience, that a presidential campaign requires."

There were other factors as well. He had scant support among Democrats—and therefore, potential financial support—finishing last among all contenders with 8 percent in one major poll.

"I think a properly run campaign would have an excellent chance of winning next year," Gore said. "I think people are most concerned year in and year out with the issues here at home, and I think the economy, quite frankly, could dominate the election cam-paign next year."

Gore's announcement came just as an attempted coup against the Russian government of Mikhail Gorbachev collapsed. Bob Squire, Gore's old friend and media consultant, noted the timing and said, "Two things happened today: Gorbachev and Clinton were liberated."

*   *   *

The first concrete sign that the Democratic nomination might be worth having came in November, 1991, in Pennsylvania when Democrat Harrison Wofford, a former Peace Corps official and college president, defeated former Governor and U.S. Attorney General Richard Thornburgh in a special Pennsylvania election to fill the seat of the late Senator H. John Heinz. Wofford had tapped into blue collar resentment against stagnant wages and rising unemployment, and had made an issue out of the need for a national health insurance program. He had begun the campaign about as far behind Thornburgh as any recognizable Democratic contender had been against Bush.

But it was only Arkansas Governor Bill Clinton who seized that momentum and survived both the allegations of Gennifer Flowers that she had a long-standing affair with Clinton, and the discovery that he had cynically evaded the draft and had smoked, but not inhaled, marijuana. Clinton's theme was "change," which allowed him to pick off support from both the left and the right of the Democratic Party.

Gore had spent the better part of the winter and spring selling his book and watching the campaign with some fascination. Questioned about the Gennifer Flowers story that began with her paid article in the supermarket tabloid, *The Globe*, Gore told interviewer Larry King, "I have a lot of respect for Bill and Hillary and their family, and I don't have any respect for the paper that the rest of the press is quoting in this whole matter." The American people, he said, "would like to see the issues discussed in this campaign.

We've got a recession. We've got a global ecological crisis. We've got unemployment rising."

During the coming campaign and throughout his vice presidency, Gore would earn praise for his loyalty to Bill Clinton, and Clinton would demonstrate enormous generosity in delegating authority to the vice president. Yet when it came to issues of character, Gore never went beyond the rather tepid endorsement of this preassociation response. Not during Whitewater, nor the campaign fundraising scandals, nor the myriad "bimbo eruptions"—including the Monica Lewinsky affair—did Gore once say, "I know Bill Clinton. I know Bill Clinton's character. And the Bill Clinton I know would not do that." Always, it would be: The president has said this. I believe the president. Other things are what are really on people's minds. So let's get on with the nation's business.

King also asked Gore about the Number 2 spot on the ticket. "Well, I have no interest in being vice president of the United States," Gore replied. "I'd like to be president," said Gore, "and I may never have a better chance to run than the one I passed up this time. I understand that clearly, but even if that's the case I'll not have second thoughts."

Gore soon received a call from Warren Christopher, the future secretary of state and head of a team appointed by Clinton to interview possible vice presidents. They met on May 12 for just under an hour, and talked about Gore's views of other candidates, including Florida's Senator Bob Graham, who apparently headed the field. Christopher also asked Gore whether he would consent to go on the list of possible vice presidents. Gore said he needed to think about it.

*   *   *

While Clinton had been winning the Democratic nomination, Gore had been sparring with the Bush administration on global warming. The president's Council of Economic Advisors had reviewed the literature, met with a variety of climatologists, and concluded in 1989 that "there is no justification for imposing major costs on the economy in order to slow the growth of greenhouse gas emissions." Yet the White House continued to support the UN's effort to impose a global solution to an uncertain problem.

The next major international forum would be the United Nations Conference on Environment and Development (UNCED) in Rio de Janeiro, Brazil, in June 1992. Maurice Strong, the Canadian businessman designated secretary general of the conference, noted that two of the conference's major issues would be developing a strategy to combat global warming and conserving "biodiversity," partly through the "environmentally sound management of biotechnology." That meant that UNCED was a political disaster in the making for the Bush administration, which both needed to support the UN, while frankly doubting that global warming was a serious problem and being opposed to heavy regulation of biotechnology. One of the administration's top critics would be Al Gore, who attended the conference as the official representative of the Democrat-controlled U.S. Senate.

Why did Gore seek to criticize and embarrass his own country's government in an international forum? The only answer is that Gore saw bigger issues at stake. The late political scientist, Professor Aaron Wildavsky of Berkeley, provided a possible motive when he suggested that global warming was "the mother of all environmental scares." In Wildavsky's view, "Warming (and warming alone), through its primary antidote of withdrawing carbon from production and consumption, is capable of realizing the environmentalist's dream of an egalitarian society based on rejection of economic growth in favor of a smaller population eating lower on the food chain, consuming a lot less, and sharing a much lower level of resources much more equally." In other words, the threat of global warming led naturally to the prescriptions of *Earth in the Balance*, prescriptions that, in Gore's view, were good for mankind regardless of the reality of the threat. Global warming made them more urgent, but they were always necessary.

The Rio Earth Summit attracted 180 countries, 40,000 participants, 9,000 journalists, and 100 heads of state. Secretary General Strong called it "the most important conference in the history of humanity." A member of the U.S. delegation termed it a "circus." Environmental Protection Agency Administrator William K. Reily, a personal embodiment of George Bush's campaign vision of a "kinder, gentler" America, led the U.S. delegation.

Altogether, 154 nations, including many not present in Rio, signed the Framework Convention on Climate Change—essentially a nonbinding commitment to roll back carbon dioxide emissions to 1990 levels by the year 2000. The United States declined to sign, saying that a rollback of that scale would have meant a 60 percent reduction in projected fossil fuel usage by developing countries, while China, India, Brazil, Indonesia, and Mexico inevitably expanded their use of oil and coal.

Neither did the United States sign the Convention on Biological Diversity, which committed wealthier nations to provide financial support to poorer ones in an attempt to save plant and animal species threatened with extinction. The reason was one provision requiring unwanted biotechnology regulation, and another that would have subordinated intellectual property rights to the whim of international bureaucrats.

Even though the United States was a nay-sayer at the conference, Reily concluded, as did most observers, that the event was significant. "It marked the arrival of the international environmental issue as one which will engage questions of trade, energy, technology transfer, bilateral funding, multilateral organizational commitments and structures." It also "created a new and compelling rationale for engagement and cooperation between North and South." Developing countries now had a "new rationale for demanding concessions from richer countries: how they use their forests and burn fossil fuels, or whether they conserve their species all matter to people in developed countries who will pay to influence new policies."

Environmental protection, if not yet the "central organizing principle for civilization" Gore sought, was becoming a legitimate issue of foreign policy. While key players in the developing world—China and India, for example—gave no indication they were prepared to restrict fossil fuel use to prevent excessive carbon dioxide concentrations, many Western countries were prepared to do exactly that. And if the conference did not create an environmental "Marshall Plan," it did create a new paradigm: "Your Money or My Spider's Life."

So while Gore's vision was being adopted by the world, Gore, in daily Rio press briefings, carped at the recalcitrant Bush administration, comparing its performance to "a Greek tragedy" in which the bleak outcome was dictated by the character flaws of the key players at the conference.

When he returned home, Gore kept up the assault, charging, to the Senate Foreign Relations Committee, that "the Bush administration was, throughout these negotiations, the single largest obstacle to progress. In the end, our intransigence meant that the final agreement is completely devoid of any legally binding commitments to action."

*   *   *

While in Rio, Gore agreed to join Clinton's "short list" of vice presidential hopefuls. Later in the campaign, when Gore was asked why he had accepted after ruling it out earlier, he replied, "I thought about it. I reframed the question to take the personal ambition part out of it, because I didn't want to do it in that sense. I didn't expect it. I didn't seek it. When I said yes, the question to which I answered yes was, 'Were you willing to give your country a better chance to change?'—not, 'Do you want to run for vice president?'" Compare these tortured, self-aggrandizing words to those of Albert Gore, Sr., who, some years earlier, had offered his own reflections on what it is that motivates men to seek elective office: "At the root of all incentives to run for public office must be human ego: a desire for the approval of others, a yearning for self-expression and self-assertion; love of power and attention; zeal for success, for control and contention; concern for issues and the public trust."

Two weeks after Al Gore, Jr.'s, return from Rio, Bill Clinton made the choice official.

CHAPTER FOURTEEN

THE RUNNING MATE

AMONG THOSE CLOSEST to Clinton, the feeling was that he wanted Gore all along and that the search exercise was largely *pro forma*. Clinton admired Gore's intelligence and his grasp of issues. As Betsy Wright, perhaps Clinton's closest personal confidante, later recounted, Clinton "talked about how much he learned from him, how smart the guy was, how well he thought everything out. The governor liked the intellectual stimulation even of the arguments on points where they disagreed."*

It was Wright's conviction that the choice was based almost entirely on Clinton's assessment of Gore. "I think that probably in the history of this country there has probably never been a less political selection," she said. But Clinton did admire one political skill of Gore in particular: his ability, like many a successful candidate, to stay "on message." If Gore's career suggests nothing else, it clearly defines him as a man not easily distracted.

There were other political advantages. Clinton knew that Gore would prevent the Gulf War from becoming an opposition

---

* The Joan Shorenstein center at Harvard's Kennedy school holds a valuable symposium after each presidential election at which the campaign staffs of all candidates review their work. Ms. Wright's comments, and several others in this chapter, came from an edited transcript of the 1992 meeting.

213

issue and, with luck, could even turn it into a net plus for the Democratic ticket. As a Vietnam veteran, Gore could blunt at least some of the "draft dodger" catcalls against Clinton.

Clinton was also aware of Gore's standing with environmental activists. Clinton's own environmental record in Arkansas was marginal, soiled, among other things, by charges that he'd been overly lax in regulating chicken waste disposal because of the financial clout and political support of Arkansas's Tyson chicken company.

Finally, on cultural issues from welfare to the death penalty, Gore was a solid moderate, the sort who could blunt Republican charges that Democrats were soft on crime and indulgent of people unwilling to work. In short, Gore could help Clinton win back the "Reagan Democrats" who were less than impressed by George Bush's "globalism" (his "new world order"), his retreat on his no new taxes pledge, and his wobbliness on "social issues" where occasionally strident rhetoric seemed a cover for an administration more comfortable in the middle of the road, casting doubts on the administration's sincerity.

Gore knew he would have to shift left on abortion rights. He would have to mute differences over the line item veto, which Clinton wanted and Gore opposed. But generally the two were a good fit, having been partners in the centrist Democratic Leadership Council and the Progressive Policy Institute, and having a new, moderate Democratic image.

The official call from Clinton came at 11:15 PM on July 8, formally offering Gore the Number 2 spot. Gore, who was with Tipper and the children in Carthage, accepted immediately. The Gore family was invited to Little Rock, where Clinton would make the announcement and the two families would provide reporters with a photo-op at the rear portico of the Governor's Mansion.

The event would be a strategic turning point to the campaign. The country was becoming increasingly disenchanted with the Republicans. The Los Angeles riots of April 29 appeared to show that race relations were foundering. There was a need for change.

On May 1 the unemployment rate was announced at 7.8 percent, the highest since 1984. Another need for change. And on May 19, speaking in San Francisco, Vice President Dan Quayle said the Los Angeles riots were the product of "a lack of family values" and attacked "Murphy Brown" for having a child out of wedlock. Criticizing a television character who consistently finished a close second to Barbara Bush in the "most admired" category showed an administration not in tune with the American public. And when the administration struck out at Ross Perot's third party candidacy— Bush spokesman Marlin Fitzwater called him a "monster" and Marilyn Quayle likened him to a seller of "snake oil medicine"—the administration appeared desperate, if not hysterical in its attempts to beat back its challenges. George Bush himself was running away from his record, telling Barbara Walters of ABC News he regretted having agreed to the tax boost two years earlier. "That was a mistake, because it undermined to some extent my credibility with the American people."

With the Republicans self-destructing in one of the worst-run campaigns in recent American history, Clinton and Gore and their families stepped into the sunshine behind the Governor's Mansion in Little Rock to introduce themselves as a team to the American public. As Betsy Wright said: "[T]he two of them standing there together looked like change."

Change across the board. Change from the certainties of World War II to the ambiguities of Vietnam; from the "long twilight struggle" against "the evil empire" to an age of moral relativism; from Depression-era sensibilities to the self-absorbed "Boomers"; from the civil rights struggle to the vagaries of affirmative action; from rock to rap; from steak and eggs to tofu; from belching smokestacks to endangered species; from JFK to Oprah; from George Bush, who lost his daughter to leukemia and worked through his grief in the privacy of his family, to Al Gore, who saw his son hit by a car and wallowed in the experience in the pages of his book—and who would do so again before a television audience numbering in the tens of millions.

Clinton and Gore had already jogged together on the morning of the announcement, the governor, sipping McDonald's coffee, noting with satisfaction that the fitter senator "didn't run me into the ground."

At the announcement, Clinton praised his running mate as "a father who loves his children and shares my hunger to turn this economy around, to change our country and to do it so that we don't raise the first generation of children to do worse than their parents." He promised that Gore would "assume a strong role in the Clinton administration, a role of genuine leadership in the areas of his passion and expertise." In this, Clinton would prove totally true to his word.

Clinton, his running mate, and their families then set out by chartered bus for New York City and Madison Square Garden. The bus tour was the idea of David Wilhelm, the quiet, effective manager of the Clinton campaign. Wilhelm saw it as a way of presenting the two candidates as a team, but far more important, as a way to cut through the heart of such states as Ohio, Illinois, and Pennsylvania that would be crucial to Democratic chances in November. The bus was also tailored to Clinton's campaign style. "[T]he president was at the White House and Ross Perot was in television studios and Bill Clinton's great strength was the energy that he derives from and gives back to average folks," Wilhelm would recall. "What better way of doing that than the bus trips?"

Gore had lengthy sessions with Wilhelm and Clinton's other key political advisors: the ferocious campaigner James Carville, pollster Stanley Greenberg, and the ubiquitous George Stephanopolous. Betsy Wright presented Gore with a "tutorial" on the Clinton campaign, explaining its theory and strategy, with briefings on hundreds of issues and mini-issues. Gore was exhaustively prepared on how to respond to specific questions. Elaborate "Q & A" exercises followed, until the "board of examiners" felt he was ready. "So immediately, day one, he was as good as he turned out to be," Mark Gearan, who managed his vice presidential campaign, recalled. Carville offered even higher praise: "He was, in my opinion, the best: somebody disciplined on the message, as good a national candidate as I've ever seen out of either party. It's extremely rare for a Democrat, but he had unbelievable message discipline."

En route to New York, the two candidates and their families stopped at the Smith County Courthouse where both Albert Gore, Sr. and Jr., had first declared their candidacies for Congress. Now the senior Gores were on hand along with thousands of well-wishers crowding the adjacent streets. Former Governor of Tennessee Ned McWherter introduced Gore, declaring his friend to be "as Tennessean as a bluetick hound dog." In sweltering heat, the two candidates—their shirts drenched with perspiration—traded friendly jabs to the shoulders, betraying a sense of personal affinity that went beyond mere political alliance, and which would survive the many ups and downs of business in the White House.

Their next stop, the Democratic Convention in New York, was a triumph. AIDS victims and homeless veterans, women and minorities, working pols and working poor all had their say in a preemptive counterpoint to a GOP gathering that by comparison would appear mean-spirited, hard-bitten, and lacking direction. As if the occasion were being manipulated by the Big Democrat in the Sky, Perot chose to withdraw from the race on July 15, the day the convention voted to nominate Bill Clinton. What on its face might have seemed a blessing for the Republican campaign in fact gave Clinton-Gore an overnight boost of 14 percentage points, while Bush gained only 3. Never again would Clinton trail George Bush.

Perot would later reenter the campaign, but his only effect was to play havoc with the Republican base that was also looking for "change" from a stale administration that provided no clear vision— or what Bush called "the vision thing."

Clinton, in his acceptance speech, ticked off a short list of purported differences between himself and George Bush.

"George Bush... has no game plan to compete and win in the world economy. I do.

"He won't take on the big insurance companies to lower costs and provide health care to all Americans. I will.

"He never balanced a budget. I have, eleven times...."

"He doesn't have Al Gore. I do."

For a southern Baptist, the core of Gore's speech had the cadence of a Yom Kippur confessional at an orthodox service, only Gore was reciting the sins of the Bush administration rather than his own.

"They have taxed the many to enrich the few... and it is time for them to go.

"They have ignored the suffering of those who are victims... of AIDS, of crime, of poverty, of ignorance, of hatred and harassment. It is time for them to go.

"They have nourished and appeased tyrannies, and endangered America's deepest interests while betraying our cherished ideals. It is time for them to go.... "

Then there was the reprise of little Albert's brush with tragedy, some father-son moments of public bonding, and the gathering of the Clinton and Gore clans on the podium.

Initially, Democratic plans called for the Clintons and Gores to resume their bus trip with the Gores peeling off during the second day to return to Carthage and put their lives in order. Instead, the Gores decided to remain on board for the entire four days, a tribute both to the trip's political efficacy and the personal relationships that were being cemented. The tour captured surprisingly large audiences wherever it went. In one Ohio town, for example, a farmer advised the candidates that if they proceeded to the local crossroads store they would find a crowd of perhaps four hundred waiting for them. When they arrived, they found ten thousand people wanting to say hello.

The bus tour also proved brilliant in giving jaded members of the political press corps a fresh perspective on the campaign. Tired of tarmac-to-tarmac schedules and perfunctory photo-ops, the bus tour gave the journalists more sustained access to the campaign's principals and their managers as well as some quality time with local bankers, farmers, hardware store managers, nurses, and service station mechanics who could provide "color" and quotes. Perhaps the gushiest piece by a reputable journalist came from Joel Achenbach of the *Washington Post*. Datelined "somewhere in the heartland," he called the bus trip "the most daring invasion of unfriendly turf since Lee crossed the Mason-Dixon line on his way to Gettysburg." By the end of the piece Clinton and Gore had become "Butch and Sundance," with Gore willing not only to come to Clinton's aid on matters like draft-dodging, but catering to his ego by jogging slowly and throwing miniature golf matches.

Gore was developing into a powerful asset for the Clinton ticket, but not surprisingly, campaign staffers with Clinton, Gore, and at the DNC saw *Earth in the Balance*, Gore's environmental tome, creating some potential vulnerabilities, particularly when Gore and Dan Quayle came face to face in the vice presidential debate. This concern led to an incident that in Roy Neel's words, "caused Al to get as angry as I've seen him in the 25 years I've known him."

The trouble started when staffers, seeking to anticipate the kind of attacks Republicans might launch, conducted what amounted to opposition research on the book. Ideas and arguments flew over fax machines located at DNC headquarters in Washington, the Clinton-Gore operation in Little Rock, and wherever candidate Gore happened to be along the campaign trail. The final memo, dispatched by a DNC staffer named Jonathan Sallet, included the following points, with appropriate citations (omitted here):

"Al is not qualified to be vice president.

"He has no principles. He admits he has voted for programs in which he does not believe....

"—He's apparently guilt-ridden about the role of men in society and, perhaps as a result of his own weakness, believes America as a whole is psychologically dysfunctional....

"—He is a bad scientist who doesn't care enough to get his facts straight. The fact is, we can't be certain that global warming or the level of CO_2 or even the changes in the ozone layer pose a threat as burdensome as the cost of Al Gore's proposals.

"Al is a radical environmentalist who wants to change the very fabric of America.

"He criticizes America for being America—a place where people enjoy the benefits of an advanced standard of living.

"He has no sense of proportion: He equates the failure to recycle aluminum cans with the Holocaust—an equation that parodies the former and dishonors the latter.

"He is a Luddite who holds the naive view that technology is evil and wants to abolish automobiles....

"If Al Gore has his way, we would give up America's jobs and destroy the economy."

As the memo and comments about it were being circulated, one staffer apparently hit a single wrong digit on a fax number, and the entire package wound up in the office of a surprised Republican representative, Dick Armey, then Minority Whip. Armey could not bring himself to believe the Clinton-Gore team could inadvertently make so big a "mistake," and suspected he was somehow being set up. So rather than say anything about the material, he sent the fax to the *Wall Street Journal* which published the memo in its entirety together with a jabbing editorial.

"I can't remember Al's precise language, and I'm not sure I would tell you if I could," says Neel. "But he was furious. The irony is we did a more devastating job tearing apart *Earth in the Balance* than the Republicans did."

On October 13 Gore, Quayle, and James Stockdale—a retired admiral and former POW running as Perot's vice presidential candidate—debated in Atlanta. The presidential candidates had already gone through two similar exercises and had one more scheduled. The consensus was that Clinton had gotten the better of the president, who appeared as though his heart wasn't in the contest. But Perot had been the most impressive of the three, making it clear that he would remain an important if not yet fully defined factor in the race.

For Gore, whose ticket was coasting with a double digit lead in the polls, the Number 1 priority was not to get hurt, while the second was to score a few points consistent with the overall Clinton message, "Let's put people first."

That was pretty much the way things worked out. Gore and Quayle were veteran Senate colleagues who had spent dozens of hours debating foreign and domestic issues. Both were formidable extemporaneous speakers, both well prepared, and neither could easily be surprised. "We have an environmental crisis, a health insurance crisis, sub-standard education," said Gore. "It's time for a change." In the sort of petty demagoguery common in such events, he accused Bush and Quayle of having "taken our tax dollars and subsidized the moving of U.S. factories to foreign countries," omitting the fact that the program he was describing was part of the Caribbean Basin Initiative for which he had voted in the Senate.

Quayle, in a passing attempt to tap Gore's environmental vulnerability, accused him of endorsing a $100 billion transfer of resources to the Third World, when in fact Gore, in endorsing an environmental "Marshall Plan," had simply mentioned that the original plan cost $100 billion in 1990 dollars.

Repeatedly Quayle cited inconsistent positions by Clinton. He claimed this was endemic to Clinton's character. "Three words he fears most in the English language: Tell the truth," said Quayle. He returned to the theme again and again, urging Gore to defend Mr. Clinton's character. Gore never took the bait; he and his handlers had decided in advance that it was better not to let the matter ripen into a full blown campaign issue discussed by both sides.

Unfortunately for both candidates and the millions watching at home, the evening's dominant theme was neither Gore nor Quayle, nor either's attacks on the two principals, but Stockdale's fumbling performance. Clearly the distinguished scholar and war hero had lost a step or two since his leadership at the "Hanoi Hilton." And the chances are that even in his prime he was not cut out to produce clever political sound bites. Further, in some areas he was simply ill-prepared, or, in his own words, "out of ammunition." He did, however, become the only candidate in the history of such affairs to turn his hearing aid off in the midst of the debate. The early post-debate polls showed an even division between Gore and Quayle. Later ones gave Gore an edge, but these may have reflected sentiment on the general campaign rather than the debate itself.

Gore enjoyed a loving press throughout the campaign. Reporters wrote of how Tipper—she of porn rock lyrics fame—flirted suggestively with her husband along the tour, and how Gore himself mimicked rock singer James Brown—"I feeeeeeeeeeel good!"—on airplane flights, the same ones on which he would use a food tray as a snow board and surf down the aisle during take-offs. No longer the man who "gave wood a bad name four years ago," Gore was seen as positively relaxed, loose, liberated perhaps by the wisdom that he was in a no-lose situation. "Either he gets to be a heartbeat away from the top job, and a natural successor to President Clinton," wrote Jonathan Freedland in the *Washington Post*, "or he becomes a front-runner for 1996, as uncoated with blame as Lloyd Bentsen is for 1988."

Yet, then as later, Gore's metamorphosis seemed incomplete. In 1992 observers would occasionally see "the stiff programmed, packaged policy dweeb that has remained his evil twin for years." Four years later, despite additional coaching and practice, it could still be written that "When Gore vanishes behind his public mask, he seems to undergo a wild, almost violent act of self-compression. The athlete's body language suddenly broadcasts a lack of fluency: His arms dangle lifelessly from his shoulders, and he seems to have no joints at all above the waist."

*　　　　*　　　　*

Al Gore's major foreign policy address of the campaign attacked Bush on the Persian Gulf. In a September 29 speech at the Center for National Policy, a centrist Democratic think tank, Gore charged, "His poor judgment, moral blindness, and bungling policies led directly to a war that never should have taken place."

"Coddling tyrants," said Gore, "is a hallmark of the Bush foreign policy."

Gore also charged that, "because of his naiveté and lack of candor, U.S. taxpayers are now stuck with paying the bill for $1.9 billion President Bush gave to Saddam Hussein...." That was a complete distortion of events, but par for the campaign course.

Far more devastating was Gore's claim about American high tech exports to Iraq—that "there were 162 items that were licensed for sale despite their potential nuclear applications." He identified computers like those used in U.S. missile test ranges; high-tech equipment Iraq put to use on its Condor II missile; other materials intended for use as components for the Iraqi "super gun" intercepted by British authorities; machine tools, lasers, and other equipment used in the manufacture of Scud missile casings; technology and equipment for fabricating shapes out of glass that are useful in nuclear weapons manufacture; and even equipment for a detergent factory used to make chemical weapons.

Soon, charged Gore, "our sons and daughters were to be sent to risk their lives facing a threat that had been built up through U.S. technology and U.S. tax dollars by our own president, who now summoned them to battle."

The text of the Gore speech was accompanied by fifty-six footnotes, one of the more pedantic exercises in recent political history, most citing articles in the press. But pedantry is not erudition. Many of the reports cited were themselves the product of shabby journalism. The essence of the press allegations was that the Bush administration intentionally helped Iraq purchase arms by permitting the diversion of funds from $1 billion in agricultural loans made by the Commodity Credit Corporation (CCC) for the purchase of grain, and by looking the other way as the Atlanta branch of Italy's Banca Nazionale del Lavoro (BNL) illegally loaned $5 billion to Baghdad, much of which was also used to purchase sophisticated weapons. As the latter transaction came to light, it was further alleged that two attorneys general—Richard Thornburgh and William Barr—had orchestrated a coverup to prevent links between the Atlanta BNL branch, the Italian government, and Washington from coming to light.

The source for much of the agricultural loan story was a seventy-four-year-old Democratic representative from Texas named Henry Gonzales, whose long service as a constructive populist had been undermined in recent years by chronic irascibility coupled with a penchant for recommending the impeachment of Republican presidents—Reagan over the invasion of Grenada and the Iran-contra affairs, Bush over the dispatch of forces to the Persian Gulf. Suggestions of Justice Department hanky-panky came mainly from the district court judge presiding in the Atlanta case, a John Sirica wannnabe named Marvin Shoob.

The stories were false in their entirety. The $1 billion *loan* turned out to be a $500 million *credit*, only $392 million of which had been drawn by Iraq when the Bush administration suspended the deal in April 1990. Moreover, none of the money involved was ever advanced to Iraq in the form of cash: Iraq ordered rice from the seller, who then received payment from a U.S. bank. Iraq was obligated to pay for its purchase over a three-year period. The CCC was prepared to pay the U.S. bank if the Iraqis defaulted. Iraq got grain, not money. And since the program had been working since 1983, Iraqi installment payments from past credits exceeded the total of new credits advanced by the Bush administration by $455 million. So there was neither actual nor even theoretical potential during the Bush presidency for Iraq to divert any CCC money to arms purchases.

Regarding the Atlanta transaction, about $4 billion in loans were advanced by BNL to Iraq. The loans were illegal because they exceeded the limits authorized by the parent Rome bank and had not been disclosed to federal bank examiners as required by law. Of this amount, $1.5 billion involved CCC agricultural credits finalized during the Reagan administration. Both FBI investigators and federal prosecutors concluded that the crime was perpetrated by the Atlanta BNL manager, Christopher Drogoul, several of his bank subordinates, and at least four Iraqi nationals. The evidence was that the parent company—BNL Rome—was an innocent victim. At no point was there even a scintilla of evidence that the Bush administration had known of the illegal transactions, let alone approved them.

When Drogoul agreed to plead guilty to more than sixty counts of illegal activity, insisting that his Rome superiors had no involvement in the plot, Judge Shoob all but accused prosecutors of seeking to cover-up the involvement of higher ups in the effort to finance Iraqi weapons purchases. Interestingly, neither the extension of substantial credit to Iraq by a U.S. bank, nor the use of such funds by Iraq to purchase weapons would—standing alone—have contradicted prevailing U.S. policy that precluded only the sale of weapons to Iraq by Americans, or the acquisition by Iraq of weapons of mass destruction.

Three Justice Department reviews, including one that would later be conducted by the newly installed Clinton administration, together with separate assessments by congressional committees with oversight responsibility for intelligence or agriculture, would all conclude there had been no wrongdoing, no cover-up by anyone from the Bush administration. Yet a frenzy of television, newspaper, and magazine reports and editorials appearing through Election Day and even beyond condemned the Bush administration for its culpability in the CCC and BNL affairs.

The Republican response was perfunctory. Marlin Fitzwater, not quite ready for prime time, was the designated hitter. "This is another effort by the Democrats in Congress to rewrite history to conceal their opposition to the war," he harrumphed. Bush, in the days ahead, would fire his own accusations regarding Clinton's failure to tell the truth about his draft avoidance efforts or his organization of anti-war demonstrations while a student at Oxford in the late 1960s, and the GOP would run several television spots targeting the same matters. But, in the main, the Bush campaign spent more time attacking the tax increase it had backed than recounting its foreign policy successes.

History will, of course, recall, even if the voters did not, that George Bush successfully managed American foreign policy during the break-up of the Soviet Empire in Eastern Europe and secured Soviet acceptance for a re-unified Germany to enter NATO. He had backed Mikhail Gorbachev's reform efforts, would wind down the Cold War, and had mended fences with Boris Yeltsin, as that former Communist advanced toward power in Moscow. He had negotiated the important North American Free Trade Agreement, ensured that the results of free elections in Nicaragua were respected, and liberated Panama from the evil clutches of Manuel Noriega. He had brilliantly put together an international coalition that expelled Saddam Hussein from Kuwait with minimal loss of life and few political complications, and had sought to parlay that success into a broader Middle East peace.

These were remarkable achievements. Yet, Al Gore, the pious moralist from Tennessee, had managed to put Bush on the defensive over an alleged international conspiracy, the evidence for which was non-existent.

But Gore was on a roll now. In Lexington, Kentucky, on October 15, he suggested that the reelection of Bush could unleash a Watergate-type scandal which could paralyze a second term Bush White House. "George Bush is presiding over a cover-up significantly larger than Watergate," he told a gathering of the National Editorial Writers Conference. Watergate began as a "two bit burglary," but "Iraqgate includes the largest bank fraud in American history," Gore said.

The following day in Marietta, Georgia, Gore plummeted to levels of demagoguery that might even have embarrassed Joe McCarthy. "This is a larger cover-up than Watergate ever was," he told supporters at a private lodge. "It involves the biggest bank fraud, it involves $2 billion of the American taxpayers' money that we're stuck with. It involves the decision by George Bush to arm Saddam Hussein and to lead him to miscalculate and launch a war that never should have taken place and would not have except for the poor judgment and bad foreign policy of George Bush, and he ought to be held accountable for it."

Iraq was not the only place where Gore found the administration's policy toward technology transfers objectionable. In 1989, following the brutal Chinese government suppression of the Tiananmen Square demonstrations, the Bush White House suspended plans for China to launch U.S. satellites. The following year China asked for and Bush agreed to a waiver permitting the launch of a U.S. satellite on a Chinese Long March rocket. In 1992 Gore joined a number of senators who wrote the administration claiming China was using the program to "gain foreign aerospace technology that would be otherwise unavailable to it."

In the closing days of the campaign, Gore criticized the administration for permitting the Chinese to launch five additional U.S.-made satellites. "President Bush really is an incurable patsy for those dictators he sets out to coddle," said Gore.

The Clinton-Gore team was generally critical of Bush placing economic and political considerations ahead of human rights, particularly as it applied to China and its "most favored nation" trade status. They pledged, if elected, to make visible progress on human rights the centerpiece of their relationship with Beijing. They would wind up de-linking human rights from trade while presiding the most lax supervision of technology transfers to China of any post-war Presidency.

*   *   *

On November 2, 1992, Clinton and Gore were elected president and vice president of the United States. They had polled 43 percent of the popular vote to 37 percent for Bush and 19 percent for Perot. In the electoral college, their vote total was 370 compared to 168 for Bush and zero for Perot. Clinton strategists believed the choice of Gore as vice president had been more than vindicated. They felt his presence on the ballot had made the difference between victory and defeat in Georgia, Tennessee, and North Carolina, and had helped considerably in Colorado, New Mexico, and Montana. More than that, it had helped Clinton define his message of change with stability and moderation, a message that seemed to attract Democrats in the Northeast and Midwest who had become habitual defectors in presidential elections.

Further, Clinton knew that in Gore he had a man of considerable intelligence, an aptitude for hard work, and a deep sense of personal loyalty. As media man Bob Squire had told him months earlier, "He will not stab you in the back, even if you deserve it."

CHAPTER FIFTEEN

"THE GREATEST
VICE PRESIDENT IN HISTORY"

BILL CLINTON AND AL GORE now had an exalted respect for each other's political instincts. Over time, the staffs of the two men would overlap, and Gore's personal recommendations could be decisive. But not at first.

Almost immediately, Gore had to fight a preinauguration battle to keep Hillary Rodham Clinton from taking the vice president's traditional office space in the White House. And Gore was deeply frustrated at the Clinton team's early incompetence: making bad appointments, often placing people in jobs for which they were obviously unqualified or insufficiently vetted.

On the Clinton transition team, Harold Ickes, who had run Jesse Jackson's 1988 presidential campaign, and Susan Thomases, Hillary Rodham Clinton's friend and advisor, were never close to Gore. Gore was not happy to see either of them playing major head-hunter roles immediately following the election. As the process got clogged with nanny problems, ethnic and racial quotas, even a former Playboy bunny, Gore became irate. "We're off to a bad start," he complained to staffers, "The whole operation shows a lack of discipline and preparation. It's like trying to run the 100-yard dash and put your track shoes on at the same time." Gore thought the president had made a mistake by giving so much free reign to people like Ickes and Thomases who would not be part of the White House chain of command once the administration got under way. He told his own people that the delay in naming a chief-of-staff was slowing down the entire process.

Thomases arrogated to herself the role of "official office space designator" for the new administration. She suggested that Gore would be able to function perfectly well from a fine suite of offices in the Old Executive Office Building, leaving the one about eighteen strides from the Oval Office for Hillary Rodham Clinton. "This was never going to be an issue," recalls Roy Neel. "Whatever some staff person thought, that office was going to go to the vice president."

After naming Thomas F. "Mack" McLarty his chief-of-staff, Clinton organized a meeting with Gore, Neel, and McLarty to make sure all were in sync on the prominent role he wanted the vice president to play. Several important arrangements grew out of that session: the president-elect and Gore would lunch privately together once a week. Further, Gore would play an active role in foreign policy. In practice Gore would have major responsibility for nuclear arms control and co-chairmanship of "commissions" with the heads of state of Russia, Ukraine, Egypt, and South Africa. He would shape policy and advise on appointments for environmental and communications issues. Neel, Gore's chief-of-staff, would also serve as a personal assistant to the president—he eventually became the president's deputy chief-of-staff—a good way to keep Clinton and Gore on the same page. Leon Fuerth, Gore's longtime national security assistant, would, as a senior member of the National Security Council, participate in all meetings of cabinet-level national security officials. This was an impressive, perhaps unprecedented portfolio for a vice president and would be augmented in the early days of the administration with responsibility for "reinventing government." Aides to Gore say it did much to cushion what otherwise might have been a bumpy and competitive relationship with the first lady, the "two," as in Bill Clinton's campaign line of "two for one."

The Clinton and Gore staffs would—during the course of the two Clinton terms—prove fungible. Gore's chiefs-of-staff, first Neel, then Jack Quinn, and legislative affairs director, Thurgood Marshall, Jr., would move to important positions on the Clinton staff. Bruce Reed, Gore's 1988 speechwriter, was already helping to formulate domestic policy for Clinton. Franklin Raines, the Office of Management and Budget director, and future Clinton chief-of-staff Erskine Bowles, were friends of the vice president. Even Rahm Emanuel, the ultimate Clinton loyalist, was politically in tune with Mr. Gore.

President Clinton valued Gore's Capitol Hill experience and trusted his advice on dealing with Congress. He also immediately envisioned Gore as his eventual successor. "At the first cabinet meeting," recalls Neel, "the president was very direct in addressing Gore's role. 'Look, let me get one thing settled off the bat,' he said. 'When the vice president speaks, assume he's speaking for me.'"

Despite this kind of support, there were some rough moments, even after the choppy preinaugural days. Just as Gore had been critical of the administration's slap-dash appointment process, so too was he privately appalled at the "Travelgate" fiasco, when the administration fired seven members of the White House Travel Office on contrived charges of financial improprieties. Billy Dale, the longtime manager, was dumped unceremoniously and replaced with a twenty-five-year-old distant cousin of the president, Catherine Cornelius. The press quickly discovered that the Clintons' Hollywood friends, Harry and Linda Thomason, had actively sought White House travel business for their consulting firm. There were also suggestions that the White House had been all too eager to help the FBI develop what turned out to be spurious evidence of wrongdoing by the travel office staff. Moreover, while aides publicly denied Mrs. Clinton's involvement in the affair, an internal White House memorandum showed that she had insisted on replacing the Dale team. Dale was later indicted on questionable charges of financial impropriety, but was acquitted by a jury after only two hours of deliberation. Seven months after his dismissal, the White House was still seeking to obtain confidential information about him from the FBI, claiming, ridiculously, that he was being considered for a White House pass.

A former senior member of Gore's staff says that Gore "was appalled by what he saw as stupidity and ineptitude. He complained there were too many people in the wrong jobs. He said there were too many political friends and associates in the White House, and elsewhere in the agencies. He felt that people like McLarty, [Bernard] Nussbaum [White House Counsel, who resigned shortly after Travelgate broke], and [David] Watkins [White House Director of administration] were all in over their heads." But Gore said nothing publicly. To the contrary, whenever Clinton or his wife were under attack, Gore reminded his staff to say nothing critical of the president or first lady.

Gore made ample use of his power over personnel appointments in environmental jobs. Carol Browner, a veteran of his Senate staff known for an uncompromising approach to environmental issues, became the new head of the EPA with its powerful mandate in the areas of clean air and water regulation. Kathleen McGinty, a younger firebrand from his Senate staff, was named chairman of the President's Council on Environmental Quality, a position that effectively made her the administration's liaison with the nation's environmental movement. Far less appreciated—except by those directly affected—is how the Gore mandate translated into the daily business of applying environmental policy, not only in the areas of clean air and water, but also public land management, wetlands policy, protection of endangered species, coastal zone management, fish and wildlife management, and similar issues. Since Gore would not have time to manage these responsibilities on a day-to-day basis, it was his appointed environmental true believers in senior regulatory positions who controlled daily policy. They quickly gained a reputation as zealots.

"What Gore's people never seem to understand," complains a former senior Interior Department official from the Jimmy Carter years, "is that you need to cooperate with industry, agriculture, and state and local government when you are fashioning rules to govern the use of land in this country. It can't work in an environment of edict and confrontation which is what these people seem to strive for, or they don't think they're tough enough. And I think that's the basic message they're getting from Gore."

*   *   *

Gore's major project of the first Clinton term—particularly the first two years—was what the White House described as "reinventing government." Despite the grand title, the issue was a consolation prize after Hillary Clinton preempted Gore on health care reform, and after Senior Presidential Advisor George Stephanopoulos and Office of Management and Budget Director Leon Panetta denied him his choice of welfare reform, convincing the president to postpone the issue until the second Clinton term, when they hoped it would wither. Stephanopoulos, a liberal refugee from the staff of Richard Gephardt, was not a Gore fan and even regarded Gore as a rival for Clinton's ear. He and others hostile to Gore regarded reinventing government as a political sinkhole in which the vice president would founder, away from the media glare, locked in a death grip with the powerful government workers unions.

President Clinton announced Gore's assignment to considerable fanfare on March 13, 1993, as part of the administration's commitment to modernization and change. Gore pledged a comprehensive report within six months. Yet the initial "reinventing government" team consisted of only two people: Gore and a capable woman named Elaine Kamarck, who had joined Gore's staff the very morning of Clinton's announcement, and who thought she had accepted a somewhat broader portfolio, that of domestic policy advisor. A veteran of past Carter, Mondale, and Babbitt campaigns, she was also from the party's moderate wing, having come directly from the Progressive Policy Institute.

Gore and Kamarck understood that a lot of spadework had already been done. Under President Reagan, the Grace Commission had recommended scores of ways for government to become more efficient and customer friendly. But the unions and a Democratic Congress had blunted any meaningful effort at reform. David Osborne and Ted Gaebler had written a surprise best-seller book on the subject and would serve as consultants, conducting seminars for the Gore team.

Another recruit was John Sharp, Texas Controller of Public Accounts, who had initiated a project in his home state that, at the federal level, would become the National Performance Review (NPR). Sharp had saved enough money through commonsense reforms to enable Texas Governor Ann Richards to scuttle a planned tax increase. For example, by having state employees tend to their own office plants, Sharp had saved an estimated annual $630,000.

As project director for reinventing government, Gore and Kamarck selected Bob Stone. As deputy assistant secretary of defense for installations, Stone had a reputation for cutting red tape and encouraging "customer service" in his department. The first NPR report bragged that at the Department of Defense, Stone had "reduced a four-hundred-page construction manual to four pages and cut eighteen different sets of housing regulations to one."

Gore demanded the White House show commitment to his project by approving a large staff. He wound up with just over two hundred—about half the size of Hillary Rodham Clinton's health care team—selected almost exclusively from federal agency personnel. The staffers' recommendations were submitted to Gore or Kamarck, who whittled them down for presentation in the first report.

*   *   *

John Sturdivant, president of the American Federation of Government Employees (AFGE), was a soft-spoken air force veteran with a deft political touch. Of the 2.9 million civilian government employees in 1993, about two-thirds were unionized and 700,000 were in AFGE.

"You know, this is a union that draws on all one's political skills," he said in his Washington, D.C., office in the spring of 1997, one year before his death from leukemia. "Thirty percent of our people vote Republican. We have some of the most conservative white people in the country as members—bureau of prison folk, DOD civilians, immigration officials. To last ten years as president, I have to know the things that unite us."

Early in the process, the leaders of the key government unions, principally Sturdivant and John Tobias of the National Federation of Federal Employees, decided not to fight the idea of reinventing government, concentrating instead on protecting union jobs and making sure unions were involved if major changes were made in how jobs were to be done.

"I was not scared by the cutbacks," Sturdivant insisted. "This was a crossroads for us. Polls showed the people didn't like how government works. We can't look at private industry—autos, computers, manufacturing—and see what's gone on there and then have me make the case that we can't slim down. Also, I knew the big targets would be middle-managers, not front-line workers."

Sturdivant and the others at first found Gore and Kamarck difficult to deal with. "They treated us like a group worthy of outreach but not part of the decision-making process." That changed dramatically with a meeting at Independence Hall in Philadelphia in

June 1993, attended by company executives from Xerox, Cadillac, General Electric, Harley Davidson and others who had managed downsizing and reorganization during the 1980s. Their message to Gore: if you have unions, bring them into the process because nothing you try will work without their cooperation. Just in case Gore and Kamarck needed that point underlined, Sturdivant went public with an op-ed page piece in the *Washington Post* warning, "There will be no reinventing government, there will be no fundamental change, there will be no bold leaps, only bureaucratic tinkering around the margins, without fundamental changes in the union's role in the workplace."

"I think the vice president and Ms. Kamarck knew exactly what I was talking about," said Sturdivant. "We have refined obstructionism to a high level of efficiency. We could file a suit, seek arbitration, file an unfair labor practice, leak to the *Washington Post*. We have many tools, many tools."

Gore and Kamarck took the lesson to heart. Indeed, as Don Kettl, the foremost academic authority on Gore's project, observed, "Building a partnership with the unions thus became the centerpiece of the National Performance Review's relationship with government employees, and the core of union relations was to be a new National Partnership Council (NPC)." The NPC included representatives of the three largest federal employee unions, a representative from the AFL-CIO Public Employees Department, seven agency heads, and a representative of the vice president.

The "partnership with labor" turned out to be a limited partnership. Gore never brought managers and other nonunion employees to the table in anything like the way he courted labor. The unions were appeased, the managers, run over.

Gore and Kamarck also decided that his report would lack credibility with the public and Congress unless it reduced the size of government by a specified amount. The figures his staff came up with were a reduction of 252,000 personnel by the year 2000, which would save the government $108 billion a year. The entire cut would come from the ranks of middle managers. Not a single union job was found expendable. Gore chose to affront logic, not political reality.

Gore reached the figure rather crudely. As Robert Stone, the project director, would explain, he started by counting 670,000 middle manager civilians in government and assumed arbitrarily that only half were needed. From the resulting figure—335,000—one-quarter of the cuts were restored on the assumption that the 25 percent of those cut were people who performed services vital to the reinvention process such as setting goals and measuring progress. Subtracting one-quarter, or 83,000, from the 335,000 cut brought Gore back to 252,000, his final number. (Currently, the number of federal civilian employees is down by about 350,000 since Gore began his work, but cutbacks in certain programs and departments mandated by the Republican Congress make it difficult to credit Gore with more than the initial 252,000.) This would be achieved by a combination of normal attrition and congressional legislation authorizing a buy-out for anyone in the target group willing to leave government.

Gore and Kamarck also took advantage of the ongoing cutback of civilian Department of Defense employees. A second factor was the schedule of military base closures urged by the respective services as a way of saving as much money as possible for weapons modernization and force readiness. Overall, nearly three-fourths of the positions eliminated would come from the defense establishment, which lost 16 percent of its total civilian jobs. While a handful of agencies suffered proportionally larger cuts—most due to special circumstances—no other cabinet department suffered cuts that large, or even came close. As of January, 1996, by which time the bulk of the cuts which could reasonably be attributed to Gore's work had been made, the government-wide average was under 11 percent.

Because the fix was in with labor, Gore and Kamarck essentially shunned the help of a category of people who could have been of great assistance to their effort. As Kettl observed, "Middle managers play a critical role in the reinvention effort. They occupy the key positions throughout the government that determine how well programs work. They are the project managers, branch chiefs, and section heads who shape programs and the behavior of their agencies. They model the behavior of their subordinates."

The $2.8 billion buy-out deal also came under criticism. Seventy-two percent of those accepting the offer were already eligible for early retirement. Many who would have left now stayed around only long enough to get the added bonus. Kamarck claims, "Most of these people who took the bonus were old bureaucrats who would have obstructed change had they remained in their jobs." But the bonus also attracted many of the more capable middle managers whose common denominator was confidence in their ability to get jobs outside government.

Gore did nothing to make it easier for managers to fire, transfer, or suspend lazy, incompetent, or otherwise unproductive employees, again because the unions would have fought that. And, for the same reason, as well as the potential opposition from minority leaders, he did nothing to elevate formal hiring or promotion standards. According to a 1998 study by the Merit Systems Production Board: "When we asked supervisors to tell us to what extent the quality of applicants had worsened or improved in the past three years, we found that their assessment of applicant quality had fallen for just about every type of job category."

John Leyden was the national AFL/CIO official given the reinvention portfolio and has watched the process from the beginning with a high degree of sophistication and inside knowledge. In his view, the cuts were cushioned not only by the buy-out but because many of the supposedly eliminated jobs were "privatized"—shifted to private sector jobs under contract to the government—many without so much as a change of location. By Leyden's count,

150,000 of the "lost" jobs were lost in name only, the identical positions now being performed under contract by the "private" sector. Kamarck has heard this criticism since the first round of cuts and argues that cuts have also been made in contracting out work. But since federal spending as a percentage of the gross domestic product has continued to rise, Leyden's assessment may be on target.

From the perspective of mid-1997, Leyden—like most who have closely monitored reinvention—saw significant changes in procurement across the government, but big changes in methodology only in a handful of agencies, the Social Security administration and Customs being two of the best. "Most managers took the attitude, 'This too shall pass, like TQM [total quality management]," he says. "At the Pentagon, Treasury, FAA [Federal Aviation Administration], HHS [Health and Human Services], and other big ones, we haven't seen much change."

A more damning criticism comes from John Deutsch who watched Gore's project as undersecretary of defense and, later, director of the CIA. Deutsch lost popularity at the White House after telling Congress the "unvarnished truth" about how Saddam Hussein had emerged stronger after one of Bill Clinton's feather-duster spankings—a few cruise missiles aimed at Iraqi air defenses—than he had been before. And what is the unvarnished truth about reinventing government? "It amounted to a lot of talk by Al Gore and Elaine Kamarck," he says. "I don't think it made much difference in the way the government works." Nor do about two-thirds of all government employees sampled by Gore's team in 1998.

After getting battered by the unions Gore threw in the towel on yet another area of reform—the heavily subsidized maritime industry. Not only does the industry receive $215 million in direct subsidies each year, but the protectionist Jones Act forbids foreign ships to haul cargo between U.S. ports at a $600 million annual cost to American consumers. A Gore reinventing government task force was prepared to recommend ending the subsidies and rescinding the

Jones Act. But after word of the recommendations leaked, the unions threatened to confront Gore publicly. Gore scuttled the recommendations and instead urged only that a new commission study the problem.

Gore also dropped a proposal that would have allowed states to permit private contractors to handle Social Security disability claims, a function that now employs upwards of 12,000 government workers, again in response to union pressure.

"The vice president has had to handle the whole reinventing thing carefully," President John Sweeney of the AFL-CIO told the author. "He has fought us on NAFTA and fast-track. But he has tried very hard to stay on good terms with us, and he still has a fighting chance for considerable union support in the Democratic primaries. If he had tried to run over us on reinventing government, I don't think that would be true."

Small wonder that when Sturdivant came to the White House for the release of Gore's first Reinventing Government Report, "Creating a Government That Works Better and Costs Less," Gore told him only half-jokingly, "I had to go home and change my shirt. The unions took the other one."

Still Sturdivant acknowledged that neither he nor his fellow union leaders would have sat still for the same sorts of changes had they been recommended by a Republican. "We'd never have taken this from the Reagan administration," he said.

Kamarck agrees. "There was a lot about reinventing government that was Nixon goes to China," she says. "The unions would sabotage Ronald Reagan, not Bill Clinton and Al Gore."

Gore's report, containing nearly four hundred recommendations culled from the work of his task forces, was well written and filled with the kind of colorful examples of government waste that journalists love. There was, for example, the "ash receiver, tobacco," with nine pages of regulatory specifications—forcing the real price of the ashtray up from $4.00 to $54.00, compliments of the General

Services administration. Also, the broken steam trap that the Sacramento Army Depot held off replacing until it could save $10 by buying in bulk, while thousands of dollars worth of steam escaped. And the complaints of government airline travelers forced to take circuitous routes, sometimes at excessive fares, because their departments were denied the option of shopping for themselves.

Gore plunged onto the talk show circuit to push his program, breaking ashtrays and reciting punch lines written to make him look like a "regular guy." What's not to love about a fellow who wants to eliminate the Tea Tasters Board and a costly dairy farm run by the Naval Academy? True, a few colorful anecdotes do not reform make. But the personnel cuts recommended by Gore and Kamarck were—to a point—real. There was some honest talk about instilling the notion of customer service in federal employees. And the reforms in the procurement area were long overdue. Gore noted that 142,000 government employees were involved in the procurement process while the Federal Acquisition Regulation controlling procurement ran to 1,600 pages with 2,900 additional agency-specific regulations. "The numbers document what most federal workers and many taxpayers already know. Our system relies on rigid rules and procedures, extensive paperwork, detailed design specifications, and multiple inspections and audits. It is an extraordinary example of bureaucratic red tape."

As time passed, Gore understandably paid less attention to reinventing government and more to other political and policy questions. Bureaucracies formed within the various agencies to carry on the reinventing government work, the results differing vastly from place to place. Serious people who examined Gore's reforms found many of them picayune. In a devastating *Atlantic* critique in February 1995, management guru Peter Drucker branded the recommended changes so trivial that outside of the federal government most would not even be announced, "except perhaps on the bulletin board in the hallway. They are the kinds of things a hospital expects floor nurses to do on their own; that a bank expects branch managers to do on their own; that even a poorly run manufacturer expects supervisors to do on their own—without getting much praise, let alone extra rewards."

Drucker then sounded what would become the dominant theme of most critics of Gore's effort, the failure to ask fundamental questions about the role of government in society. "Every agency, every policy, every program, every activity, should be confronted with these Questions: What is your mission? Is it still worth doing? If we were not already doing this, would we now go into it?"

Except for such mini-recommendations as ending the subsidies for mohair production and honey and eliminating the position of federal tea-taster, Gore, in round one, had deliberately avoided any basic inquiry into government missions. But after Republicans gained control of Congress, Gore sought to preempt the "meat-axe" Republican approach by asking the basic questions himself. Among the questions he posed to the agencies at the beginning of 1995 were: if the agency in question were eliminated, "how would the goals or programs of your agency be undertaken—by other agencies, by states or localities, by the private sector, or not at all?" For a while, Gore's effort and Republican reforms seemed to complement each other.

But the government shut-downs of 1995-96 led to a hardening of positions, a drawing of lines in the sand, and abandonment by the Clinton-Gore administration of any pretense of making government smaller by scaling down its powers, missions, and programs. George Nesterczuk, the majority staff director of the House Civil Service Subcommittee, observed that Gore's 1995 round of proposals "included more that 186 new recommendations for agency actions and 121 regulatory reforms. Unfortunately, as Congress proposed to enact its version of [reinventing government] through appropriations bills and various balanced budget acts during the latter half of 1995, it found the administration less enthusiastic about serious reforms. In exercising the veto over specific reduction measures, Clinton seriously undermined the credibility of his own reform agenda."

To this charge, Kamarck basically pleads "guilty," but with an explanation. "As much as we wanted to kill something big—even for political reasons—we found no political will to do it. The business of the agencies is based on policy, and people in this country basically want protection in lots of areas. And every time they read about another e-coli episode they want more protection." As an example Kamarck cites Republican calls for the abolition of the Department of Commerce. "But when you look at it," she notes, "85 percent of the cost and personnel of Commerce is in three areas: the census, the patent office, and the weather bureau, all of which have support even among Republicans. After that you have plenty of insignificant, dumb little programs with very tenacious constituencies."

Gore kept his hands off most of his own pet projects and departments. The EPA, for example, was hardly touched, though in 1995 it was sternly rebuked by a panel from the National Academy of Science for low scientific standards and lack of peer review for its work.

An even more egregious example was the IRS, whose ponderous inefficiencies, brutal tactics, and porcupine-like resistance to oversight—even by its nominal superiors in the Treasury Department—were all exposed by congressional inquiry rather than by Gore and his task force. Reform and changes in senior personnel eventually did come, but not because of anything for which Gore could take credit.

Nor could Gore come up with a single idea for reinventing the Superfund, one of the earliest products of his congressional career, and one of the least efficient government programs on the books.

Pointing to the personnel cutbacks and procurement reforms achieved, and here and there the glimmer of a new agency ethic of serving the "consumer," Gore may claim with at least a semblance of justice to have reinvented government. But at the end of the day he did little to change it.

*   *   *

Gore's moment of singular triumph during the first Clinton term was his smashing victory over Ross Perot in a November 9, 1993, debate hosted by Larry King on CNN. The subject was the merits of the North America Free Trade Agreement (NAFTA) which eliminated most tariffs on trade involving the United States, Canada, and Mexico. The debate, the idea of Gore's chief-of-staff Jack Quinn, carried some political risk. Through his half-hour infomercials during the 1992 campaign, Perot had become a veteran of the extended television spiel, and he was rather good at it. He had also performed capably in the presidential debates. And as Clinton and Gore were learning daily through graphic media depictions of Mexico's labor conditions and environmental practices, it is easier to demagogue the case against a treaty like NAFTA than it is to dem-agogue the case for one.

White House alumni of the period recall that many senior presidential staff and advisors recommended against a Gore-Perot match-up. Political consultant Mandy Grunwald, for example, said that Gore's presence on the show would give Perot status he currently lacked. "Nobody takes him seriously anymore," agreed George Stephanopoulos. "Why should we?"

Grunwald and Stephanopoulos thought the White House should send some "policy wonk" to the show. But Gore felt passionately that he could beat Perot convincingly, and, with the support of Neel, Quinn, and David Gergen—Clinton's Republican-in-residence—Gore took his case directly to Clinton, who backed his vice president.

The administration knew that NAFTA was in trouble. NAFTA was a creature of the Bush administration, and during the 1992 campaign Clinton had given it only qualified endorsement, pledging he would first modify the agreement to prevent Mexico from turning its cheap labor and lower environment standards into commercial advantage. After deciding to back the treaty the administration took months negotiating provisions, allowing it to claim it had met its campaign commitments. As that process unfolded, Clinton devoted most of his attention to his economic package and health care, while Gore busied himself reinventing government.

At the same time Perot was starting to spend money reacquainting the country with the "giant sucking sound" of jobs fleeing to Mexico. The AFL-CIO, reinvigorated by President John Sweeney's confident activism, was mobilizing national opposition to the treaty. And Speaker Richard Gephardt, whose protectionist themes had helped shape the 1988 presidential campaign, was organizing Democratic anti-NAFTA forces in the House. Belatedly, Clinton entered the contest, bidding for votes by peddling everything from photo-ops to trade centers. Still the nose-count in the House was perilously close. Not until Gore's public flogging of Perot did the measure gain the momentum needed for victory.

The debate itself was an exercise in demagoguery, distortion, and irrelevance. Perot claimed his position was one of free trade modified only slightly by the need to address Mexico's appalling labor conditions and shabby environmental standards.

Gore never really addressed the point. Instead he offered anecdotal nonsense, a list of treaty endorsements, and some rather nasty *ad hominem* attacks on Perot.

Gore cited the support of five living former presidents, and involved his boyhood chum, Gordon Thompson, then working at a tire plant in Elmwood, Tennessee, on the treaty's behalf. He rapped Perot for allegedly profiting from a "free trade zone" run by the City of Fort Worth at the Dallas-Fort Worth Airport. ("If it's good for him why isn't it good for the rest of the country?") After Perot displayed pictures of Mexican slums and exploited workers, Gore struck back with pictures of his own, "pictures of Mr. Smoot and Mr.

Hawley," authors of the protectionist legislation of the late 1920s that is widely blamed for contributing to the subsequent worldwide depression.

In much of the debate, Perot was on the defensive. But when Gore claimed that twenty-two independent studies had projected that NAFTA would produce more American jobs, Perot attacked. A lot of the increase in exports, Perot claimed, would be high-tech components, such as radios, to be installed in products, like automobiles, that would be manufactured in Mexico and then reimported into the United States.

Throughout the program, Perot appeared grumpy and flustered, like a slugger kept off balance by an opponent who jabs, clinches, sticks his thumb in your eye, and punches your kidneys through twelve rounds. The Texan never mobilized his arguments into a coherent presentation. He never sought to quantify NAFTA's damage—if any—to the well-being of American citizens or to convey the likely benefits of his own "social tariff." He reacted with anger to Gore's sleazy attacks. More than anything, he seemed uncomfortable in the rough-and-tumble world of Washington debate, anxious to be back among people and things he owned, yearning to retreat inside one of his half-hour infomercials where there were no adversaries, no interruptions, and where the numbers meant any darned thing he wanted them to mean.

As for Gore, after sixteen years debating legislation in committee and on the floor of the House and Senate, holding town meetings nearly every weekend, confronting opponents on the campaign trail, he knew what to do. He didn't get flustered. He marshaled his facts well, sensed the amount of demagoguery he could get away with, knew enough to bring everything back to the guy on the assembly line or the working mom trying to make ends meet, and had a feel for the kinds of issues the press would find appealing.

"Al was confident and relaxed," recalls Roy Neel. "The White House worked hard to prepare for Perot. We took him seriously.

But I could tell looking at Al that he knew he had this guy beat early on. After the event, there was no big show of emotion. He just knew things had gone very, very well." At a time when Bill Clinton was still searching for a presidential identity, Al Gore appeared to be the administration's rising star.

The contrast in the political fortunes of the two men grew even more pronounced as the midway point in the first Clinton term approached. Clinton and his wife were pecked by scandal—Whitewater loans, billing records from Mrs. Clinton's law firm that disappeared as fast as Travel Office employees (only mysteriously to reappear), FBI files that wound up in the hands of a beefy former bar-room bouncer with no apparent credentials for the security job he held. By contrast, Gore seemed squeaky clean.

Bill Clinton got hung up on national health insurance. Al Gore reinvented government.

Bill Clinton wanted to put gays in the military. Al Gore used his foreign policy lead to negotiate nuclear missiles out of the Ukraine and fissionable material out of Kazakstan.

Gore was hawkish on Bosnia where Clinton failed to act.

Gore favored a bold response to Saddam Hussein's attempt to kill George Bush, Clinton wanted a distant and likely ineffective cruise missile strike.

Gore wanted to proceed with welfare reform. Clinton plunged into reforming health care, and for a moment it appeared his administration might drown because of it.

Bill Clinton spoke much and accomplished little. Al Gore spoke little, but, as with his NAFTA debate against Ross Perot, accomplished much.

To some observers, the contrast ran even deeper. Bill Clinton, under the influence of liberals like Hillary Rodham Clinton, Ira Magaziner, and George Stephanopoulos, was abandoning welfare reform, abandoning middle-class tax relief, and abandoning the moderate New Democratic approach to government that had given life to his candidacy.

Because of this leftward turn, Clinton was proving a liability in the 1994 congressional campaign. Democratic candidates often shunned his visits to their state. Republican ads routinely "morphed" their Democratic opponents into a likeness of "Bill." Gore, on the other hand, was virtually ignored by the GOP, as he stumped nationwide for Democrats, often with no member of the national media on his plane. So Gore was hardly tainted when the Republicans triumphed, capturing both houses of Congress.

Many wondered whether Gore should challenge Clinton for the presidency in 1996, to restore the Democratic Party to the moderate path it needed for success. The bellwether *New Yorker* ran a lengthy article by Peter J. Boyer boosting a Gore push for power.

Like Democrats across the country, Gore realized the extent of the November debacle. Not only were incumbent Democrats upset in numbers greater than usual, but in the House and Senate, Republicans won every open seat. Senator Harrison Wofford of Pennsylvania, whose election had signaled the start of the health care debate, lost this time to a conservative Republican, Rick Santorum. Governorships fell like target dolls at an amusement park; among the nation's ten largest states, only the governor's mansions in North Carolina and Flordia remained in Democratic hands. State legislatures followed suit. The outlines of a political realignment appeared to be emerging, particularly in the South, where white voters were forging a new identity with the Republican Party and where even sitting legislators elected as Democrats were defecting in historic numbers. And nowhere were the results more catastrophic than in Gore's home state of Tennessee where both Senate seats—including the one he had relinquished in 1992 to become vice president—fell to the Republicans. The governorship and state legislature were captured by the GOP, and two seats in the House of Representatives were also lost.

But those who urged Gore to begin asserting his independence completely misread the man they wanted to play hero. Albert Gore, Jr., is a team player who believes in the chain-of-command. When the *New Yorker's* Peter Boyer asked whether he would be satisfied running for president on the Clinton record, Gore replied, "Absolutely. If I decide to run for president at some point in the future, I will be happy and honored to be judged by the accomplishments of Bill Clinton's administration. And I *ought* to be judged on that basis if I ever run, in significant measure because I've worked so hard as a part of this team."

Clinton knew he needed a bold stroke to regain his political equilibrium for his 1996 reelection campaign. He found that stroke in a friend who had helped him in Arkansas, bringing the gifted, if flawed, Machiavellian figure of Dick Morris into the White House.

Gore saw Morris as a potential ally. He told Morris he would support him so long as Morris endorsed Gore's environmental program and so long as Morris stayed away from his Republican friends and former clients—most especially so long as he promised not to leak to Trent Lott. Morris agreed.

Morris quickly confirmed that a media man's greatest talent is the ability to see the obvious. What was obvious to Morris, and to most Americans, was that the man elected as a New Democrat needed to come back to center from his extreme leftward drift on national health care, gays in the military, and other issues.

Morris recommended that Clinton commit himself to welfare reform and a balanced budget by a certain date. He also advised Clinton to come out unequivocally against affirmative action—advice Clinton did *not* take because he wanted to avoid a primary challenge from Jesse Jackson.

Morris urged a massive ad campaign to repair damage to Clinton's image, to be followed by Democratic National Committee ads that could be thinly disguised Clinton-Gore reelection spots. The senior political team—which included the president, Gore,

Dick Morris, Leon Panetta, Harold Ickes, George Stephanopoulos, White House Political Affairs Director Doug Sosnik, and Peter Knight, Gore's former chief-of-staff, now a Washington lobbyist— would continue to meet regularly throughout 1995. The media plan was approved at a meeting on September 20, 1995. Ickes, a leftist, hated Morris, but was so excited about using Democratic National Committee (DNC) money to bolster Clinton, he claimed co-parentage of the idea. And Gore and Morris would work so closely together that Clinton would accuse Morris of having "made the vice president your employee."

The drive to raise huge sums of money quickly was directed not only at beating the Republican candidate in November, but at scaring off primary challengers. "One, we had to do it very fast to demonstrate the kind of political strength that the president had," said Peter Knight. "But also, to give us the money that we needed to communicate our message whenever we wanted to do that. All of us know how expensive that can be."

When it came to raising the money that would be circulated through the Democratic National Committee, Ron Klain, Gore's new chief-of-staff, noted in a memo that Gore should tell Clinton, "we can raise the money—*but only if*—the president and I actually do the events, the calls, the coffees, etc...." The president would be more than an equal partner when it came to "events" and coffees. But with a few exceptions, the phone calls fell to Gore.

In late 1995 and early 1996, Gore made fifty-two calls—completing forty-six—from official White House telephones. He generated up to $795,000 in political contributions. Most of the "call sheets" providing names and descriptions of the would-be donors, specific financial objectives, and thumbnail sketches of the approach to be used, were prepared by Peter Knight. While the list included a handful of Gore's own friends—Nate Landow, for example, was asked to ante up $25,000 (he delivered it to the DNC that same afternoon)—it also included veteran contributors to Democratic causes and candidates who had never been close to Gore. Indeed, some of them he barely knew. This absence of traditional intimacy strongly influenced the tone of many conversations. Instead of the candidate inspiring the inspired with a fervent invocation of shared values, Al Gore—the number two man in the executive branch—seemed more like the Sheriff of Nottingham coercing tribute from those needful of his protection. When Bob Woodward of the *Washington Post* later contacted many of those who had been "Gored," he would report a sense of disillusionment bordering on anger. One "donor" termed the vice president's approach "revolting." Another claimed it had "elements of a shakedown." Those from businesses dependent on government contracts or subject to heavy regulation were particularly affronted. According to one, "It was like dealing with a mafioso."

Whatever his method, Gore's fundraising role became so prominent, he soon earned the nickname among the campaign hierarchy, "Solicitor-in-Chief."

CHAPTER SIXTEEN

PURGES

TO BE "GORED" could mean being shaken down for contributions. But it could also mean other sorts of hardball—specifically, purging people whose opinions Gore considered heretical or who were a potential political liability to him.

For example, Gore's accession to the vice presidency seemed, if anything, to intensify his ardor on the issue of global warming, and he tried to interest the media in running stories on how scientists who were skeptical of it were merely tools of industry. Two ABC News *Nightline* producers appeared ready to take the bait. But when Gore tried to seal things with a personal call to anchor Ted Koppel, the move backfired.

On February 24, 1994, Koppel introduced the program by describing the Gore call. As Koppel recounted it, "The vice president suggested that we might want to look into the connections between the scientists who scoff at the so-called greenhouse effect, for example, and the coal industry. There was also a connection to the Reverend Sun Myung Moon's group, and with Lyndon LaRouche's organization." In fact, Gore's staff had provided *Nightline* with documents which "suggest that Fred Singer has been receiving support from the Reverend Sun Myung Moon's Unification Church...."

Gore accusations were true enough. For instance, a magazine of little influence in the global warming debate was apparently a LaRouche front; one prominent skeptic, Professor Patrick Michaels of the University of Virginia, was executive editor of *World Climate Review*, funded by the Western Fuels Association.

But, on the other hand, it was also true that the vast majority of Professor Michaels' research money came from public funds, and that in almost every case, the global warming skeptics were noted experts in their field and their scholarship had gone through the peer review process essential for academic legitimacy. Moreover, their professional standing was no more suspect than, for example, those working on grants from federal agencies staffed by Gore loyalists, or, for that matter, scholars knee deep in the movement of environmental activists. As Professor Fred Singer noted in his interview with Koppel, "I would simply point to the fact that every environmental organization I know of gets money from Exxon, Shell, Arco, Dow Chemical, and so on."

Indeed, in 1993, the dozen largest environmental activist groups had a collective income of $600 million. In 1994, the year of the *Nightline* broadcast, the nation's oil and automobile companies contributed more than $2,760,000 to the activist organizations. (Big Oil displayed either a generous soul, or the belief that extremism in defense against nuclear energy is no vice.)

Koppel found Gore's methods puzzling, noting, "There is some irony in the fact that Vice President Gore, one of the most scientifically literate men to sit in the White House in this century ... is resorting to political means to achieve what should ultimately be resolved on a purely scientific basis."

*   *   *

Another "heretic" who quickly found himself excommunicated

by Gore and his staff was William Happer, Jr., the Bush-appointed director of energy research at the Department of Energy. Happer had been asked to stay on by Clinton's Energy Secretary Hazel O'Leary at least through July 1993, largely to fight for renewed congressional backing for the super conducting super collider. The multibillion-dollar Reagan-Bush project, briefly adopted by the Clinton administration, involved construction of a particle accelerator designed like a fifty-mile "racetrack" which, by engineering proton collisions, promised scientists their best look ever at the composition of atoms. But Happer was purged from the department with the speed of an accelerating proton after telling both Gore's staff and Congress that better surface measurements were needed before leaping to conclusions on the effects of ozone depletion in the stratosphere. It had long been the Gore position that chloroflourocarbons burn through ozone "like an acid," allowing more ultraviolet-B (UV-B) rays to reach the earth's surface, exacerbating the risk of skin cancer.

But in his April House testimony, Happer said, "As an individual, I think that there has been an exaggeration of the dangers of ozone depletion and climate change." Noting that surface UV-B measurements were at best ambiguous, he cautioned, "One of the problems with ozone is that we don't understand how the UV-B is changing at ground level, and what fraction of the ultraviolet light really causes cancer." To Happer, the big mystery was why a rather sharp depletion of ozone levels in the stratosphere—3 to 5 percent over a dozen-year period beginning in 1979—had not been reflected on the ground where a century's worth of depletion had amounted to only 5/18 of a single percentage point increase in UV-B levels. Since such factors as the season and latitude are far more important than stratospheric ozone levels as determinants of radiation, even the 3 to 5 percent would have resulted in no more radiation increase than a New York City family would experience by moving to New Brunswick, New Jersey, about sixty miles to the south. But the samplings of recent years strongly suggest that the loss of stratospheric ozone has not resulted in increased earthly exposure to UV-B.

In the Bush administration, Happer's views were prized for lending balance to often emotional debates. For example, Robert Watson, head of NASA's "Mission to Planet Earth," who had detected global warming in the summer of 1988, warned at a 1992 meeting of Bush's Federal Coordinating Council on Science, Engineering and Technology that the ozone crisis had reached the point where there was real danger of "an ozone hole over Kennebunkport." That happened to be Bush's vacation retreat and the site of the meeting in question. Watson went on to detail the threat to man, fish, fowl, and beast. Happer angrily protested Watson's assessment, calling his ozone scare talk "bullshit." He noted that the seas off the coast of Ecuador—the world's richest fishing area—receive "a thousand times more UV-B radiation than does Antarctica at the height of its ozone hole season."

Gore, however, got wind of the Kennebunkport prediction and advertised it as something akin to Divine retribution for the Bush administration's sinful lack of action on the environment. The hole never happened, but Watson was named associate director of environment in the new administration's Office on Science and Technology Policy.

Having already argued the ozone point with Gore's aide, Kathleen McGinty, Happer had been identified as the political equivalent of an infidel. By the end of April, he was out. Representative George Brown, Jr., the Democrat who, as chairman of the House Committee on Science, Space, and Technology, had interrogated Happer on numerous occasions, offered one explanation: "Happer marches to a different drummer than Al Gore. Will is a pure scientist. Al Gore is a politician."

Safely back at his academic home in Princeton, Happer joked, "I was told that McGinty has an enemies list and that I was on it." In a more serious vein he said, "It seems to be an act of treason to propose that there is a great deal of interesting and useful research that needs to be done on the origin, extent and effect of greenhouse gasses."

*   *   *

Perhaps the strangest Gore purge involved the Harvard-based speechwriter, Richard Marius, a Tennessee farm boy and former Christian minister who had become a gifted writer and teacher. Liberal, politically passionate, of uncompromising integrity, and with an ego that thrived on peer rather than public recognition, Marius had watched Gore's vice presidential acceptance speech at the 1992 Democratic convention, and concluded it was "as graceful as an effort to ice skate on a wooden floor." He promptly contacted his old Tennessee friend, Roy Neel, of the Clinton staff, volunteering his services as a speech writer. Soon he was busy pounding out words for the vice president.

In March 1993 Gore's office asked Marius to work on a speech for Gore to deliver at Madison Square Garden on April 18 to commemorate the fiftieth anniversary of the uprising against the Nazis by the Jews of the Warsaw ghetto. En route to Washington, Marius dwelled on an unforgettable image of the event, "a photograph of a young boy with hands raised over his head, walking at the head of a long, doomed line of Jews marching out of the smoke and ruin of the Ghetto when the Nazis had finally reduced it in May 1943. On the side of the street a leering Nazi trooper held a rifle."

Marius played with this image to produce a memorable oration. As Gore later recited:

> I am always arrested by the image of one frightened
> little boy. He wears a coat that reaches to his bare knees
> over his short pants. On his head is a wool cap as if some
> mother had dressed him to ward off the morning chill on
> his walk to school. Yet here he is, trudging at the head of

a weary column of doomed humanity, his hands lifted in the air in a gesture of harmlessness under the scornful laugh of a German soldier who holds an automatic rifle in his hand.

This child is not on his way to school. He is going to his death....

Before that image, words fail. We are reduced to silence—silence filled with the infinite pool of feeling that has created all the words for humility, heartbreak, helplessness, and hope in all the languages of the world.

How could the human race have allowed such a calamity as the Holocaust to fall upon us? What terrible darkness lies coiled in the human soul that might account for this venomous onslaught in the middle of a century that was hailed at its birth as a 'century of progress?'...

The story of the Warsaw ghetto is sacred text for our time. It warns us of the unfathomable power of evil, the pestilence of the human soul that for a time can dissolve nations and devastate civilization....

But the uprising in the ghetto also warns tyrants wherever they rule for a season that a fierce, bright light blazes eternal in the human breast, and that the darkness can never put it out....

Marius read his draft in the vice president's office to Gore, his foreign policy advisor, Leon Fuerth, and Marla Romash, his press secretary. "When I finished reading, Leon was so overcome with emotion that he had to leave the room for a few moments," Marius later wrote. "The VP and I sat there with tears in our eyes. Marla looked on with an expression of astonishment."

But a few weeks before the April 18 date, Romash called Marius with troublesome news. Not only had Martin Peretz—Gore's close friend and former Harvard mentor—submitted a draft of his own, he had "exploded" upon learning that Marius had also written a speech, complaining to the vice president that Marius was an anti-Semite.

Peretz' complaint dealt with a book review Marius had written for the March/April 1992 issue of *Harvard* magazine. The book was called, *A Season of Stones: Living in a Palestinian Village*, by Helen Winternitz. In recounting the book's description of the excesses of Shin Bet—Israel's secret police—during the sustained period of Palestinian civil unrest in the late 1980s known as the Intifada, Marius wrote:

> Many Israelis, the Holocaust fresh in their memory, believe that that horror gives them the right to inflict horror on others. Winternitz's account of the brutality of the Shin Bet, the Israeli secret police, is eerily similar to the stories of the Gestapo, the *Geheimstaatspolitzei* in Nazi-occupied territories in World War II—arbitrary arrests in the middle of the night, imprisonment without trial, beatings, refined tortures, murder, punishment of the families of suspects.

It is easy to see why many Jews and others would regard the Marius analogy as a stupid and offensive caricature of the truth. For one thing, support among many Israelis for the temporary detention of suspected terrorists, and interrogation techniques that may at times be harsh, or even brutal, springs not from memories of the Holocaust that deprived them of sisters, brothers, and parents a generation ago and a continent away, but from terrorist bombs and bullets that do the same even today.

Further, on its worst day, the actions of Shin Bet do not approach the mass deportations, tortures, and murders of the Gestapo.

And finally, while the security agencies of free and democratic societies like Israel—and the United States—can be guilty of shocking excess, their actions are not rooted in the sort of racist or nationalist fanaticism that characterized Nazi Germany. Gestapo agents were executing a state policy of genocide. No remotely similar state policy informs the actions of Shin Bet agents today.

Despite this single instance of rhetorical overkill, Marius has a long personal record of opposition to anti-Semitism. His writings have explored and condemned the anti-Jewish bias of Martin Luther as well as the occasional fundamentalist of today who would declare Jews and other non-Christians ineligible for Salvation. Nor is Marius a knee-jerk supporter of Israel's regional enemies. "I do not in any way romanticize or idealize the Arabs with their tyrannical, woman-hating governments and those rich Arab classes in countries like Kuwait where two-thirds of the population sat out the Gulf War in luxury hotels abroad and where a peonage akin to slavery is common," he has written. Marius's personal history is one of passionate advocacy for the underdog underlined by the sort of moral certainty that often flourishes in the tenured environment of academia. And it is possible today to find many Jews inside Israel who would share his repugnance at Shin Bet methods, and who feel its excesses derive from the wrongful Israeli occupation of Palestinian lands on the West Bank and Gaza.

Marius told Ms. Romash that he would not defend himself against Peretz' anti-Semitism charge, but that he would cease writing for the vice president if the Holocaust speech were not used.

With the addition of a few paragraphs taken from an otherwise uninspiring draft submitted by Peretz, the speech was delivered as Marius wrote it, to wide acclaim.

From his base at Harvard, Marius continued to write for Gore and Tipper. Once Gore told Marius's wife Lanier, "Your husband's the best." After a high school commencement address Marius had written for Tipper, Gore told him, "You're our savior."

In early 1995 Marius contacted Lorraine Voles, who had

replaced Marla Romash as communications director, indicating he would like to take a period of leave from Harvard and write speeches for Gore through the 1996 campaign. Voles vetted the proposal through Jack Quinn, Gore's chief-of-staff, who in turn got enthusiastic approval from the vice president. Marius was told the job was his at a salary of $70,000 a year. He gave notice to Harvard, got his leave, rented his house, and even bought two suits from J. Press, spending $750 for the pair.

In early July 1995, as Marius prepared to head for Knoxville, where he conducted an annual writing seminar for teachers, Skila Harris, Tipper Gore's chief-of-staff, asked him to write a speech for a family values conference Mrs. Gore would be addressing in Nashville. The evening before her speech, Tipper told the press it would be very special. "I've worked hard on it," she said.

On Sunday, July 9, at 7 AM, Voles called Marius in Knoxville. "Richard, I have some very bad news," she said. "As you know, we have very close relations with the Jewish community...." She told him that during the past week, several in that community had complained bitterly about his appointment. She said the vice president had now read Marius's 1992 book review of *Season of Stones* and had decided he could not hire him after all.

"I have never had an anti-Semitic thought in my life," Marius protested.

"I know you haven't," said Voles. She told him the vice president's staff hoped he would continue writing for Mr. Gore "but on a contractual basis" rather than as a "political appointee."

She also asked him to provide a cover for the vice president. "We will expect you to say that this was your own decision. You can say you changed your mind. And we'll say the same thing."

Former members of the vice president's staff confirm that "Marty Peretz put the death sentence on the Marius appointment." Most felt Marius had been wronged and that the vice president had acted to keep Peretz happy rather than to protect his office.

Marius, of course, believed this was all Peretz' doing. And as shock turned to reflection, he concluded he would neither continue writing for the vice president nor lie about the circumstances of his dismissal. "It sounded something like this," he would write. "'Hey I'm not going to marry you after all. Some important friends of mine think you're wicked and evil and malicious, and I can't afford to be seen with you in public or to acknowledge you in any way, although I know you're none of these things, but hey babe! You give me great sex. So let me pay you now for what you've been giving to me for nothing. Just keep it secret.' Well, alas, I don't lie, and I don't have a red light hanging in front of my computer or my yellow pad. And I don't give a good goddamn if people attack me when I'm right on a moral issue."

Marius has no regrets. In a letter to the author, he wrote, "I consider myself lucky not to be part of the trashy behavior that's part of this administration's life—though I voted for that sleazebag Bill Clinton in both his presidential elections."

*   *   *

At times the heavy-handedness of Gore's agents reached down even to civil servants. Henry Miller was the director of the FDA's Office of Biotechnology, which kept track of the development of new organisms for use in agriculture and industry, such as the splicing of plant genes to produce a species resistant to pests, or able to produce twice the fruit of ordinary plants.

Miller, an MIT-trained biologist, participated in the development of government policy on biotechnology during the Reagan and Bush administrations. Along with a special committee selected by and from the National Academy of Science, he concluded that biotechnology could "contribute substantially to improved health care, agricultural efficiency, and the amelioration of many pressing environmental problems," that the process involved no unique hazards, that its products "are like any other new organism," and that the assessment of risk, and hence the need for regulation, should focus on the *product*, and not the *process*. That put him on a collision course with activists brought into government by Gore, including Jerold Mande, appointed to a senior political position at the Food and Drug Administration.

Gore himself appears to have been of two minds about biotechnology. On the one hand, he recognized its potential in the areas mentioned by the National Academy of Sciences. On the other, he had a rather quaint notion that the end result of all this work would be to drive the family farmer from his land. He once wrote that his fear was not that biotechnology would not work, but that in the food supply area, it would work too well. "Few expect that by accident we will set loose some genetically defective 'Andromeda Strain.' Given our past record in dealing with agriculture, we are far more likely to drown ourselves in a sea of excess grain." Of course, more efficient production would also mean the potential to eradicate starvation and malnourishment worldwide, less land devoted to agriculture and more available for reforestation, fewer pesticides and fertilizers, and a generally cleaner environment with lower levels of carbon dioxide.

Given his stated belief in the safety of biotechnology, Gore's endorsement of Jeremy Rifkin's diatribe, *Algeny*, is hard to fathom. Gore described the book, a wild attack against genetic engineering, as "an insightful critique of the changing way in which mankind views nature.... This important book raises the questions that must be addressed as we achieve an ever-greater ability to control nature and as we move rapidly toward the ultimate technology: human genetic engineering."

Steven Jay Gould, who teaches geology, biology, and the history of science at Harvard, offered a somewhat less enthusiastic critique: "I regard *Algeny* as a cleverly constructed tract of anti-intellectual propaganda masquerading as scholarship. Among books promoted as serious intellectual statements by important thinkers, I don't think I've ever read a shoddier work."

The quality of Rifkin's science was perhaps even better illustrated in a subsequent treatise, *Beyond Beef*, where he suggested that men who eat beef are more likely to beat their wives than those who don't. Meat, he claimed, "is a means of conditioning women to accept a subservient status in society."

On February 26, 1993, just over a month after the inauguration of Bill Clinton and Al Gore, Henry Miller was asleep in his room in a Tokyo Hotel. Later that day he was scheduled to deliver a noncontroversial paper at a conference sponsored by Japan's Science and Technology Agency. Shortly after midnight, he was awakened by a call from his secretary who told him that Commissioner David Kessler did not want him to deliver the speech.

When Miller came home, his superiors told him that the White House had reacted badly to an article in the *Journal of the American Medical Association* he had written about the dangers of over-regulating biotechnology.

Jerrold Mande, Gore's appointee at the FDA, decided to make Miller an "unperson." Miller had always received rave reviews from his superiors and, being a civil servant, was difficult to fire. But Mande arranged for Miller to have the same large office, the same salary, the same secretary, but nothing to do. Miller soon tired of the passive abuse and retired from government service.

Today, in his office at Stanford's Hoover Institution, Miller says he regards Al Gore as America's answer to Trofim Denisovich Lysenko, the favorite biologist of both Stalin and Khrushchev, and a notorious figure in the history of Russian science. Lysenko insisted that environmental factors cause structural changes in organisms, which are then transmitted to offspring. To Soviet leaders the idea was magnificent. Wheat cultivated in their "worker's paradise" would evolve into super-crops; human beings into the "New Soviet

Man." The concept was forced upon two generations of terrorized Soviet academicians, undermining the teaching of legitimate scientific theory in the country.

Miller is dismissive of Gore's understanding of science and scientific truth. "One can only hope," Miller has written, "that in January 2001 Mr. Gore will be able to assume the job for which he seems to have been preparing all his life: instructor in 'creation biology' at West Tennessee River Delta Junior College."

Gore's old law professor, James Blumstein, offers a similar if less sarcastic assessment of his former student. He acknowledges some sharp differences with Gore over the years. For example, "He favored barring the sale of organs for human transplant purposes, while I concluded permitting their sale could be a way to ease the terrible shortages in supply," Blumstein recalls. "Also, I would share some of his environmental objectives without the hard religious fervor and close-mindedness he has exhibited."

According to Blumstein, "Part of Al Gore's make-up is a moralistic streak that makes it hard to have a diversity of viewpoints. Secular religion can be a real threat to liberty." And Al Gore can be a real threat to those who disagree with him.

CHAPTER SEVENTEEN

CONVERTING RETREAT INTO ADVANCE

IN MOST ADMINISTRATIONS the vice president is a satellite traveling in the same orbit as the president and destined to share the same political fate. During most of the first three years of the Clinton presidency, Gore's situation was somewhat more complex. Clearly the two men were close. No president had ever delegated greater responsibility to his vice president than did Bill Clinton.

Former White House officials note that Clinton derived satisfaction from his friend's achievements and good press. He valued Gore's advice, trusted him as the voice of experience in dealing with Capitol Hill, gave him highly visible roles in several domestic projects, and reserved a place of importance for him in the conduct of foreign policy. "Clinton needed Gore," maintains a friend who has worked closely with Gore in both government and political undertakings. "No one else in the White House had anything like his experience and areas of expertise."

Gore's assignment as co-chairman of special bilateral commissions with the heads of state of Russia, Ukraine, Egypt, and South Africa resulted in his persuading Ukrainian President Leonid Kravchuk to return to Russia what had once been Soviet nuclear missiles stationed on the perimeter of its empire. This made it easier for Gore then to convince Kazhakstan to relinquish more than half a ton of bomb-grade uranium to the United States. On the other hand, his relationship with Russian Prime Minister Viktor Chernomyrdin, a subject of uncritical approval by much of the White House press, provided disappointing results. An inept, corrupt troglodyte, Chernomyrdin became the agent through which the administration funneled financial and technological assistance to Russia. But he proved a poor vehicle for implementing reformist ideas on economic and political renovation desired by Washington. Nor, before his dismissal in the spring of 1998, did Chernomyrdin show much ability to expand U.S.-Soviet trade, which continued to languish.

Worst of all, Chernomyrdin was a crook. It is no secret that many of the billions of dollars funneled to Russia through him by the United States and other members of the International Monetary Fund wound up in Swiss bank accounts. By the time President Boris Yeltsin sought to reappoint Chernomyrdin in 1998, the Soviet stock market had collapsed, the economy was *in extremis*, and political power appeared to be flowing back toward a Duma dominated by seasoned Marxists. That Duma rejected Chernomyrdin in favor of Yevgeny Primakov, a mischievous left-winger who had spent much of his career in the Foreign Ministry bolstering Moscow's alliances with terrorist states and movements hostile to American interests in the Middle East.

In November 1998 the *New York Times* reported that by 1995 the CIA had accumulated what they considered to be "conclusive evidence of the personal corruption" of Chernomyrdin and sent it to the White House, expecting the administration to take appropriate steps to protect American interests. "Instead, when the secret CIA report on Mr. Chernomyrdin arrived in the office of Vice President Al Gore, it was rejected and sent back to the CIA with a barnyard epithet scrawled across its cover...." The kindest interpretation is that Gore, a diplomatic neophyte, had become so infused with a sense of self-importance regarding the "Chernomyrdin channel," that he was simply unable to process bad news about his Russian chum, however well-documented it might have been.

The magnitude of Gore's error was underlined in an important article on the situation in Russia written by the distinguished observer of Moscow affairs, David Remnick, in the January/February 1997 issue of *Foreign Affairs*. Remnick wrote that "Chernomyrdin represents a longed-for predictability aboard, but to Russians he represents the worst of Yeltsin's government: corruption, privilege, and an almost delusional disregard for the public."

*   *   *

Just as Gore practiced absolute loyalty to Clinton in his public statements, and demanded the same of his staff, he was no less cautious inside the White House about avoiding any visible conflict with presidential policies. In cabinet meetings he never opposed the president and would rarely take a position on a matter of importance until he had discussed it in private with Clinton. Where differences became known, it was often because Clinton himself referred to the vice president's views in framing the issue. For example, when the administration warned the Serbs that further attacks on Sarajevo would invite allied bombing, Defense Secretary William Perry found that Gore wanted to go further than the president and issue a similar ultimatum for other locations. Perry was strongly opposed to conducting the strikes beyond Sarajevo favored by the vice president because there were no UN forces on the ground to serve as forward observers identifying targets. But he learned of Gore's position only through his own discussions with the president, the vice president not wishing to make himself a center of internal opposition to a

Clinton directive. In the end, Clinton rejected Gore's advice and backed the more limited measure urged by Perry.

*   *   *

The 1994 election proved a turning point for the political fortunes of the Clinton administration, but not in the direction many had forecast. Doctrinaire liberals on the White House team, who had won most of the debates during the first two years, began losing them as the third year progressed. Liberal political operatives like James Carville and Mandy Grunwald no longer had the freedom they had enjoyed earlier to wander in and out of policy debates as they saw fit. Dick Morris, hated by the White House cadre of liberals, became Mr. Clinton's most influential advisor, quickly forming an alliance with the vice president. Reinventing government, barely mentioned by the Clinton team after its initial unveiling, now became the president's darling. Clinton was surprised when a Peter Hart poll showed that the effort to streamline government and make it work more efficiently drew enthusiastic nationwide responses.

Since taking office, Gore had advocated steps to balance the budget, the first goal being to cut the deficit. Clinton resisted and, in the spring of 1995, authorized George Stephanopoulos and Laura Tyson, chairman of the Council of Economic Advisors, to conduct background briefings for reporters suggesting that such a commitment could slow the economic upturn and throw people out of work. By June, however, Morris had convinced the president that he would never recover his political popularity by continuing to fight for a budget deficit. Soon the White House announced that Clinton was ready to reduce the deficit to zero by the year 2002; the remaining difference with Congress involved whose "scoring" would rule—the Congressional Budget Office or the administration's own Office of Management and Budget. A period of bipartisan compromise ahead seemed at least plausible.

Gore was already working closely with Republicans on

telecommunications reform, another area where Clinton had given him the authority to make policy decisions on his own. Beginning in the early 1980s, he had held hearings highlighting the difficulties computers were having communicating with each other, and had begun urging the creation of an "information superhighway" to match the growing sophistication of the machines. This was compatible with the goal of the legislation, which was to transform the entire communications industry, breaking down the barriers to free market competition in all telecommunication venues, paving the way for the overnight technology revolution—from outmoded and expensive, to modern and affordable.

Under the plan, the seven regional "Baby Bells"—products of a 1982 antitrust decree—would be able to compete for long distance service as soon as they could achieve real competition in their local markets. At the end of the day, the hope was to have a substantially unregulated competitive market in local and long distance telephone services, television broadcasting, and cable.

While Gore's role in shaping the legislation gets generally good reviews from legislators who worked with him, one notable critic has charged him with abandoning his principles in exchange for communications industry campaign contributions. Throughout the 1992 campaign, Gore championed a publicly funded information superhighway, comparing it to the interstate highway system his father had sponsored in the 1950s. At Clinton's Little Rock economic summit in December, he declared, "[W]ith the advanced, high-capacity network, like the National Research and Education Network, it does seem to me that government ought to play a role in putting in place that backbone, just as no private investor was willing to build the interstate highway system, but, once it was built, then a lot of other roads connected to it. This new, very broad-band high-capacity network... ought to be built by the federal government and then transitioned into private industry."

One year later, Gore had reversed himself 180 degrees:

"Unlike the interstates, the information highways will be built, paid for, and funded by the private sector.... And so I am announcing today that the administration will support removal, over time, under appropriate conditions, of judicial and legislative restrictions on all types of telecommunications companies: cable, telephone, utilities, television, and satellite."

In his investigative book on the 1992 presidential campaign, *The Buying of the President*, Charles Lewis of the Center for Public Integrity saw evidence of a quid pro quo for Gore's switch: "On the exact date of his speech, Gore's Democratic Party received $92,000 in soft-money contributions from key industry players. MCI wrote twenty-three checks to the DNC between 1991 and 1994, averaging $11,696.96 per check. Among those checks was one for $50,000 written on December 21, 1993, the same day that Gore changed his position. On the following day, MCI kicked in another $20,000. Other major donors to the Democrats that day were Comptel, $2,000; NYNEX, $15,000, with another $10,000 the following day; Sprint, $15,000; and U.S. West, $10,000. Total giving over the two-day period from the industry was $132,000. Earlier that month, Bell Atlantic, whose average annual soft-money donation to the Democrats is $10,000, made a $50,000 contribution to the Democratic Party on December 7, 1993. Shortly thereafter, Gore's longtime assistant Roy Neel became head of the U.S. Telephone Association, one of the industry's most aggressive lobbying firms."

Defenders of the vice president say he yielded on the issue of public ownership because private industry eventually built most of what he had wanted government to fund. In addition, Republicans, who now controlled the key committees, would have it no other way. Neel, one in a never-ending line passing through the revolving doors of government service to the world of private influence and wealth, claims to have recused himself on all matters related to the telecommunications bill until he was permitted by law to lobby. Neel's job on Gore's staff was taken over by Greg Simon, who has now also found his place in the world of private Washington consulting.

In view of the image of moral superiority he frequently projects, it is useful to be reminded from time to time that, when money talks, Al Gore, Jr., listens.

*   *   *

There is little doubt that Gore's personal idiosyncrasies made the closing negotiations over the telecommunications bill more difficult than they otherwise would have been. For example, on two occasions, Republicans rebelled against Gore's alleged attempt to limit their role in hammering out the details. After one highly productive meeting of White House aides with Republicans Thomas J. Bliley, Jr., congressman from Virginia, and Senator Larry Pressler of South Dakota, and Democrats John Dingell, congressman from Michigan, and Senator Fritz Hollings of South Carolina, Gore excitedly and prematurely announced that a breakthrough had been reached. Resentful Republicans responded by stalling final passage for weeks.

Gore failed to learn from the mistake. In June 1997 broadcasters closeted with Senate Commerce Committee Chairman John McCain, House Telecommunications Subcommittee Chairman Billy Tauzin and others, seemed on the verge of an agreement to rate programming both in terms of the intended age group for which a program was directed and the level of sex, violence, or profane language in the program. During these delicate negotiations, Gore publicly called on the parties to provide "reliable information about the level of violence in Y-7 rated programs" (programs intended for children seven and younger). Suddenly the broadcasters felt coerced and the negotiations collapsed in acrimony. One senior Republican staffer complained, "The vice president's grandstanding was the straw that broke the camel's back."

Still, the administration heralded the achievement of telecommunications reform with a glitzy Library of Congress celebration. It fit neatly into the Clinton-Morris reelection scenario of accomplishing things that were important to middle-income Americans— and what could be more important than the tube, the phone, and the Internet?—in ways that defied ideological tagging and didn't cost very much. The hero of the hour was the man who had heralded himself as a "raging moderate" since entering Congress two decades earlier, Al Gore, Jr.

The job of implementing the act now fell to Federal Communications Commission Chairman Reed Hundt, a reliable Gore ally and friend since their St. Albans days. Hundt helped bring down a broadcast industry effort to write technical standards for digital TV that would have been fine for broadcasters, but not the computer industry. He also led efforts to smash the power of the international cartel that keeps overseas telephone rates at least three times higher than they would be in a competitive market, and conducted auctions of frequencies for cellular phones and other digital services that brought at least $20 billion into the federal treasury.

In one blatantly political move, Hundt sought to help Clinton and Gore implement a campaign promise to link all elementary and secondary schools in the country to the Internet. So hyped was this initiative that in one joint appearance at a California school, the president and vice president paraded along a corridor unrolling a spool of electrician's wire, masquerading as Internet cable, painted red, white, and blue for the occasion. The school effort would cost an estimated $10 to $20 billion a year to implement fully, but is capped at $2.25 billion. To finance the remainder, Hundt proposed a thinly disguised tax on phone service, which promptly became a political football when critics branded it "the Gore tax."

Congress opposed the tax. States that had chosen not to offer "an Internet in every classroom" complained about Washington's unfunded mandate. And states that had already installed school Internet systems, often with financial help from private industry, resented a "Gore tax" that benefitted other states. The controversy over Gore's federal solution to a non-problem took some of the gloss off what was, on the whole, an admirable telecommunications initiative.

*   *   *

Clinton proved himself an effective counter-puncher against the Republican Congress. Together with Gore, the congressional Democrats, and organized labor, the president successfully caricatured the Republican agenda as cutting benefits for the middle class to finance a massive tax break for the rich. Clinton positioned himself as the champion of a *compassionate* balanced budget. His "mend it, don't end it" approach to affirmative action kept Jesse Jackson satisfied, and the Republicans off-balance. And President Clinton proved no less effective at neutralizing foreign policy issues. A commitment to expand NATO to include Poland, Hungary, and the Czech Republic met Republican demands even if some security experts questioned the wisdom of isolating Russia.

Clinton could also point out, on the world stage, that America's intention to respect "legitimate" civilian rule in Haiti had been achieved without carnage, albeit with no lasting benefit to the Haitian people either. And Clinton's gifted diplomat, Richard Holbrooke, had achieved at least a temporary peace in the Balkans.

The Republicans could have taken some credit for dragging the Democrats to the right, but this too was neutralized by Al Gore's and Republican Speaker of the House Newt Gingrich's mutual antipathy that blocked overt compromise, and by Gingrich's confessed inability to understand and outmaneuver Bill Clinton. So the Democrats took all the credit for their popular centrist position and left the Republicans looking like unhelpful, carping critics.

These accumulated successes would provide the Clinton-Gore administration with a useful buffer when, in mid-1996, its policy in Iraq began to disintegrate. The problems commenced with an intramural dispute among "protected" Kurdish factions. One of the faction leaders invited help from Saddam Hussein, who unleashed a large armored attack inside a Kurdish enclave demarcated by America and its allies. In the process, Saddam, smashed a major U.S. intelligence operation working to build a political and military infrastructure to challenge him. Saddam's execution of its leaders was an international humiliation for the United States. Within a year, Saddam was routinely defying UN weapons inspections, and American policy towards Iraq appeared to be vacillating between appeasement and empty threats. A surprisingly stiff December, 1998, bombing campain launched by the President provided uncertain results.

*   *   *

The author was among the correspondents covering the Republican convention in San Diego and the Democratic convention in Chicago. I spent most of each evening walking among the delegations on the convention floor. Compared to the Republican wake in San Diego, Chicago was an emotional fiesta. Republican delegates had reveled in Nancy Reagan's touching tribute to her husband and Elizabeth Dole's well-staged presentation of hers. But in private conversations, much of the talk was about whether Senator Bob Dole and his running mate Jack Kemp would lose badly enough to jeopardize the GOP hold on Congress. Republican Speaker of the House Newt Gingrich and Senate Majority Leader Trent Lott were already seeking accommodation with the White House, passing bills to increase the minimum wage, ease the portability of health insurance, and achieve bipartisan welfare reform. The Republicans were actually trying to ride on Clinton-Gore's coattails as friends of the administration.

There was no such defeatism among the Democrats. Not even the news that Dick Morris, the president's political guru, had been caught entertaining a prostitute at his Washington hotel put a damper on anyone's spirits. "These things have a short half-life," presidential advisor Mickey Kantor assured me when I ran into him on the convention floor. "No one's going to impute Dick's problem to the president." Early in the convention I asked a leading California Democrat how his state looked. "Big win," he replied. "California is the most pro-choice, pro-environment, and antismoking state in the country, so there's no reason for Dole to even show his face out there." And what about Clinton and Gore? "We love 'em both. Gore maybe even better because he's so comfortable in Silicon Valley."

"I almost feel like this is three conventions in one," said a woman delegate from Texas. "We're nominating Clinton once and Gore twice. That keeps us in the White House all the way to 2008." Gore spent many of his "off duty" hours visiting state and other caucuses in the hotels. Wherever he was sighted, delegates would chant, "Twelve more years."

"Let's not get ahead of ourselves," Gore would respond demurely. "Let's not rush things."

Never had I seen a convention where the vice presidential candidate got so much quality time, both on the floor and on television. Never had I seen a president more generous in sharing the spotlight during his moment of triumph, so willing to talk about his running-mate as an equal member of his team. Never had I seen a transition from one man to another so artfully played, yet with no transition actually taking place.

Gore was to deliver his major address before the president spoke, another indication that Clinton, rather than fearing that he might be upstaged by his vice president, regarded Gore's success as an essential ingredient of his own. Now the floor, easily navigable most of the time, became a pressing mass of humanity as delegates, alternates, guests, and anyone who could gain access squashed against each other to the point where the simple act of breathing became a luxury.

Gore's speech began with a deadpan offer to display his version of the popular "macarena," followed by silence as he stood statue-like for what seemed like half-a-minute, after which Gore asked, "Would you like to see it again?" Then came the mandatory "We shall not let them" litany of social and political crimes the Republicans would commit if again allowed custody of the White House.

But the speech will forever be remembered for Gore's stark evocation of his sister's 1984 death from lung cancer, including his final moments visiting her in the hospital, "savaged by that terrible disease."

"She couldn't speak, but I felt clearly I knew she was forming a question, 'Do you bring me hope?'

"All of us had tried to find whatever new treatment or new approach might help, but all I could do was to say back to her with all the gentleness in my heart, 'I love you.'"

Gore continued: "And then I knelt by her bed and held her hand. And in a very short time, her breathing became labored and then she breathed her last breath.... And that is why until I draw my last breath, I will pour my heart and soul into the cause of protecting our children from the dangers of smoking."

To the author, squeezed into involuntary embrace on the packed convention floor, the moment was overpowering with emotional intimacy. Each word landed with searing sensation. Immediately, one shared Gore's fury at those accountable for the tragedy, admiring him for the courage to part with memories so wrenching, precious, deep, and personal.

But just as suddenly, I found myself uneasy about what had occurred. Quickly I remembered the speech four years ago when Gore's son's near-tragedy outside the ball park had been vetted before a live audience of thousands and a television audience in the tens of millions, all partaking in what was, after all, a political event. I remembered too that when a reporter had asked Al, Jr., and Tipper about the taste of baring so private a moment at a political convention, Tipper had replied, "That happened to us, in public, and we dealt with it in public. We kept as much private as we could, but it's become part of our lives, and it's part of who we are and very much a part of who Al is, and I think that it was courageous of him to reveal that. He's a very different person in many ways because of that trauma, and if you want to know him, you have to know what happened." Empathy suddenly gave way to a suspicion that my emotions and those of millions of others watching this event on television had been cruelly exploited. And that gave way to anger that Gore had violated the privacy of his loved ones for the purpose of exploiting the rest of us. Soon I began to wonder about the convention in the year 2000 that would likely nominate him. Whose privacy would be invaded by Gore's need for simulated empathy? Whose illness, whose accident, whose death, whose rape, whose murder would be described in gruesome detail so that Albert Gore, Jr., could jump-start his fall campaign for the presidency by overcoming his image as a political stiff?

Gore claimed he had found a mission the moment his sister died, but reporters saw little evidence of it in the days, weeks, and months after Nancy Gore Hunger's death or in his 1988 campaign for president when he had spoken of his personal knowledge of and admiration for tobacco farming.

Indeed, only a year after his sister's death Gore was testifying before Congress in support of protecting domestic tobacco growers from foreign competition. His concern was not with cancer patients, but with the economic well-being of tobacco farmers. "So what we are really talking about when we are talking about this program is a program that benefits hundreds of small family farms in the southern United States and elsewhere," he said.

Asked by reporters to explain the seeming inconsistencies, Gore said, "I felt the numbness that prevented me from integrating into all aspects of my life the implications of what that tragedy really meant."

In response to that exercise in New Age double-talk, Ed Gillespie of the Republican National Committee jibed, "Some of us thought it had to do with the North Carolina presidential primary, but that must have been a mistake."

* * *

Riding a booming economy and a world that by historic standards seemed positively sedate, Bill Clinton and Al Gore were coasting to an easy reelection by the time Gore debated Jack Kemp in St. Petersburg, Florida, on October 9, 1996. The vice presidential debate was sandwiched between the two presidential debates, the first of which left Dole running a distant second to Bill Clinton, unable to match him in policy wonking.

So Republican hopes rested with Kemp. But Kemp refused to go for the jugular on character issues where Republican strategists thought the administration was vulnerable. Still, on issues of policy and principle, Gore and Kemp conducted a lively and informed debate. Gore called a proposed tax cut by Dole "a risky $550 billion tax scheme that actually raises taxes on the hardest-working families."

Kemp replied that the cut "has to be viewed against the context of a $50 trillion U.S. economy" and that rather than blowing a hole in the deficit as Gore had charged, "the only hole it would blow is a hole in the plans of this administration to try to tinker with the tax code and defend the indefensible."

On abortion, Kemp reminded the audience that "we have a president who vetoed a congressional ban on the ugly and gruesome practice of snatching life away from a child just moments before he or she enters the world."

Gore quickly brought the issue back to choice. "The platform on which Mr. Kemp and Senator Dole are running pledges a constitutional amendment to take away a woman's right to choose, and to have the government come in and order that woman to do what the government says no matter what the circumstances."

The exchanges were well mannered, civil, and substantive, with the press reporting the debate as having no clear winner. Not so the Dole camp. The candidate's spinmeisters in Florida thought Gore had pulverized their man. According to John Buckley—one of the most able of them—the Dole campaign "made a decision that the only possible way to get out of St. Petersburg alive was to do a flat-out *ad hominem* attack on Al Gore, so we did. So, we came out immediately saying that Gore was an automaton and, you know, it was a victory of humanity over cyborgs."

Unfortunately, by the time Jack Kemp and Bob Dole converged in Cincinnati for the post-debate "victory" celebration, the word from Dole's plane was that the campaign was distressed over Kemp's failure to exploit the character issue and other personal weaknesses of the president.

Once again, Al Gore had become the clear "winner" of the debate. By the end of the spin cycle, he had turned Jack Kemp into Ross Perot. It had been deja vu, "NAFTA II."

But there were two worrying blips as the Clinton-Gore team cruised to reelection. First were the persistent reports from Tennessee showing Dole might carry the state. Frantically, Gore cut individual radio spots for each of Tennessee's ninety-five counties, and campaigned hard in the state. Tennessee wound up narrowly in the Clinton-Gore victory column.

Second, and more worrying, were escalating stories of Clinton-Gore campaign fundraising scandal involving foreign nationals with links to Communist China and access to the White House. The hapless Bob Dole protested: "Where's the outrage?" But the American electorate said, "Not here."

Only after the second inaugural, as new details of Gore's fundraising activity came to light, would he begin to suffer some political fallout from what had been a wild, undisciplined operation, unguided by any principle save that of expediency.

CHAPTER EIGHTEEN

"NO CONTROLLING LEGAL AUTHORITY"

IN THE SPRING OF 1998 newspapers reported that the previous year Al and Tipper Gore had donated a total of $353 to charity on income exceeding $197,000. Political opponents, talk show piranhas, and the occasional editorial writer were quick to brand him a Scrooge, a tightwad, a closet meanie, a big-spending liberal, generous only with other people's money.

The jokesters weighed in with their own cruel cuts. Comedian Jay Leno said, "It was so hot today I was sweating more than a United Way volunteer trying to squeeze a nickel out of Al Gore." A rival predicted that the popular prime time show *ER* would soon broadcast an episode where the "'jaws of life' are used to pry open Al Gore's wallet."

Had these modern day members of the Pharisee sect been privy to a document executed in the District of Columbia on November 1, 1997, by Albert and Mary Elizabeth Gore, their comments might have been a good deal more charitable. On that day, Mr. and Mrs. Gore executed a Deed of Trust (mortgage) on their farm in Carthage, Tennessee, in favor of the Citizens Bank, 407 Main Street, Carthage, as security for a loan of $214,600.

The Gores had to pay for tuition, room, books, and board for two daughters at Harvard, and tuition for their son at Sidwell Friends, a costly Washington prep school. They had also celebrated a lavish Washington wedding for their oldest daughter Karenna, followed by a big bash in Nashville. But the real family budget-buster may have been the need to hire two of the nation's top lawyers— James F. Neal of Nashville and George T. Frampton, Jr., of Washington, D.C.—to ward off the possible appointment of an independent counsel to investigate Gore's use of his White House office for fundraising calls early in the 1996 campaign. Under the ancient (1887) Pendleton Act, it is a felony for any person to solicit political contributions in any federal building.

For Gore, the plunge from Boy Scout to debtor fighting off potential criminal prosecution involved more than just financial costs. The revelations came as the country was still digesting details of the vice president's featured appearance at an April 29, 1996, luncheon fund-raiser at the Hsi Lai Buddhist Temple in Hacienda Heights, California, an event, that Gore, in successive interviews, characterized as a "community outreach event," a "finance related event," and "a political event and I knew that there were finance people who were going to be present." A creative staffer contributed the term "donor maintenance event," which had a good samaritan ring to it, like some sort of pilot methadone program. And when some of Gore's telephone fundraising escapades were revealed by the *Washington Post*'s Bob Woodward, the vice president responded with a press conference at which he sounded more like a programmed Manchurian Candidate than a Democratic candidate. He acknowledged that "on a few occasions," he had used White House offices to place the calls in question, but, seven times during the session, he mechanically asserted that there was "no controlling legal authority" interpreting such calls as a violation of the law.

Gore suffered reversals on several fronts. Republicans called for the appointment of an independent counsel to explore the question of Hatch Act violations regarding the strict separation of government and campaign operations. And the liberal establishment—perhaps thinking that anyone with access to so much big money must be a Republican at heart—tore into Gore for his myriad sins, including duplicity. The *New York Times*, for example, editorialized:

> The vice president has many gifts, but they do not seem to include candor when it comes to the business of politics. Along with the erratic recollections of the number of calls he made, Mr. Gore has shifted stories on how they were paid for and insisted implausibly that he was unaware that his now-infamous appearance at a Buddhist temple in Los Angeles had anything to do with fundraising. It cannot have been pleasant to have made so many fundraising calls and then to have invented such distorted excuses. Mr.Gore did it to make sure that Mr. Clinton remained his best political friend. But in the process, Mr. Gore became the worst enemy to date of his own presidential ambitions.

The Hsi Lai fund-raiser would have involved no illegal activity on the part of Mr. Gore or his staff unless they had consciously participated in a scheme to accept campaign contributions from foreign nationals or donors operating under false names. Far more likely, the temple violated regulations relating to its tax-exempt status, and could have been in trouble with the IRS if the DNC had not refunded the questionable contributions. Event leaders like Maria Hsia, who allegedly conspired to reimburse monks and nuns for their contributions to the DNC, might also have been legally culpable.

But the event will be recalled far more for the side of Al Gore that came to light. Fading into the mist of spin control was the highly educated and articulate nuclear arms controller, the cutting-edge intellectual projecting the impact of technology well into the next century, the committed environmentalist begging, cajoling, pressuring his country to take seriously the threat of global warming. Here instead was the shabby pol operating close to the edge of the law, turning a blind eye to the violations of others, intimately involved in planning the event yet pleading ignorance of its inevitable consequences, lying unabashedly about the nature and purpose of the event, cutting and trimming and tacking with each shift in the wind.

Gore and the Buddhists went back a long way, and always at the center of the relationship was money for the Tennessean and his campaigns. In perhaps the most impressively written and detailed section of its final report, the Senate Committee on Governmental Affairs, chaired by Gore's fellow Tennessean, Fred Thompson, traces the beginning of the relationship to the 1988 aftermath of Gore's failed presidential campaign. The cast of Asian characters included:

- Maria Hsia, the Taiwan native who became a permanent U.S. resident in 1975 at the age of twenty-four, established a lucrative business assisting Asians with immigration problems, and became a political activist and fund-raiser to build a reputation and serve potential clients.
- Howard Hom, Hsia's partner and, for several years, "significant other."
- James Riady, the son of Dr. Mochtar Riady, an Indonesian of Chinese descent, who controlled the multibillion dollar confederation of companies known as the Lippo Group. Lippo interests include "banking, finance, insurance, property development, and manufacturing interests concentrated in Indonesia, China, and the United States." At the time, James Riady was managing his father's interests in the United States.
- John Huang, James Riady's "man in America," who maintained a position with Lippobank of California—owned 99 percent

by James Riady—and whose political advice was important in helping Riady decide where to invest.

These four, among others, established a group called the Pacific Leadership Council (PLC) "as a fundraising and lobbying organization to promote their interests in U.S. politics." Most of the initial seed money came from Riady who advised that in addition to the general cultivation of sympathetic Democratic politicians, the group should work to win political endorsement for policies that would benefit Lippo interests. These included getting senators to pressure Taiwan into allowing Asian-American banks to open branch offices, getting the federal government to deposit funds in Asian-American banks, and winning support for "special, exceptional immigration cases" when necessary. One approved vehicle for acquiring friends and influence was the Democratic Senatorial Campaign Committee (DSCC), headed by Senator Alan Cranston of California. The DSCC became a leading beneficiary of PLC largesse.

But the PLC's initial forays into 1988 politics proved disappointing. Michael Dukakis, their favored presidential candidate, lost in a landslide to George Bush. And, in the California Senate contest, Democrat Leo McCarthy came up short against Pete Wilson. Determined to recoup something from the year, Maria Hsia and the others hit upon the idea of a high profile tour of Asia by a group of Democratic senators. After casting bait at a number of likely fish, the group was rewarded by only one, Al Gore. Hsia wrote the senator that were he to accept, "I will persuave [sic] all my colleagues in the future to play a leader role in your future presidential race." Gore staffers Peter Knight and Leon Fuerth urged their boss to accept. Fuerth looked upon the trip as a way of familiarizing Gore with an important part of the world. Knight saw the Asian Americans as an interesting constituency to develop on his boss's behalf as he—Knight—was about to leave Capitol Hill to try his hand at private

influence peddling. Gore, after all, did have a substantial 1988 presidential campaign debt to repay and a war chest to replenish for his
1990 Senate romp.

When corporate sponsorship for the PLC trip lagged, Eddy
Yang, one of the group's co-founders and a man who had long
enjoyed ties to the Fo Kuang Shan Buddhist Order, invited his
group to pitch in. Thus did Gore become involved with a sect whose
"Master," Hsing Yun, regarded participation in the political process
as an essential part of "spreading the Dharma," or Buddhist ideals.
Hsing Yun's view had not developed casually. Prior to escaping the
China mainland in 1949 and leading a group of seventy monks to
Taiwan, he had been interrogated on several occasions by both the
Communists and Kuomintang (Nationalist Party) for intelligence
about the other. Later he and three hundred fellow monks would be
imprisoned by nationalist authorities who suspected them of prior
cooperation with the Communists. Over time, Hsing Yun's relations with the government on Taiwan improved. But the lesson
remained. "Having experienced first-hand the inconvenience and
even danger of being perceived as an outsider and potential threat,"
the Thompson report said, "he seems to have actively sought the
trust of political authorities."

Hsing Yun absorbed similar lessons in the United States after
his followers purchased first an old Protestant church and then, in
1978, a fourteen-acre site at Hacienda Heights, where they sought
to construct their monastic retreat. There followed years of zoning
battles and other reflections of community hostility as residents,
unnerved by the prospect of a Buddhist sanctuary in their solid
upper-middle-class area, fought as though the master had proposed
to introduce a porno shop. The cornerstone for the structure was
not laid until 1986.

Thus the Gore trip was something of a coup for the group, a
great leap forward from grubby local controversy to national political respectability. Huang handled the itinerary; he and James Riady

contributed $10,000 in "seed money." Overall sponsorship of the trip was provided by "a nonprofit organization in Indonesia."

Due to the involvement of the Buddhist group, the trip included a visit to the Fo Kuang Shan Temple in Kiaoshung, Taiwan, where Gore met with Master Hsing Yun. According to one account of the meeting, Hsing Yun remarked casually, "Hey, you could be president."

Gore asked, "Do I look presidential?"

"Very much so, very much," said the master.

Hsing Yun very likely conveyed that assessment to Maria Hsia. The Thompson Committee noted that the trip to Taiwan marked the start of "an extremely close relationship between Hsia and Senator Gore," involving Hsia and her political assistant, Jeffrey Su, in numerous fundraising events for the Gore campaign. Several were in southern California, establishing a pattern that would culminate with the 1996 Hacienda Heights event. But Hsia also helped organize Asian Americans for Gore in Tennessee.

The PLC held one California fund-raiser for Gore at the home of Tina Bow, one of its founders. The event raised an estimated $20,000 for Gore and included purported contributions from several Hsi Lai monks and nuns. Gore wrote a "thank-you" letter to at least one of the monastics, and a more elaborate one to Hsia in which he noted that because his presidential campaign had delayed efforts to raise money for his Senate campaign, "Your contribution at the early stage of this effort has helped to replenish our account and will allow me to build a strong organization."

Hsia and her colleagues also participated—with Gore's encouragement—in an effort to skirt national campaign spending laws that limit individual candidate contributions to $1,000 in a primary contest and another $1,000 in a general election campaign. Under Hsia's scheme, donors would contribute "soft" money—money not tied to a specific candidate—to the Democratic Senate Campaign Committee (DSCC). The DSCC claimed the legal right to accept unlimited "soft" dollars. But Hsia arranged for the money to be "tallied" by the donors for specific candidates. Essentially, in "tallied" donations, the DSCC served as a conduit from contributor to candidate for unlimited amounts of money.

Gore was, of course, fully aware of these activities. In one typical letter to Hsia, he thanked her for "your generous contribution to the Democratic Senatorial Campaign Committee which you had tallied to me."

Hsia informed Gore that she "would also like to see you become one of the senators closest to the Asian Pacific community," a development that would require "time and a special commitment from each other."

The lugubrious Federal Election Commission finally pierced the veil of tallied contributions. In 1995 it fined the DSCC $75,000 for violating campaign financial laws.

From the very outset, then, there was little mystery about what made the Gore-Hsia relationship tick. In a word, it was money. Hsia was a link to wealthy donors from the United States and abroad, eager to develop ties with U.S. politicians. Hsia was also manifestly willing to go beyond the law to deliver cash.

When it came to immigration issues, Hsia had a direct economic stake in liberalizing the law, and Gore, for his part, offered enthusiastic support for Hsia's immigration agenda, even sponsoring one of her amendments.

To those like Hsia, Huang, and the Riady family, who had been playing big-time U.S. politics for only a few years, the election of Bill Clinton and Al Gore was like a rookie horse-player hitting the daily double in one of his first visits to the track. Clinton had been wooed in Little Rock by the Riadys and Charlie Trie, the most extraordinary Chinese restaurant owner in American history. In 1992 Trie, after consulting with Clinton, formed the Daihatsu International Trading Co. in an effort to capitalize on burgeoning U.S.-China trade. Neither this nor any subsequent ventures earned money for Trie, whose annual income hovered around $30,000. He did, however, come to know a Chinese businessman based in Macau by the name of Ng Lap Seng. Ng had close ties to the People's Republic of China. Interestingly, between 1994 and 1996 Trie managed to contribute $220,000 to the DNC. The Thompson Committee concluded that Trie used "foreign-source money that he obtained primarily from [Ng Lap Seng]" to fund all of his DNC contributions. This pattern was repeated when Trie contributed hundreds of thousands of dollars to the Clinton Defense Fund. Trie had unusual access to the White House, and even offered advice to the president on U.S.-China relations. Only a few years earlier Trie's advice to Clinton had been limited to choosing Mandarin Shrimp over General Tso's Chicken.

The soft money contributions continued to pour in—no longer through the DSCC, but through the Democratic National Committee (DNC) controlled by Clinton/Gore political operatives.

By 1993 the group was also laundering political donations through straw men and straw companies. Both John Huang and Maria Hsia laundered funds apparently donated in connection with the White House visit of Shen Juren, the head of China Resources, a firm long known by counterintelligence officials as a civilian business cover for Chinese espionage agents. The Thompson Committee offers conclusive documentation that Shen Juren met with Gore's chief-of-staff, Jack Quinn, and excerpts from a later conversation between Gore and Shen Juren strongly suggest that they had met in Gore's White House office.

In advance of Shen Juren's 1993 visit, Huang wrote two $15,000 checks to the DNC. He signed on behalf of two American subsidiaries of the Riady-owned Lippo Group. Neither of the subsidiaries, however, was operating profitably. A third check, issued days later, had a similar pedigree. Each of the checks was backed by money from Lippo accounts overseas. At the same time, Hsia—in what was to become her *modus operandi*—arranged for the Hsi Lai temple nuns to contribute a total of $5,000 to the DNC, the money quickly refunded from Hsi Lai coffers. The "middleman" in the transaction was Man Ho, the nun, who served as the temple's administrative officer. The committee majority found that, "all of these donations"—both Huang's and Hsia's contributions—"were illegal, representing money from foreign sources or money from 'straw donors,' illegally reimbursed by another party." Even more troublesome, the committee found evidence that "Hsia has been an agent of the Chinese government, that she has acted knowingly in support of it, and that she has attempted to conceal her relationship with the Chinese government." The committee majority found that Hsia had raised more than $146,000 in illegally laundered contributions, some $116,500 of which went to the Clinton-Gore campaign.

The Thompson Committee never established complicity by Vice President Gore in these illegal fundraising activities. But the committee's failure to find the link that would convict Gore might have more to do with politics than anything else. Senate Majority Leader Trent Lott imposed a December 31, 1997, limit on the jurisdiction of the Thompson Committee, in order to avoid the endless partisan bickering that typified Senator Alphonse D'Amato's Whitewater Committee. The result, however, was to encourage the White House and unfriendly committee witnesses to play for time until the deadline.

Still, it strains credulity to suggest that Gore believed the contributions from the Buddhist monks and nuns of Hacienda Heights were legitimate, or that the event at that site was anything other than a campaign fund-raiser.

The luncheon grew out of a March 15, 1996, White House meeting between Gore and Master Hsing Yun arranged by John Huang. At the meeting the master invited Gore to visit the Hsi Lai Temple. Gore said a visit might be possible as he was visiting the West Coast in April. Shortly after the meeting, Hsia wrote a letter to Leon Fuerth suggesting that Hsing Yun "could be very helpful for President Gore's reelection." Hsia wrote another letter to Gore himself announcing that "John Huang has asked me to help with organizing a fundraising lunch event, with your anticipated presence on behalf of the local Chinese community." Initially, the fund-raiser was to be followed by a political rally at the Hsi Lai temple, but the two events were quickly merged into one at the Hacienda Heights site.

In addition to these communications, internal staff documents mentioned the visit as a fund-raiser. The vice president was briefed on the event by White House political coordinator Harold Ickes. The briefing included an estimate of how much money would be raised at the event, and the briefing paper bore the names of both John Huang and Richard Sullivan, the two main DNC moneymen. As the Thompson Committee Report documents, when the event failed to generate the desired money, Sullivan complained to Huang, who reached Hsia, who made certain that the temple would raise at least $100,000 from its treasury, funneling the money to the DNC through individual monks and nuns.

The utterly unambiguous nature of the event comes through most clearly in an exchange of messages between John J. Norris, one of Gore's national security staffers, and National Security Council China specialist Robert L. Suettinger. Dated April 15, 1996, Norris's message read:

"Bob—

"Hsing Yun has invited the VP to visit the Hsi Lai Temple in LA. Hsing Yun would host a fundraising lunch for about 150 people in the VP's honor.

"Any problems with the VP participating in this event from the perspective of U.S. China relations? The event would take place at the end of June."

Suettinger's reply read as follows:

"John—

"This is terra incognita to me. Certainly from the perspective of Taiwan/China balancing, this would be clearly a Taiwan event, and would be seen as such. I guess my reaction would be one of great, great caution.

"They may have a hidden agenda."

But the perceived need for money outweighed the concerns of national security. The event took place one month after Communist China had threatened Taiwan and fired missiles over the Straits of Formosa. The "great, great caution" urged by Suettinger took the form of avoiding displays of Taiwan's flag and shunning controversial rhetoric.

On the day before the event, Huang, Hsia, and a DNC fundraiser named Maeley Tom worked at the Temple, using their cellular phones to persuade people to attend. A witness to the conversations told the Thompson Committee: "My impression was that they were kind of soliciting contributions, soliciting guests maybe."

On April 29, 1996, at 12:30 PM, the vice president arrived at the huge pagoda-shaped temple. A high school band performed outside the building. Inside the entrance hall, Hsia, Huang, Representative Bob Matsui, and DNC Chairman Donald Fowler were among the official greeters. According to the Thompson Committee Report:

> After meeting briefly in a holding room with Master Hsing Yun, the vice president walked up the Temple's courtyard, between a phalanx of monastics, to the Temple's Buddha Shrine, to which the vice president made a flower offering. From there, the vice president was escorted downstairs to have his photograph taken with VIP attendees and those who had contributed in connection with the event.

The lunch was closed to the press, highly unusual for "a community outreach event." The vice president sat at the head table with Master Hsing Yun, Hsia, Huang, and Ted Sioeng, a wealthy Belize citizen with close commercial and political ties to the Chinese government. Sioeng, who had previously contributed negligible amounts to political campaigns, generated—through family and business interests— $400,000 to DNC soft money accounts during the 1996 election cycle. The Thompson Committee concluded that "half of this figure, or $200,000, was made with money wired into the U.S. from accounts in Hong Kong." Neither the Thompson Committee, nor the subsequent House investigation conducted by Representative Dan Burton was able to establish definitively how much, if any, of this money was illegal. The combination of complex, secretive bookkeeping, inaccessible foreign accounts and an absent witness—like others, Sioeng retreated to his foreign base rather than confront U.S. investigations—precluded the committees from concrete findings of illegality.

Once the luncheon was over, the embarrassment to Gore was immediate. Reporters, who had been barred from the "closed" event, grumbled about the propriety of holding a fundraiser at a religious institution. Within days, journalists had unearthed many of the details of the fundraiser. Even after the precise nature of the event was well established, Gore continued to split hairs, insisting "no money was offered or collected or raised at the event," and claiming, "it was not a ticketed event." Maybe not, but with John Huang having stood shoulder to shoulder with the master at his White House meeting, and then at the Hacienda Heights luncheon, it was clear to all but the willfully oblivious that a money-changer was in the temple.

And in fact when, under scrutiny, the DNC rushed to return the questionable contributions, one nameless DNC staffer offered this written explanation: "It was a temple, you idiot!"

In the Clinton-Gore lexicon, the Buddhist temple "outreach" was not a "fundraiser." Also not "fundraisers" were White House "coffees" or guest evenings spent in the Lincoln bedroom, even if they were openly expected to raise hundreds of thousands of dollars. It is, after all, as the administration concedes, illegal to use the White House for fundraising events. By White House standards, if Mr. Clinton did not wake the visitors from their slumber and ask for money, the procedure could not be described as a fundraising event.

On March 2, 1997, Gore gave a press conference that bordered on the surreal. For the first time in his charmed political life, Gore was under pressure, and his instinct was to confront his problems directly. The press conference was scheduled with the barest preparation, and over the vigorous dissent of White House Communications Director Mike McCurry. Political pros worried that Gore—who had yet to consult legal specialists on campaign laws and regulations—was asking for trouble.

The pros were right.

Gore began by acknowledging what Bob Woodward of the *Washington Post* had reported the day before—that he had solicited campaign contributions over the phone, but dissented from characterizations suggesting this was a "shakedown" or somehow "repugnant." Gore went further and confessed that "on a few occasions I made some telephone calls from my office at the White House, using a DNC credit card," he said. "I was advised there was nothing wrong with that practice.

"My counsel—Charles Burson is my counsel here—my counsel advises me that there is no controlling legal authority or case, that there was any violation of law whatsoever in the manner in which I asked people to contribute to our election campaign. I have decided to adopt a policy of never making any such calls ever again, notwithstanding the fact that they were charged to the Democratic National Committee as a matter of policy."

Six additional times during the session Gore would recite the phrase "no controlling legal authority" as his mantra for explaining the calls, winning it a place alongside Nixon's "I'm not a crook" on the honor roll of political ineptitude. Nor was the fact that Gore's statements were stylistic disasters their only problem.

The "few occasions" turned out to be fifty-two calls, forty-six of which were completed, leaving the vice president's spinmeisters to explain that while the calls were many, the occasions were few.

The "DNC card" turned out on several calls to be a Clinton-Gore campaign card, or, on one occasion, no card at all.

Another Gore assertion, that the president and vice president are exempt from the Pendleton Act, had been rejected by the Justice Department nineteen years earlier and had little support anywhere outside the Oval Office.

Nor was it ever clear whether Gore had sought and received advice from Burson—newly arrived from Tennessee—that the procedure was legal *before* he made the calls, or whether that was simply a position maintained after the fact, when liability for having violated a felony statute was staring him in the face. The enduring consensus among members of the national bar is that a competent lawyer like Burson would never have advised Gore in advance of the fact that the calls were legal and appropriate. A contrary interpretation of the law—indeed a flat ban on campaign solicitations from the White House—had been the rule while Abner Mikva had been Clinton's White House counsel. Moreover, in defending a series of White House coffees for big contributors, the president had argued that the ban on fundraising at the White House had been strictly observed, saying, "We got strict advice about—legal advice about what the rules were and everyone involved knew what the rules were.... There was no solicitation at the White House."

Presidential spokesman Mike McCurry had made the identical point about the coffees: "There is a separate restriction that exists for the solicitation of funds for political activities, which cannot occur on these premises."

As for the "controlling legal authority," Gore was right in the sense that case law on the statute was scarce. But the language of the law seemed plain on its face:

> It shall be unlawful for any person to solicit or receive any campaign contribution within the meaning of… the Federal Election Campaign Act of 1971 in any room or building occupied in the discharge of official duties.

The language had been plain enough for Gore during the 1987 planning for his presidential campaign when he had insisted on meeting moneyman Nate Landow at his parents' Capitol Hill apartment rather than his senatorial office. And it had been plain enough for him in December 1995, when he visited the DNC to do his fundraising.

Still, the very same legal specialists who doubted that any knowledgeable lawyer would have advised Gore to solicit campaign contributions from the White House office, maintained that no federal prosecutor on earth would move to indict Gore under the facts that were known. For one thing, the situation at hand was not the one the law—more than a century old—had been designed to address. The purpose of the old Pendleton Act was to protect federal workers against political shake-downs, not economic fat cats from being asked to ante up.

Second, the notion of a major prosecution coming down to the vice president's choice of phones seemed designed to prove that the law is indeed an ass. Gore could have telephoned from the White House kitchen or any of a dozen other rooms with perfect impunity, but not from one of the offices. Suppose, lawyers asked, he had been using a cellular phone and had strolled from office to living quarters during a single fundraising conversation. Would he still face prosecution? Would the issue become where he had spent most of his time? What he had been talking about in each room? Perhaps that offense, it was joked, being only half as bad as raising funds exclusively from a stationary phone, should give rise only to a misdemeanor prosecution.

Then there was a quaint 1912 decision by the Supreme Court in the *Thayer* case where a solicitation was mailed from outside a federal building to a government employee inside the building. The court held that the solicitation occurs at the time it is heard or seen by the recipient. Thayer was held guilty because the recipient opened the letter inside the building. Had he waited until he left the office, there would have been no crime. Gore's people maintained the Thayer case made the location of the recipient decisive and his calls to potential contributors at their homes or offices, innocent. The better view was that Gore's presence in the White House was enough to trigger the statute, but no one could be certain how a court would rule.

Unsurprisingly, the question of hard versus soft money also came into play. Money contributed to the national party committees can be either hard (intended for use in a specific election campaign) or soft (used for anything from issue ads designed to attract voters to the party, to "get out the vote" campaigns). If Gore had been soliciting only soft money, a number of knowledgeable commentators thought he could glide by unscathed, although it would seem that a shakedown is a shakedown regardless of whether the money is hard or soft. But memoranda from Ickes to the president and vice president suggested that at the DNC, both hard and soft money needed replenishment. Gore, then, had reason to know that at least some of the money he was soliciting could well go directly to help the Clinton-Gore reelection campaign.

Just prior to her reappointment for the second Clinton term, at a time when certain fundraising irregularities were known but the complete picture was just starting to take shape, Attorney General Janet Reno decided that neither President Clinton nor Vice

President Gore had been identified with any illegal activity. Thus, she concluded, there was no need for her to name an independent counsel to investigate campaign irregularities. Prior to this pronouncement, Reno's survival had been in doubt—the White House had leaked profusely that her propensity for appointing independent counsels had left Mr. Clinton grandly displeased. Following her decision, she was promptly reappointed.

Gore's disastrous press conference put pressure on the attorney general to take a second look at the need for an independent counsel. So did the White House effort to preempt the Thompson Committee by releasing thousands of campaign documents, including a vast body of material from the office of outgoing deputy chief-of-staff Harold Ickes. The material showed beyond any doubt that—as the *New York Times* commented editorially—"the Democratic National Committee was virtually a subsidiary of the White House. Not only was Clinton overseeing its fundraising efforts, not only was he immersed in its ad campaigns, but DNC employees were installed at the White House, using the White House visitors' lists and communicating constantly with Clinton policy advisors."

Had it not been for the president's squalid effort to mislead observers by referring to the DNC operation as that "other campaign" whose sins of omission and commission were no blemish on his White House, neither the *Times* nor anyone else would have found it remarkable that throughout the campaign the DNC was at the White House's beck and call. Such coordination is neither unusual nor in any sense pejorative. Until Clinton chose to dissemble about things, no one at the White House or the DNC ever sought to conceal the fact that there was close coordination between the two.

In discussing the campaign in December 1996 at Harvard's quadrennial post mortem, for example, Knight made no secret of the fact that a key campaign goal "was to achieve integration with the

White House and the DNC. We took a look at the last four campaigns since 1976 that had tried to run for the presidency from the White House, and only one of those had been successful—-Reagan in 1984. Although that was not necessarily the model that we were going to use, certainly the failure of that integration gave us pause, and was something we felt we needed to work on."

In terms of the law, coordination and control become important only in determining whether electioneering advertisements purportedly sponsored by a third party are attributable to the candidate for purposes of federal spending limits. The Clinton-DNC ads, as well as the Dole-RNC ads, took advantage of permissive Federal Election Commission and court precedent on the issue of what counts as electioneering.

Thus, the question of control of the DNC by the White House was of potential relevance concerning only whether those in the White House who did the controlling could credibly claim ignorance of wrongdoing—such as accepting illegal foreign contributions—by those on the staff of the DNC. Common sense may well dictate skepticism of White House denials of such knowledge. But without a sufficient threshold of evidence to support such skepticism, it would be hard to sustain the argument that the attorney general *must*, under law, appoint an independent counsel.

On March 13, 1997—ten days after the Gore press conference—Chairman Orrin Hatch of the Senate Judiciary Committee formally urged Reno to appoint an independent counsel, noting the question of "whether federal officials may have illegally solicited and/or received contributions on federal property." Hatch also noted "the emerging story regarding the possibility that foreign contributions were funneled into U.S. election coffers to influence U.S. foreign policy." That reference was to a March 9 *Washington Post* article reporting that government investigators had obtained "conclusive evidence that Chinese government funds were funneled into the United States last year," and quoting one official as saying that "there is no question that money was laundered."

On April 14, 1997, Reno rejected the Hatch request. While questions of Chinese involvement and money laundering were being pursued, she said there was no current allegation of wrongdoing by a "covered" (senior) official.

As regards the raising of money from White House property, Reno maintained that "soft" money was excluded from the prohibition. The fact that much of this money went for issue ads plainly helpful to the White House did not make the money "hard" unless it contained an "electioneering message"—specific language urging a vote either for or against a particular candidate.

Gore was not yet out of the woods. As Reno was preparing her response to Hatch, the Thompson Committee was deposing witnesses in preparation for the public hearing phase of its work. One of those questioned was Joseph Sandler, the chief counsel to the DNC. He told the committee that in analyzing the vice president's "call sheets" to determine the result of his phone solicitations, he and other DNC officials confirmed that some of the money had been deposited in "federal" or hard money accounts. Sandler surmised that Gore was ignorant of this fact because he had been asking for donations that on their face exceeded the legal hard money limits.

On September 3 the *Washington Post* struck again, this time with a report that $120,000 from the Gore calls, representing eight of the forty-six donors who had responded positively to his solicitation, had gone into the DNC's hard money accounts. One donor was quoted to the effect that the call "was clearly focused on the reelection campaign of Clinton and Gore."

Now Reno had no choice but to initiate a sixty-day inquiry into whether Gore's conduct had apparently crossed the threshold requiring appointment of an independent counsel. Astoundingly, the legal beagles at the public integrity section of her Justice

Department, whose sole reason for being was to ferret out the truth on such matters, had been scooped by reporters a few blocks away. Once again Reno—one of the more over-rated public servants of her generation—had come up short.

Gore needed help in a big way. To underline his point that he had done nothing illegal, he had until then avoided retaining private counsel. But now he hired two of the nation's best, Jim Neal of Nashville, a grizzled, brilliant veteran of the Watergate wars, and George Frampton of Washington, who had served as Jacob Stein's chief deputy in the independent counsel investigation of Ed Meese. Neal and Frampton understood that the two key issues were what Gore had told his donors and what he himself had understood was to be done with the money. Accordingly, they contacted those on the list one by one. And, as often happens when experienced attorneys "interview" prospective witnesses, the resulting accounts proved helpful to their client. In fact, after conversing with Neal or Frampton, nearly all donors recalled Gore talking about the need for the DNC to produce media spots designed to counter the GOP assault on issues central to the Clinton presidency. The two attorneys had succeeded in gathering evidence tending to put the solicitations on the "soft money" side of the ledger. Neal and Frampton then contacted the Justice lawyers, urging they interview the same donors. Key issue number one was soon under control.

The two lawyers took a similarly preemptive approach on the question of the Ickes memoranda about the need to raise hard and soft money for the DNC, making Gore available for an interview by Justice Department lawyers. Gore knew that the critical question was not what was in the Ickes memoranda, but what was in his head. In his interview with Justice Department investigators that took place November 12, 1997, Gore said he could not recall having read any memoranda discussing the segregation of DNC contributions into hard and soft money accounts. He said further he had been under the impression he was soliciting only soft money. He emphasized that he did not as a matter of practice read Ickes memoranda that were to be discussed at meetings. This inattentiveness to written material would have been so out of keeping with Gore's near obsessive tendency to over-prepare for every session as to raise profound questions regarding his veracity. But Neal and Frampton undoubtedly reminded the lawyers at Justice that in every instance, Gore had solicited contributions exceeding the $20,000 hard money limit federal law permits any one individual to donate to a political committee to aid a specific campaign. Hence, they maintained, Gore must have thought he was raising soft, not hard money.

The combination of the donors who remembered and the vice president who forgot gave Reno the hook she needed to reject once again the appointment of an independent counsel. She found no convincing evidence that the vice president knew that some of the funds he solicited were headed toward hard money DNC accounts. Nor in a case this tenuous did she find those "aggravating factors" that should be present to warrant investigation by an independent counsel. These might include coercion, a willful attempt to flout the law, or substantial misuse of government property or resources. Reno said she found "no evidence in the investigative results that any of these factors were present."

Reno's decision was opposed by the director of the FBI, Louis Freeh, who argued in a memorandum to her that she was misinterpreting existing law. In an effort to restore public confidence in her unimpressive investigation, Reno then recruited tough West Coast prosecutor Charles La Bella to head the inquiry into the campaign finance scandal. After a useful eighteen months that produced indictments of Charlie Trie, Johnny Chung, and Maria Hsia, La Bella departed, also persuaded that an independent counsel should be appointed to review the entire campaign finance issue. He left behind an approximately one hundred-page memo for the attorney general's edification.

The two documents paved the way for a new conflict, this time pitting Reno against Representative Dan Burton, the "take no pris-oners" Indiana Republican whose investigating committee subpoe-naed the memoranda. When Reno initially ignored the subpoena, Burton and his fellow Republicans voted to hold her in contempt. Behind the scenes, the parties explored possible compromise as the attorney general took yet another look at the grounds for appoint-ing an independent counsel to review the Gore fundraising calls, among other matters.

This time, she had one additional piece of evidence harmful to Gore—handwritten notations from his former Deputy Chief-of-Staff David Strauss, which indicated "hard" money may have been discussed at a key November 21, 1995, political meeting attended by Gore. Once again Gore had to face Justice Department lawyers. And once again Reno decided to launch a ninety-day "preliminary" inquiry to determine whether an independent counsel should be appointed to discover whether Gore had broken the law.

Thompson and his fellow committee Republicans had been disappointed at the attorney general's earlier refusals to appoint an independent counsel, and their final report contains an erudite argu-ment disputing her legal conclusion. But Thompson himself had acknowledged in a moment of total candor, "Everybody in this town knows... nobody's going to be prosecuted on these phone calls." (The calls, true. But the cover-up?)

Public statements on both sides notwithstanding, the battle between Thompson and his committee Republicans on the one hand, and Janet Reno on the other, was never really over Al Gore's calls. On the facts of the case, it would be tough to find a single informed prosecutor in the country who would recommend indict-ment. Every Republican senator on the committee knew that, as did every professional staff member.

The Republicans wanted an independent counsel because recent history has shown that the investigations can last for years while the areas investigated expand like the bellows of an accordion.

An independent counsel appointed to see whether Al Gore should be prosecuted for carelessness at the margin of an arcane and hoary statute might soon be searching for evidence of complicity by Gore, or even the president, in far more serious campaign fundraising abuses, such as the knowing receipt of illegal foreign contributions. Well into the year 2000, those investigations likely would have continued, casting a dark shadow over the Gore presidential campaign. Particularly damaging would be proof that Clinton-ordered changes in America's high-tech export policy with China were influenced by contributions from favored corporate contributors or from illegal Chinese contributions.

*   *   *

The Hacienda Heights and telephone solicitation incidents were defining events in the political odyssey of Albert Gore, Jr. Before them, he had been viewed as something of a model political citizen whose deep sense of probity extended to public as well as private life, the dutiful puritan loyally serving a president of rather more elastic moral standards. Now Gore seemed to be the one taking political shortcuts, including some disdained by his boss.

As in the darkest moments of his 1988 campaign, he again became the butt of jokes, this time about Buddhists and phone solicitations, his support for lesbian actress Ellen DeGeneres's "coming out," his thinning hair, and his exaggerated account of how he and Tipper provided the models for Erich Segal's *Love Story*. Russell Baker compared Gore to "the fat boy in the schoolyard," because "tormenting him is so much fun that nobody can resist."

Gore had also shown weakness and vulnerability under pressure. His serial explanations of the temple fundraiser seemed better designed to provide material for *Saturday Night Live* than to persuade a skeptical public that he was genuinely unaware of the nature of the event he had attended. He had rejected sound political advice against rushing into a public defense of the phone conversations and had turned the resulting press conference into an exercise in self-parody.

Sources who worked for Gore say he was stunned and hurt by the reaction to his press conference and related problems. He responded by hiring a press aide—Larry Haas—to handle all questions dealing with the temple and fundraising issues, and no longer stepped in front. He fell in line with the well-practiced White House damage control effort. Later, he would hire private counsel to ward off demands for appointment of an independent counsel. Like the president and other Democrats, when all else failed, Gore could always turn his rhetorical guns on the Republicans for opposing efforts to ban soft money from political campaigns. On several occasions Gore would also attempt to strike a "business as usual" pose, traveling abroad, battling or compromising with Republicans on budget issues, even resuming a busy schedule of fundraising and other political events. But he never fully succeeded in putting the nagging questions behind him.

Because of his new-found controversy, Gore was no longer the inevitable choice to succeed the president. He still had massive fundraising and organizational advantages over any Democratic challenger, perhaps enough to scare the Kerrys, and even Gephardt out of the race. But a well-known challenger with a reputation for both high intelligence and integrity of character, like former Senator Bill Bradley, could put himself in a position to surprise Gore, even in the expensive, front-loaded delegate selection process that lay ahead.

Gore now became a special target for gleeful Republicans and others long annoyed by the squeaky clean image of a man many privately regarded as a "holier than thou" hypocrite. The easiest target was, of course, his now notorious "no controlling legal authority" press conference, where he proclaimed pride in what he had done— and promised never to do it again. The most brutal example of what might be called "Gore deconstructionism" was a portrait presented by Tucker Carlson in the conservative *Weekly Standard*. Carlson began by calling Gore "shifty and disingenuous" and proceeded downhill from there. Picturing the vice president as a self-promoting publicity hound, Carlson hit some fair targets—Gore's pandering to both sides on the abortion question, his environmental extremism, and his disgraceful 1992 campaign comparison of George Bush's failure to support the Kurds against Saddam Hussein with Stalin's keeping the Red Army out of Warsaw in 1945, "postponing liberation deliberately to give the Nazis just enough time to finish butchering the Polish resistance."

Gore also suffered embarrassment from the conduct of past and present associates. In 1987 Marvin Rosen, a leading Florida fundraiser, introduced Gore to Howard Glicken, CEO of a Miami-based precious-metals trading company called Metalbanc. Glicken became the 1988 Gore campaign's chief Florida fundraiser.

According to a 1997 *Wall Street Journal* investigative report, Glicken and his executive vice president, Harry Falk, had both been fired from earlier positions with a Miami bank after taking large "commissions" on a loan, commissions the bank regarded as kickbacks. And in 1991 Falk was convicted of laundering drug money though Metalbanc. Glicken was granted limited immunity in the case and testified for the prosecution. By virtue of a deal with the government, one of Glicken's businesses—Jillian's Entertainment Corporation, which owned a chain of upscale billiards parlors—surrendered $375,000 in cash and stock.

Glicken's relationship with Gore remained intimate following the 1988 campaign. The *Wall Street Journal* reported: "Mr. Glicken and his wife have thrown book parties for both Mr. and Mrs. Gore at their home in Coral Gables. Mr. Glicken once arranged a weekend for the Gore family on exclusive Fisher Island near Miami. The Glickens put vanity license plates on their two Jaguars reading 'Gore 1' and 'Gore 2.' Mr. Glicken sometimes shows snapshots of a $6,000 billiard table that he arranged to have donated to the vice president's home.

"Mr. Gore, for his part, has arranged for Mr. Glicken to come to the White House for events or meetings, including a visit with the vice president's national security adviser. Mr. Glicken has also flown on Air Force One, attended one coffee with Mr. Gore and another with Mr. Clinton, witnessed the Israeli-Palestinian peace-signing and joined the U.S. delegation to Peru's presidential inauguration."

This would be heady stuff for a billiards baron, but Glicken left that business in 1993, when, following the election of Clinton-Gore, he joined the Washington office of a Boston consulting firm, the Commonwealth Group, and began recruiting clients from Latin America. But neither his shady background nor sudden metamorphosis to influence-peddling raised any warning flags with the vice president.

To the contrary, at Gore's insistence, President Clinton considered Glicken for a federal appointment in 1993. Following an FBI background check, the appointment was never made. But in 1994 the Commerce Department gave him a seat on one of its trade missions to South America. In 1996 he raised about $2 million for the Clinton-Gore reelection effort and that year formed his own Miami-based company, Americas Group, which brokers deals involving U.S. and Latin American companies. He would sometimes advertise his access for clients by escorting them to events for big campaign donors involving appearances by the president or vice president.

As of mid-1997, Glicken had, according to the *Journal*, visited the White House seventy times, "mostly to see officials who now say they can't recall why...." In 1997 the Federal Election Commission (FEC) developed evidence that Glicken may have generated at least $20,000 in illegal contributions from a German national, Thomas Kramer, who owns several south Florida businesses. Strangely, FEC counsel recommended against pursuing the matter because it was "unclear" Glicken would settle, given his newfound notoriety and close relationship with Gore. The vice president thought mention of his name by the FEC was gratuitous and complained about it publicly.

In July 1998 Glicken agreed to plead guilty to two misdemeanors in connection with the Kramer transactions, with the understanding that the punishment would be limited to a fine.

Gore, while denying he had known anything about the 1985 Falk trial, had already distanced himself from Glicken, making certain his friend did not show up at Florida fundraisers where he, the vice president, was the featured attraction. Now, in response to the criminal matters, Gore's office released a statement which was at once businesslike, but warm. It read, "Vice President Gore regrets that Howard and his family face these difficulties. The vice president recognizes both the seriousness of the charges against Howard and the fact that Howard has taken responsibility for his actions."

Even Gore's closest fundraiser friends were nonplussed by the vice president's uncritical acceptance of Glicken's insinuating approach. Within this circle, Glicken was regarded as an aggressive glad-hander with little discretion, certainly not someone to be trusted. His sudden entrance into the influence-peddling business raised warning doubts among a group of people not themselves known for excessive timidity. Some felt that in his calculated blindness to Glicken's past, Gore had suffered a severe lapse in judgment.

The entire matter had also disturbed Gore's longtime mentor, friend, and defender, Martin Peretz, whose impatience with the relationship was apparent even before the last misdemeanor chapter. "Howard Glicken is a punk, and I'm not going to defend that relationship," he said.

At times, poor background work seemed little more than a synonym for the Clinton-Gore team's insatiable appetite for money. In November 1995 Cuban-American fundraiser Vivian Mannerud encountered a man named Jorge Cabrera at a Havana hotel. Cabrera, a veteran drug trafficker who had suffered two felony convictions in the 1980s, thought that hobnobbing with some senior political figures was the sort of public relations therapy he needed. Mannerud had a proposition: help the Clinton-Gore campaign and you'll get to attend a dinner honoring the vice president.

Returning to Miami, Cabrera wrote a check to the DNC for $20,000 from an account that included proceeds from cocaine smuggling. Within two weeks of the contribution, he was invited to the promised dinner at the home of longtime Democratic fundraiser Jerome Berlin. There he got himself photographed shaking hands with Gore. He also received a set of vice presidential cuff links and a bottle of wine with Mr. Gore's picture on the label. He later attended a Christmas reception at the White House hosted by Hillary Rodham Clinton.

But Cabrera did not have long to enjoy his readily-purchased respectability. Within months he was back in federal prison serving a nineteen-year sentence for drug smuggling. A spokeswoman for the vice president said Gore was "disappointed" at the turn of events. "He never wants to be associated with people who break the law," she said.

Even more embarrassing was the account of how Gore's two heaviest hitters, fundraiser Nathan Landow, and former chief-of-staff and 1996 campaign manager Peter Knight, had been involved with the efforts of two impoverished Indian tribes—the Cheyennes and Arapahos of Oklahoma—trying to recover the Fort Reno lands confiscated by the federal government in 1869. As later set forth by the Thompson Committee, Democratic fundraisers essentially sold the tribes a White House audience with the president for a pledge of $100,000 to the DNC.

After they had coughed up "only" $87,000—from a fund used for "funeral costs, heating bills and general assistance for needy tribal members"—they were pressured into spending another $20,000 on a presidential birthday fundraising tribute. The tribes were soon put in touch with Gore's longtime friend, Nathan

Landow, who allegedly offered to use his weight with the administration on their behalf in exchange for 10 percent of any settlement price for development of the land and 10 percent of any revenue from gas or oil extraction for a period of twenty years.

Landow also recommended the Cheyennes and Arapahos enlist Gore intimate Peter Knight, at a retainer of $100,000 and legal fees of $10,000 per month. Tribal leaders recall a profanity-laced tirade from Landow when the Indians came to the meeting unprepared to finish the deal, and Landow threatened to derail their project. Meanwhile, associates from Knight's pricey law-lobbying firm of Wunder, Knight, Levine, Thelen & Forscey continued to seek the tribes' account.

After a scathing report of the affair appeared in the *Washington Post* on March 10, 1997, the DNC refunded the tribes' contribution, claiming concern that the money might have come from their welfare fund. The DNC also wanted to dispel the "link in the minds of the tribe's members that they needed to give this money in order to be heard on an official government matter." Landow also dropped the project after publication of the *Post* story. He maintains that his main motive in the affair was to throw some business to Knight, and that his own "cut" would have come only *after* the return of the Fort Reno lands, and only *if* the tribes decided in favor of commercial development. Doing good for Native Americans is one thing. But after all, a buck's a buck.

Peter Knight would soon find himself under far more intense scrutiny in an endeavor that—even by Washington's familiar "revolving door" standards—seemed to carry an awful stench. Knight had entered the world of influence peddling shortly after Gore's unsuccessful 1988 run for the presidency. His fortunes took a turn for the better following the 1992 presidential election when former Gore colleagues like Carol Browner at the Environmental Protection Agency, Reed Hundt at the Federal Communications Commission and Tom Grumbly at the Department of Energy, assumed powerful administration jobs. He has remained extremely close to his former boss, handling fundraising efforts for the chair in environmental studies named for the late Nancy Gore Hunger at the University of Tennessee, and the facelift to the vice president's public residence at the Naval Observatory. During the 1992-93 transition period, he served as deputy director of personnel, placing Gore loyalists in senior positions throughout the bureaucracy.

Among Knight's later private sector clients was Molten Metal Technology. Its CEO, Bill Haney, was a 1988 field coordinator for the Gore campaign. Its vice president for governmental affairs, Vic Gatto, is a former Harvard classmate of Gore's. Founded in 1989, Molten Metal offers technology for the cleanup of radioactive and other hazardous waste by heating the wastes in an iron vat to a temperature of 3,000 degrees Fahrenheit.

During the Bush administration, Molten Metal was among a few dozen enterprises competing for future nuclear cleanup missions, working under a contract worth $1.2 million. Then the company retained Knight under an unusual lobbying arrangement that paid him not only $7,000 per month, but also gave him the option to buy at least 40,000 shares of Molten.

Knight was worth the price. As reported by *Time* magazine's Michael Weisskopf, "When the company needed credibility to build early capital, Knight arranged for [Tom] Grumbly of the Energy Department to attend the plant's ribbon-cutting ceremony, at which he touted the firm and suggested it could qualify for up to $200 million in grants from the department. When Molten sought equal billing with incinerators as a clean-up method for toxic waste, [Carol] Browner met with the company's top executives and later signed off on a regulatory classification, rare for a process not yet in full commercial operation."

Not only did Knight ensure access for Molten officials to top Washington policy-makers—rare for a small firm—he continued to deliver them as if on command. Gore himself visited the company's

Fall River, Massachusetts, plant on Earth Day 1995, declaring the company "a success story, a shining example of American ingenuity, hard work, and business know-how, all being used to clean up our environment, and at the same time provide jobs and economic growth."

For that bit of business, Haney wrote Knight thanking him for "orchestrating" Gore's trip. "I should have asked for the Pope or the Stones," he gushed. "You hardly seemed to break a sweat in bringing the vice president to Fall River."

But what drew even more attention was the series of political contributions made by Molten and its officers juxtaposed with increases in its Department of Energy contracts, all in the face of some serious questions being raised within the government regarding the value of its technology.

On March 22, 1994, Haney contributed $50,000 to help endow Gore's sister's chair at the University of Tennessee. Two days later, Molten made a $15,000 contribution to the DNC. That same day, it received a modification from Department of Energy, raising its government contract by $9 million.

On September 29, 1994, Molten contributed $2,500 to the DNC. The following day a "stop work" order was lifted and the contract extended for a period of months.

On January 30, 1995, Molten contributed $15,000 in soft money to the DNC. Sixteen days later the company signed a $5 million contract modification with the Department of Energy.

Molten and its officers pledged a total of $50,000 to the Clinton-Gore campaign, leading Knight to write that their participation "will give you a special place of significance with the vice president and put you first in line."

Molten money continued to flow. On June 14, 1995, Molten officers and employees contributed $10,000 to the Clinton-Gore Primary Committee. That same day, the company signed a $10 million contract modification with the government.

On February 27, 1996, Molten made a $15,000 soft money contribution to the DNC, following that up with a $10,000 contribution on May 7. On May 10, 1996, the company signed an $8 million contract modification with the Department of Energy.

Influence peddling is nothing new in Washington, nor is the coincidence between political contributions and access to the public treasury. What sets the Molten Metal case apart is, first, the extraordinary "bang for the buck" achieved by the company, both in terms of Department of Energy business and the personal involvement of senior administration people, up to and including Gore himself. Second, and far more disturbing, internal reviews for the Energy Department suggested the Molten waste treatment process was nothing special. One 1992 report for the Department of Energy noted that the extremely high temperature used by Molten would make nuclear and other materials more volatile, possibly escaping from the plant in the "off gas stream." Further, the process would not get rid of sufficient radioactive waste to permit commercial or most Department of Energy reuse. In short, "there is no significant advantage offered by this particular technology over the others that would justify its preferred development over them."

Later reports were similarly negative. Michael Weisskopf of *Time* magazine noted that "In January 1994, the Lawrence Livermore National Laboratory reported that the process was probably inappropriate for the kind of waste at most nuclear weapons sites. By late 1995, a technical peer-review panel said the department should cease funding Molten Metal at the end of the fiscal year. Another Energy Department Panel concluded last December [1996] that Haney's technology poses environmental and safety risks and might not be cost-effective."

Things finally caught up with Molten Metal Technology. At long last, it lost its Department of Energy contract. Shareholder lawsuits charged company officials with misrepresenting the commercial potential of the technology and with using insider information to dispose of their stock at artificially high prices. The Department of Justice began one investigation; the House Commerce Committee, another.

Spokesmen for Gore, Knight, and Molten Metal all expressed shock—shock that anyone could suggest linkage between the political donations of the company and its officers and the award of government contracts.

True to his history of deep personal loyalty, Gore made no effort to distance himself from his friend when Knight came under scrutiny. "Peter is one of the most honorable, honest men I have ever known in my life," he told the *New York Times*. "The partisan attack against him has hit way wide of their intended mark. He's a great friend."

Knight, Gore friend and former FCC Chairman Reed Hundt, Tennessee developer Franklin L. Haney—a former aide to Al Gore, Sr.—and Robert A. Peck, placed first by Knight as a Hundt assistant, and later in a senior General Services Administration job, figured in another lucrative but politically embarrassing enterprise known as the Portals Project.

The Portals are part of a commercial development in remote southwest Washington, D.C., in which Haney had purchased a controlling interest. At issue was whether the Federal Communications Commission would be ordered by the General Services Administration to move to the Portals, as well as the terms of any lease the General Services Administration would sign on the Federal Communication Commission's behalf with Haney. In 1996 Haney would contribute $230,000 to a variety of Democratic political causes. His Washington lawyer was Knight.

Business Week would later report that Knight sought to ensure that the Federal Communications Commission moved to the Portals, and that a lease signed before Haney bought control would be changed to establish a fixed date for the start of rental payments, allowing Haney to pre-sell bonds and use the proceeds to finance the project.

In November 1995 the General Services Administration ordered the Federal Communications Commission into the Portals. Two months later, the General Services Administration signed a lease authorizing rental payments to begin in July 1997, a change that resulted in the government paying nearly $16 million in rent for an empty building.

On January 7, 1996, the day the lease was signed, Knight signed a $1 million bill to Haney for legal services rendered in 1994 and 1995. Federal law prohibits contingency payments on government contracts. Haney's office told *Business Week* the payment to Knight was not a contingency fee. The fact that the invoice was written on the same day as the lease signing was "just a coincidence."

In September 1998 Knight was testifying before the House Commerce Committee still trying to explain the "coincidence," insisting that the $1 million was not for the Portals project alone, and certainly not a contingency payoff on Portals, but for three years of work on about a dozen projects, including Portals.

But House Commerce Committee members noted that this explanation was flatly contradicted by a 1995 letter of engagement signed by both Knight and Haney that committed Knight to billing Haney on a project-by-project basis. This obviously didn't happen, given that there was only one million-dollar bill.

Knight replied that arrangement had been superseded by an oral agreement reached later the same year. Not a shred of documentation supported that claim. Knight conceded that $1 million "is a significant sum of money."

"But," he added, "it is not a huge payment by Washington law firm standards."

Such was the big money world available to Al Gore's associates in what Clinton and Gore promised would be the "most ethical administration in history."

CHAPTER NINETEEN

DEBACLE IN KYOTO

GLOBAL WARMING was Al Gore's issue. He had raised it from the academic fascination of a single scholar to the leading environmental issue on the international agenda. He had held hearings on it, written a book about it, convinced activist groups to adopt it as a cause, funded research efforts to study the threat, and led the assault to discredit scientists who dissented from what he declared to be the mainstream or orthodox view. Now charged with responsibility for determining the Clinton administration's environmental policies, Gore regarded it as his mission to get the country to embrace a treaty that would limit carbon emissions to levels far below projections.

But Gore found many in the new administration as skeptical of the global warming campaign as had been the Bush White House. Treasury Secretary Lloyd Bentsen and Department of Energy Secretary Hazel O'Leary both objected to obligatory carbon emission standards, the former because of its impact on the economy in general, the latter because it would adversely effect employment and profits in the energy industry.

But President Clinton did not want to humiliate his new vice president on his core issue, nor did he wish to alienate the "green" constituencies that had been drawn to the ticket by Gore's presence. Accordingly, on Earth Day 1993, Clinton announced that the U.S. would sign the Framework Convention on Climate Change and the Convention on Biological Diversity, which had been rejected by the Bush administration at the earlier Rio Summit.

In the autumn of 1993 the administration issued a "Climate Change Action Plan," advertised as a means of stabilizing "greenhouse gas concentrations in the atmosphere at a level that would prevent dangerous anthropogenic interference with the climate system." Since no one had yet been able to define the level at which carbon dioxide emissions became "dangerous," the formulation clearly had the virtue of flexibility. In reality, the extremely modest series of voluntary measures recommended for industry, public utilities, and major energy consumers was calculated to give the administration some breathing space while a committee called the Conference of Parties (COP), established by the Rio Accord, nudged the world community toward more decisive action. At COP's first meeting in Berlin in the spring of 1995, Timothy Wirth, the undersecretary of state for Global Affairs and a close personal friend of Gore, acknowledged that U.S. carbon dioxide emissions in the year 2000 were likely to be 30 percent higher than in 1990.

The meeting adopted what would, to U.S. legislators, become the "poison pill" of the global warming controversy: an exemption for all "developing countries"—essentially the non-Western world, other than Japan—from the need to limit their carbon dioxide emissions.

At the next COP meeting in Geneva in July 1996, Wirth, following Gore's instructions, urged the establishment of binding standards for industrialized nations to be signed at the UN Framework Convention on Climate Change meeting in Kyoto, Japan, in December 1997. That was the place and time established by the UN for reducing the various negotiated accords to one or more binding treaties. Kyoto thus became the focus of lobbying efforts by environmental activists, governments, political opposition parties, climate scientists, and potentially affected businesses and industries.

At this point Gore did not hold a promising hand. He had taken a "crisis" that many scientists said did not exist and prescribed a remedy from which as many as 134 countries—including the likes of China, India, Pakistan, and Brazil—were exempt. Further, the 1996 report of the UN's Intergovernmental Panel on Climate Change (IPCC) was far less alarmist than its 1990 predecessor. True, the report's executive summary contained a sentence stating that "the balance of evidence suggests that there is a discernable human influence on the global climate." But now, instead of a 3.6 degree Fahrenheit warming by 2050, the IPCC was predicting a 3.6 degree Fahrenheit warming by *2100*, a substantial modification. And the scientists admitted their computer models could not account for the extremely modest temperature rise of the past century. One possible explanation is that the computer models have not been able to account accurately for the incidence of cloud formation and its impact on temperature. Another is that the earth, with its soil, plants, and oceans, is managing to absorb or "sink" more of the carbon than the experts had expected.

In companion reports, the IPCC predicted that "global agricultural production could be maintained... in the face of climate change," with more abundant production in the higher latitudes, and that globally, "fisheries production is expected to remain about the same."

One of the most remarkable statements by the IPCC related to the impact of global warming on weather extremes. Recall that Gore had heard the cracking glass of *Kristallnacht* during the hot summer days of 1988. And in 1991 George Mitchell, the Senate majority leader, had warned that "climate extremes would trigger meteorological chaos—raging hurricanes such as we have never seen, capable of killing millions of people; uncommonly long, record-breaking heat waves; and profound drought that could drive Africa and the entire Indian subcontinent over the edge into mass starvation." Yet in its 1996 report, IPCC conceded, "Knowledge is currently insufficient to say whether there will be any changes in the occurrence or geographical distribution of severe storms, e.g., tropical cyclones."

The clarification about tropical storms provides a key to understanding much of the global warming debate. Most climate scientists *do* accept the notion that greenhouse gases caused by the burning of carbon are likely, over time, to produce some warming affect. But few can say how much. Many suggest the consequences are as likely to be positive as negative. And many scientists and economists maintain that the costs of adapting to any change are both easier to achieve politically and more efficacious scientifically than trying to avoid the problem through a crash carbon diet.

If the projections for global warming were hedged and vague, projections by many economists regarding the impact of a deal that would impose binding carbon dioxide cuts to below 1990 levels by the year 2010 were hard and pessimistic. Harvard economist Robert N. Stavins projected costs equivalent to a carbon tax of $150 per ton that would equal an annual $200 billion drain on the economy, approximately the cost of complying with all other existing environmental regulations. In its internal deliberations—never published—the Administration estimated that a tax of $100 per ton of carbon burned would be required, which would equal a tax of about $80 per ton on coal and 25 cents per gallon of gasoline. This would more than triple the delivered price of coal to utilities over a decade and adversely affect coal-mining, steel, and such electricity-intensive industries as aluminum and chemicals. Some of these industries could be forced to relocate to other countries, and U.S. exports would be more expensive.

But while the economists worked from sober, reliable models, Gore could not resist the temptation to turn natural disasters to political advantage. When in 1997 the Red River flooded Grand

Forks, North Dakota, Gore told reporters, "People in Grand Forks, North Dakota, who had to move out of their homes because of the flooding don't think global climate change is such an abstraction anymore."

Of course, global warming likely had nothing to do with it, making Gore's statement a piece of shameless grandstanding, or science by *belief* rather than *fact*. Most climatologists share the view of Patrick Michaels of the University of Virginia who predicts that in those areas where some warming may occur, principally the northern latitudes, "precipitation will likely decrease due to milder fluctuations between daytime and nighttime temperatures." According to Michaels, "Excessive snowfall, the product of cold weather, not warm weather, set the stage for the Red River flood." In linking the Grand Forks disaster to global warming, Gore appears to have been practicing "junk science," a term he would use from time to time to deride the work of scholars not willing to march in lockstep with his global warming views.

But it was important for the White House, in its support of Gore, to mobilize public opinion behind the emerging Kyoto consensus to cut carbon dioxide emissions. At one point, a throng of TV weathermen was invited to the White House so Gore could present them with his updated *Earth in the Balance* lecture: The earth's population is exploding. Too many people are pouring too much carbon dioxide into the atmosphere. And unless we take drastic action, carbon dioxide and the other greenhouse gasses could cause enough global warming to threaten the well-being of our entire planet. Reporters covering the event said a majority of the audience remained skeptical. Gore had been impressive, but not persuasive.

In late June 1997 the president placed his own prestige on the line, delivering a major address to the "Rio plus five" meeting in New York that pushed all the expected fear buttons regarding the consequences of global warming in the absence of concerted world action. But in important respects, the performance was a throwback

to the middle-of-the-road approach of George Bush. Western
European leaders Tony Blair, Helmut Kohl, and Jacques Chirac
scolded the president for failing to endorse binding cuts in carbon
dioxide emissions or to adopt a specific program designed to achieve
such results. Domestic environmentalists were no happier. On the
other hand, those wary of the Kyoto process had little cause to cel-
ebrate, fearing the president—hounded by Gore—would eventually
adopt the activist agenda.

On July 25, 1997, the Senate passed Resolution 98 saying the
United States should sign no treaty that failed to hold developing
nations to the same standards as the industrialized nations, or which
produced serious harm to the U.S. economy. The vote was 95 to 0,
the clearest possible warning to President Clinton and Vice
President Gore that they were moving toward the kind of accord the
Senate would never accept.

Nonetheless, at Gore's insistence, the president indicated the
United States would bring to Kyoto a binding promise to cut carbon
dioxide emissions to 1990 levels within the next ten to fifteen years.
He threw into the domestic pot a proposal to spend $5 billion over
the next five years on tax breaks to encourage energy efficiency and
the development of new fossil fuel technologies. The idea was con-
cededly short of anything that could possibly accomplish the stated
objective, but having previously been forced to back away from a
floated plan to impose new carbon taxes plus a host of other energy
levies, Clinton and Gore were anxious to avoid immediate controversy.

Still there was strong resistance to Kyoto within the administration—particularly from the Treasury and Department of
Energy—and from Republicans, alert to a potentially winning political issue. The White House started to leak word that there might
be no agreement at all in Kyoto without developing country participation in the carbon dioxide cuts. As the December meeting drew
near, U.S. negotiators reported back to Gore that the developing

countries, led by China, were not going to come around on the issue. And the Europeans were still demanding cuts in carbon dioxide emissions beyond anything the United States had previously said it could agree to. If he were going to come away with a signed treaty at Kyoto, Gore would have to accept provisions that would preclude Senate ratification. If Kyoto produced no treaty, the international effort to come to grips with global warming could collapse.

"At this point, Al's intention became simply to keep the Kyoto process alive," recalls a former senior member of his staff. "He had been pointing to global warming as a potential crisis when no one else even knew there was a problem. He believed that over time the public could be educated to demand solutions. So if Kyoto produced a treaty that the Senate wouldn't ratify, Al wouldn't be happy, but he wouldn't see that as final defeat. The only final defeat would be for Kyoto to come and go with no agreement."

The explanation is convincing to a point, but it does not fully account for the intensity of Gore's feelings on the subject. This, after all, was the man who had publicly proclaimed a clash between Western civilization and environmental survival, who had concluded that America was "dysfunctional" because of the environmental damage it was producing, who demanded an end to the internal combustion engine, who experienced deep guilt because he ran his car's air-conditioning system, and who had heard echoes of *Kristallnacht* in the hot summer of 1988. On this issue, Al Gore, Jr., was, to put it charitably, a true believer, or less charitably, an extremist.

He was also the person counted on by environmentalists to represent their interests. Carol Browner at the Environmental Protection Agency was a valuable friend who clearly had the courage of Gore's convictions, but his policy-making power was superior to hers. Kathleen McGinty, young, smart, and more inclined in her job at CEQ than she had been earlier to seek consensus on questions like land use regulation and clean air policy, was a marvelous liaison between environmentalists and the White House, but again, her

most important role was to deliver Gore on the issues that counted.*
And now, during the run-up to Kyoto, several situations converged
that environmentalists and their friends in the media used as litmus
tests of Gore's continuing commitment.

The first involved Champion Paper and the Pigeon River.
While Gore's intervention on behalf of Champion during the 1988
campaign had made life difficult for the EPA, since the early 1990s,
the EPA and Champion Paper in Canton, North Carolina, had
more or less achieved a *modus vivendi*. The company was still pumping water with 250-400 units of color—the equivalent of 86,000
pounds—into the Pigeon River each day. But by the time the water
reached Hartford, Tennessee, it was down to 50 units—clean by
EPA standards—with no exceptions for the tides.

The improvement had not come cheaply. By 1994 Champion
had spent $330 million modernizing its plant. This reduced its water
intake by 35 percent and its color discharge by 75 percent, and further resulted in far less chlorine and dioxin discharged into the river.
In the process, some seven hundred jobs were phased out, leaving
the company with 1,300 workers. Champion warned that expensive
new standards imposed in an effort to achieve marginal river quality
improvements would force it out of Haywood County altogether.
With annual wages averaging $48,000 per employee, that was a mat-
ter of dire concern to those directly or indirectly dependent on the
plant for their livelihoods.

But by now the cause had been adopted by the national environmental movement, particularly the well-heeled American Canoe
Association headquartered in Fairfax, Virginia, and its high-pow-
ered, politically sophisticated director, David Jenkins. Jenkins knew
that east Tennessee was overwhelmingly Republican and that
elected officials there were not a bit adverse to embarrassing Vice
President Gore. In addition, the governorship was now in the hands
of Republican Donald Sundquist. When, in October 1996, North

---

* McGinty has since left government service.

Carolina, with EPA approval, gave Champion five additional years in which to continue operating under the standards applicable since 1991, Jenkins invaded east Tennessee with the idea of winning the fight once and for all. "We got every mayor, every city councilman, every county official, every state representative from the area to endorse strict color standards in North Carolina, not thirty-seven miles downstream in Tennessee," says Jenkins. "We got Governor Sundquist's backing too. The national media got hold of the issue. Getting EPA to reopen the case and tighten the standards became a test of Gore's commitment to the environmental movement."

Newsweek slugged its story, "Gore's Pollution Problem." Knoxville's Mayor Victor Ashe—Gore's 1984 Senate campaign opponent—joined the Tennessee Wildlife Resources Commission in urging the state to appeal the EPA ruling. Columnist Frank Cagle of the *Knoxville News-Sentinel* charged that during the 1988 campaign, "Gore was running for president and sold out his Tennessee constituents in return for North Carolina votes in the Super Tuesday primary."

"Gore's alleged hypocrisy on tobacco cannot compare to his hypocrisy on the environment and the issue of cleaning up the Pigeon River," the columnist wrote. "Gore has gotten a free ride on the Pigeon River because environmental groups are uneasy about attacking the poster boy for environmental causes. I think it's time that the environmental groups that have given Gore so much support and so much cover on this issue call in their debt."

Gore responded to the pressure, telling EPA Director Carol Browner, his former staffer, to urge reconsideration of the Champion permit. Talks began involving the EPA, Champion, and North Carolina and Tennessee officials. Before they were completed, Champion announced that its Canton plant was for sale. The company subsequently reached agreement, approved by the EPA to meet the fifty-unit standard by the time the flow reached a site called Hepco, a North Carolina encampment consisting of a dock and a few shacks, about seventeen miles downstream. After Hepco, two pristine streams merge with the Pigeon, which then runs through a big lake dammed for electric power. By the time it reaches Hartford, Tennessee, the color unit indicator was expected to read in the twelve to twenty range.

Jenkins of the American Canoe Association was delighted. "Gore came through for us this time," he says. But for the workers at Champion, the result was ominous. Early in 1998 they put in a bid for the plant, pledging their pension funds as collateral for the effort to save their jobs. The company found the bid too low and rejected it.

*   *   *

Gore was also under pressure from environmental activists to rescue Carol Browner's audacious plan to revise Clean Air Act regulations. Browner had announced plans to implement Clean Air Act standards for ozone and particulate matter (soot) so stringent that few of the nation's major metropolitan areas would be able to meet them. From the moment she announced those standards, Browner's effort ran into a firestorm of protest, not only from "the usual suspects"—the energy and heavy manufacturing industries—but from mayors and state and city environmental commissions, liberal members of Congress, scientists, and economists—including some from the White House.

Those hardest hit by the new standards would be precisely the places most in need of an infusion of economic activity, the inner cities. Nineteen areas—most in urban centers—were already in noncompliance with existing Clean Air standards. The Browner edict would increase that number overnight to 141, making it almost impossible for new industries to locate in these places and, perhaps, driving existing ones out. Municipal officials the country over also charged that Browner's environmental calculations were one-sided. Her standards would push new manufacturing plants into remote areas, which would mean new road-building, heavier automobile usage, and more traffic accidents. Also not calculated were the health effects of unemployment and poverty on people in big cities, like Chicago, who otherwise would have had jobs.

Browner estimated the cost of compliance at $2.5 billion. But Alicia Munnell of the President's Council of Economic Advisors claimed those figures were based on only partial compliance and that the real number was closer to $60 billion. Nor was that the only area where Browner dealt from the bottom of the deck. Her estimates of the cost of sickness and death her initiatives would save were vastly inflated. Indeed, there was little if any medical support for her claim that the new restrictions would prevent 20,000 premature deaths each year and 500,000 cases of respiratory disease. To the contrary, the assistant director for the environment at the White House Office of Science and Technology argued internally that current data failed to support clear associations between premature mortality and soot and ozone at the levels Browner was proposing to regulate.

Erskine Bowles, the president's chief-of-staff, privately appealed to the EPA chief to adhere to a rule of reason on the issue. But Browner refused to budge and relied on Gore to make her case with the president. For a time that seemed a forlorn hope as the White House repeatedly leaked word that the administration would not adopt the recommended standards. But the leakers ignored the impact a little pressure from the environmentalists would have on Gore. Quickly they turned the issue into yet another test of Gore's fidelity. "The silence from the White House has been deafening," complained one senior lobbyist for the American Lung Association. "There's a Gore watch out. We can't find Al."

The fury of the American Lung Association was real, in part because it is paid by the EPA to be furious. That the agency funds all sorts of academic studies that miraculously support the efficacy of tougher regulations is widely known. But in a set-up that has about as much inherent integrity as, say, a pro wrestling match, the EPA doles out grants to organizations like the American Lung Association, which then use the money to sue the agency, demanding strict new edicts. In the midst of the clean air controversy, *Investors Business Daily*, citing figures compiled by the Federal Assistance Awards Data system—which tracks government grants—reported, "Between 1990 and 1994, the Environmental Protection Agency gave the lung association's national office and its various state chapters more than $4 million. In 1995, the Environmental Protection Agency gave the group close to $1 million more...." The article quoted Scott Seigel, an attorney and professor of environmental management at the University of Maryland. "Truth be known, the Environmental Protection Agency wants to be sued, because every time they are sued it expands the reach of the Clean Air Act."

In any event, the issue came to a head the same week President Clinton was preparing to address the Rio group on his plans for Kyoto. In a front-page story the *New York Times* reported, "Vice President Al Gore, one of the environmental movement's steadiest allies, is under attack from major conservation groups in an unlikely turn that carries important implications for environmental policy as well as presidential politics."

A consortium of at least eighty organizations chided the vice president for failing to bring the White House in line on either global warming or Clean Air Act standards. They branded his period of alleged inactivity "Al Gore's Silent Spring." Said Phillip E. Clapp, president of the National Environmental Trust, "The failure of the White House to provide any leadership on the clean air standards and on climate change raises real questions about what real environmental progress Vice President Gore can point to in claiming the mantle of the environmental movement in the year 2000." The environmentalists advertised that their representatives had been meeting with Dick Gephardt, Gore's putative Democratic opponent.

Gore's environmental bodyguards within the administration leaped to his aid. "There's no doubt in my mind that the vice president is in there doing what he has done on many difficult issues," said Carol Browner. Kathleen McGinty added, "I guess the problem is, you always hurt the one you love. The environmentalists have a strategy here to send a message to us because they know the vice president does care about what they say."

Gore's answer was totally candid. "Everybody knows my views," he said. "But I'm not going to publicly try to back the president into a corner. I never have done that and I never will."

Eventually Browner won Gore's intervention, and an extremely reluctant president endorsed his EPA chief on ozone and soot standards, extracting only Browner's promise to be flexible in implementing the policy.

The signal that Gore's personal involvement might also be needed to save the Global Warming Treaty came when, just weeks before the Kyoto conference, the State Department's global environmentalist, Tim Wirth, announced his retirement. He was replaced by Stu Eisenstadt, a capable and experienced diplomat, but not the sort of "brand name" Wirth, a former U.S. Senator, had brought to the post.

Gore was in frequent telephone contact with Eisenstadt, and the reports he received were pessimistic. The Europeans wanted mandatory emissions levels below what the United States had previously offered. The difference between the allies could be explained partly by the relative political strength of the European Greens, and partly by the ease with which Europe had already achieved a substantial part of the cuts through Germany's dismantling of the East German filth factories, the United Kingdom's switch from coal to natural gas, and France's substantial conversion to nuclear energy.

More important, developing nations would not consider submitting to any mandatory levels. Shu Kong Zhong, the chief economic advisor to the Chinese delegation, spoke for all the developing countries when he complained that "In the developed world only two people ride in a car and yet you want us to give up riding in a bus." Officials in Beijing called economic development a matter of "human rights," while Chen Yaobang, the head of the Chinese delegation, said, "Poverty eradication and developing the economy are still the overriding priorities of China. It's not possible for the Chinese government to undertake the obligation of reducing greenhouse gasses until the country develops."

Gore pressed on. According to aides who worked with him on the issue, he was particularly anxious to introduce a provision allowing countries to trade unused emission rights among themselves. Thus, if Russia, for example, due to its wretched economy, would likely release far less than the amount of carbon dioxide it was permitted under the treaty, it could sell the right to release those emissions to the United States, which would likely have trouble getting down to its mandatory levels. "In Al's view this would in effect allow the West to pay less developed countries to develop their economies with greater energy efficiency," explains Jonathan Spalter, who wrote Gore's international affairs speeches. "It would ease the burden on the U.S. and therefore make the treaty more acceptable to the Senate. And, if trading was applied to individual industries, it would help apply classic free market principles to the solution of a pressing environmental problem."

Most of the industrial countries were decidedly cool to Gore's trading proposal. For one thing, since the developing countries had no standards to meet, they would have no unused emission rights to sell. Second, the Europeans and others feared that the United States buying emission rights from a country like Russia would result in no net decrease in worldwide emissions. Instead of the desired reductions, they feared the United States would deliver instead a series of bookkeeping tricks, "buying" reductions that would have occurred Treaty or no.

As the talks stalled, the conference, in the view of observer

Thomas Gale Moore, an economist and former member of President Reagan's Council on Environmental Quality, "had degenerated into a mix of revival meeting and guerrilla theater." The *Wall Street Journal's* John Fialka saw it, instead, as a "cultural shoot-out: Gucci Gulch versus Timberland." Visitors saw a "conference hall full of environmental ministers, environmental activists, recyclers, bicyclists, solar-powered coffee-makers, windmill enthusiasts, and a gay English fellow who lived in a treehouse for three months to protest a shopping mall." A somewhat more traditional hospitality center was maintained by the Global Climate Coalition, represented by one hundred poised executives, most from the energy and automobile industries.

Outside the center, Greenpeace served visitors at its "Solar Fried Snack Bar." The facility included a refrigerator powered by $20,000 worth of solar panels and offered free solar-brewed coffee during periods of sunshine. The same organization also displayed a "sharp-fanged one-ton metal dinosaur built from auto parts and various flotsam from fuel tanks and gasoline pumps." Charmingly, he was called, "Carbonosaur." Another group carved ice sculptures and then shed tears at an evening prayer meeting as the faithful sought forgiveness for allowing the ice to melt.

For a brief period, Gore appeared ready to accept defeat on the issue, assuring reporters that there would be no deal "without meaningful participation by key developing countries." Finally, the White House announced that Gore would head to Kyoto in an effort to break the deadlock. The trip, via Anchorage and Yokahama, took twenty hours. Aides say Gore never slept, but huddled with Fuerth, McGinty, and Spalter working on his speech, punctuating that with calls to Eisenstadt. Upon arrival, Gore tried to present a bold face, pretending he had some cards to play, telling reporters, "I would like to make it clear that as others have said, we are perfectly prepared to walk away from an agreement that we don't think will work."

But there was still no apparent way to square the circle: finding an agreement that would be both accepted at Kyoto and ratified in the Senate. "This entire issue is fraught with political peril," McGinty acknowledged. "But this is a question of leadership."

Gore's presence did lift the spirits of the convention because it signaled that achieving an agreement remained an administration priority, which in turn meant that the United States would be moving in the direction of the developing countries and, where necessary, Europe. In his address to the delegates, Gore spoke of a commitment to the ages: "Let us resolve to conduct ourselves in such a way that our children's children will read about the 'Spirit of Kyoto,' and remember it as the place and time where humanity first chose to embark together on a long-term sustainable relationship between our civilization and the Earth's environment."

To Eisenstadt and the other U.S. delegates, Gore made clear the priority he attached to getting a deal. "I am instructing our delegation right now to show increased negotiating flexibility," he announced, "if a compromise plan can be put in place, one with realistic targets and timetables, market mechanisms, and the meaningful participation of the developing countries."

The final agreement included a binding commitment by the United States to cut carbon emissions to 7 percent below 1990 levels by 2010. For Europe the figure was 8 percent. Japan agreed to a 6 percent figure only after Gore called Prime Minister Ryutaro Hashimoto with a personal plea to accept that deep a cut.

The accord contains no commitment for developing countries like China and India. But the treaty does not bar the sort of trading in emission rights Gore wanted, leaving the matter instead for future negotiations.

The environmental forces, including the vice president, went quickly to work. Environmental activists expressed limited, modified support for what one called "a narrow victory." The *New York Times* noted sadly that nothing in the agreement would prevent carbon dioxide levels from continuing to rise, but it still believed the accord "signals business and industry that the issue is here to stay, that the ways in which energy is produced and used must change, and that these issues should be taken into consideration in planning and investing for the long term." Gore called the deal "a solid foundation for long-term efforts to protect the climate." "Make no mistake," he added, "we stuck by the president's principles and we prevailed."

A senatorial "watchdog" group in Kyoto, presided over by Senator Chuck Hagel of Nebraska, thought otherwise. Hagel noted that the United States agreed to cut its emissions to the levels Europe demanded, while exempting more than 130 developing countries, as China demanded. It was not a compromise agreement, it was a capitulation. Nor would compliance with the treaty much affect the presumed problem. Even if implemented in every detail, atmospheric carbon dioxide levels would, according to "mainstream" scientists, be twice in 2050 what they are today. And the cost of a Kyoto agreement? Economists Henry S. Rowen and John P. Weyent of Stanford University predicted that if the United States implemented the Kyoto plan, it would slash 3 to 4 percent from America's gross domestic product over twelve years. Noting the assurances of environmentalists that the cuts could be made cheaply, the two Stanford economists said, "They are dreaming. There simply is no way to cut 25 percent of our emissions without shutting down many electricity-generating and steel-making plants that use coal and without drastically scaling back gasoline use."

Republican Speaker of the House Newt Gingrich, with his predatory instinct for wounded prey, complained, "We sacrificed the future well-being of the country based on environmental correctness and inconclusive science." Indiana Republican Richard Lugar felt the president was out of options in the Senate. "He didn't make the case for fast track and he hasn't even begun to make the case on climate change. And now he has to explain how U.S. negotiators botched it in Kyoto."

Smiling like a Cheshire cat, Republican Senate Majority Leader Trent Lott invited the administration to submit the treaty for Senate ratification. That was not in the cards, of course, not only because the administration knew the Senate would likely offer far more advice than consent, but because Gore, in a more reflective moment, seemed to regard Kyoto as a work in progress. According to a senior advisor, "Al's attitude is, let's not rush into an up or down vote. Instead let the world digest its terms. Meanwhile reemphasize the education campaign by calling attention to the extent that warming can be documented." With congressional elections in the fall of 1998 and a 1999 United Nations Committee on Environment and Development (UNCED) meeting scheduled for November 1998 in Buenos Aires, there was no reason to force the issue immediately. "We will concentrate on getting the meaningful participation from these key developing countries," Gore told an interviewer, "and that will be the threshold we have to cross before sending it for ratification."

Four months after Kyoto, in an interview with Peter Jennings of ABC News, Gore was back in his inquisitor's robe, comparing scientists skeptical of a global warming apocalypse to the tobacco industry's academic whores. "Having gone through these long debates with the tobacco industry, which remind me almost exactly of this debate, I think that it is totally fair and totally legitimate to say we're going through the same kind of experience again." Challenged that he was "impugning the integrity of a lot of scientists at a lot of prestigious universities," Gore repeated his attack. "I don't want to fence on the analogy, I think the analogy is exact."

In the summer of 1998 Gore repeated the prophecies of doom he had uttered during the 1997 Red River floods. He mounted his soapbox in Florida, where brush fires had destroyed broad areas of five counties, closing two hundred miles of Interstate 95, and forcing tens of thousands of people to evacuate their homes. Gore spoke to a withered, desperate throng, calling the tragedy a powerful reminder of what global warming could do to the planet. At a time when even the most convinced believers in global warming acknowledged that its primary impact would be on winter evening temperatures in the northern latitudes, Gore could not restrain himself from wallowing in the tragedy brought on by unusually dry, summer weather in the tropics.

The thoughts of many who watched the event, or snippets of it on the evening news, were captured admirably by columnist and former Bush speechwriter Tony Snow.

> Imagine yourself sitting in that audience. A mad blaze has just reduced your home to ash. It has consumed your wedding photos. It has turned the only extant pictures of your deceased great-grandmother into glowing cinders. You last saw them spiraling upward, shedding faint sparks as they gave themselves to the clouds.
>
> You tote up your losses. You grieve for what you can never reclaim. And here comes some bozo delivering a tendentious lecture about carbon-dioxide sinks.

In August 1998 the White House announced it would not submit the treaty for Senate ratification because it was "flawed and incomplete." And while the United States signed the treaty at the Buenos Aires meeting, so many areas of international disagreement remained that the administration announced it would not be prepared to submit the treaty for Senate ratification until the year 2001, by which time, of course, at least one new President will have been inaugurated. The two major unsettled areas continue to be developing country participation, and trading rights.

With Senate ratification postponed, Carol Browner's EPA and the private Enviromental Defense fund began lobbying the automobile companies and others, insisting that with trading rights they would be able to meet any new standards imposed by the Kyoto

agreement and perhaps even turn a profit should some technological breakthrough provide them with rights they could sell to others.
The Pew Center for Global Climate Change sought, with some success, to engage oil companies and others in efforts to cut back their
own carbon emissions.

But the stark costs of the agreement never remained hidden for
long. In October 1998 the Energy Information Agency indicated in
a report to Congress that achieving the treaty's goals by 2010 would
require a more than 50 percent rise in energy prices and an 86 percent jump in electricity costs. U.S. energy consumption would have
to decline by more than 17 percent, and the Gross National Product
would drop by 4.1 percent by the year 2010. Only the truest of true
believers could imagine how an accord on trading rights would cause
a material revision in these projections while still enabling the world
to achieve the desired emissions reductions.

Less well noted was a February 1998 paper contributed to the
National Academy of Sciences by James Hansen, Al Gore's principle living mentor on global warming. In it Hansen noted that in
New York City, selected for its temperate zone location, "the temperature change there is nearly zero over the past five decades."

By contrast, a slight but statistically significant warming trend
had been discerned in the high northern latitudes, particularly
Siberia and Alaska.

Perhaps most interesting, Hansen revealed, "The growth rate
of greenhouse gas... peaked in the late 1970s... and has declined
since then. The decline is dramatic when compared with the 'busi-
ness-as-usual' scenarios, which assume continued growth of the
annual increment of greenhouse gasses." This happened despite
"moderate continued growth of fossil fuel use and a widespread per-
ception, albeit unquantified, that the rate of deforestation has also
increased."

What explains the mystery? "Apparently the rate of uptake by
carbon dioxide sinks, either the ocean, or more likely, forests and

soils, has increased"—which was exactly what many of those Gore accused of practicing "junk science" had predicted.

Hansen's report should be reassuring—that is, unless one views global warming as a biblical pillar of fire, warning our "dysfunctional" society to mend its errant ways or face the wrath of God, or Gore.

CHAPTER TWENTY

PROTECTING THE PRESIDENT-IN-TRAINING

DURING THE POLITICAL lull that spanned the period from Election Day 1996 to the start of the second Clinton term in January 1997, people close to the president let it be known that some deep thinking was going on regarding the legacy the president hoped to leave, the place in history he hoped to attain, and the rank among the panoply of presidents he sought to secure. Were history to stop with the first presidential term, his subordinates reasoned, he might be no better than a solid third-rank performer, comparable to, say, Grover Cleveland. Optimistically perhaps, the White House thought Mr. Clinton could surpass the Civil War draft dodger who fathered a child out-of-wedlock, presided over economic depression, dispatched national guard troops to break up the Pullman railway workers' strike, and set the political stage for four consecutive Republican presidential election victories while his party sought an antidote to him in the brainless populism of William Jennings Bryan.

Clinton would prefer to be ranked with more consequential predecessors. The times might not allow for a giant, a Washington, Lincoln, or Franklin Roosevelt. But what about a strong second-rank figure like Teddy Roosevelt, the redoubtable Roosevelt combined a strong domestic agenda with the ability to make the United States a significant player on the world stage. Moreover, he left some tangible mementos: the Panama Canal, the National Park system, progressive Republicanism that would long be identified with the Northeast.

Clinton's legacy, the thinking went, would be the New Democrat moderate approach to government to which he had returned with brilliant results after the sobering congressional elections of 1994. To ensure that legacy, he had to surround himself with a more ideologically homogeneous group than he had at the outset of his presidency. Next, he had to reach early accord with the Republicans on a long-term budget strategy, removing the risk of a vintage 1995-type battle that this time could result in a defeat. Finally, he had to devote whatever time and effort was needed to ensure that his party would nominate Al Gore—if possible, without a bruising primary battle, but in any case with a convincing show of support for the type of government the Clinton administration had provided.

The president thus made no pretense of seeking political balance in putting together his second term team. From chief-of-staff Erskine Bowles, the North Carolina businessman and 1988 Gore delegate, to Franklin Raines, head of the Office of Management and Budget, from domestic policy advisor Bruce Reed, a former Progressive Policy Institute and Gore staffer, to Secretary of State Madeleine Albright and Defense Secretary William Cohen—the former Republican senator—the Clinton administration was now led almost exclusively by political moderates. Gone were the likes of Leon Panetta, George Stephanopoulos, and Harold Ickes, although the latter two notched enough grand jury appearances to pass as continuing members of the Clinton White House.

The deal with the Republican Congress committing the nation to achieve a balanced budget by the year 2000 fell swiftly into place, underlining the fact that Speaker of the House Newt Gingrich and Senate Majority Leader Trent Lott had even more at stake than the president in proving divided government can work. Further, Congressional Budget Office analysis showed the economy had performed so well that tax receipts had greatly exceeded expectations.

The administration had far less success in expanding its NAFTA victory, in which Gore had played a key role. Mexico's economy collapsed in 1995, requiring a massive U.S. bail-out and leaving Mexico in an import-inhibiting recession.

By 1997 labor unions claimed that NAFTA had cost American workers more than 400,000 jobs. While convincing evidence was lacking to support that claim—indeed the total volume of U.S.-Mexican trade had reached record highs, including U.S. auto exports to Mexico—clearly the threat to close up shop and move to Mexico gave some employers collective bargaining leverage against the unions.

But what was blatantly apparent was that in the context of a spellbinding U.S. economic boom, the particular changes attributable to NAFTA were meager. As a result, anecdotal evidence became more important than NAFTA statistical breakdowns. The Florida fruit-grower who lost out to cheaper Mexican produce, the California citizen concerned about increased illegal immigration, the Texas factory worker who saw his plant move across the border—all became important witnesses in the ongoing political struggle over free trade.

Further, the institutions created to deal with labor and environmental issues in Mexico produced few noticeable results, undermining the credibility of an administration that had delayed action on the treaty in order to put these institutions into place. Moreover, the increase in commercial traffic between the United States and Mexico proved an additional complication for American law enforcement officials working to apprehend illegal immigrants and drug smugglers.

By 1997 when the administration sought "fast track" authority to conduct other free trade agreements, the anecdotes were running against NAFTA. A majority of Democrats opposed granting the president "all or nothing" authority to conclude trade deals. Republicans, whose support had been critical for the NAFTA win, were not eager to donate their votes to Clinton-Gore.

But the issue was becoming critical. Clinton had delayed pushing the "fast track" measure, inadvertently giving his leading opponents—organized labor and Missouri Congressman Richard Gephardt—an advantage in preparing for the controversial fight. Gore, against the counsel of his political advisors, went to the forefront, leaning on Democratic congressmen and publicly proclaiming that the tide had turned in favor of "fast track."

He could not have been more wrong. The possible swing votes rested with a small but critical band of GOP abortion foes in the House who said they would support "fast track" only if the president accepted an amendment restricting aid to countries that subsidized abortion counseling. Gore and the president agreed that they could not accept that ultimatum. With the vote scheduled for November 11, negotiations on the abortion issue ran well past midnight. Finally, Representative James P. Moran Jr., a pro-"fast track" Virginia Democrat, informed the White House that the Republican group would not back down. With only forty-two House Democrats prepared to support the deal, and unwilling to slight his pro-abortion constituency, Clinton informed Speaker Newt Gingrich that he wished the measure withdrawn. Gingrich, Clinton's ally on "fast track," complied.

For Gore, the defeat may have been a political blessing. With a possible Gephardt primary challenge in the works, he had been trying to preempt the alliance between the minority leader and labor on "fast track" by inserting language in the agreement preserving a separate machinery for dealing with labor and environmental issues. This was unacceptable to Republican leaders who insisted on a "clean" bill. Withdrawing the bill gave Gore time to massage the issue rather than fighting to score another "victory" over labor.

Gore took more direct steps to enhance his standing with labor. He backed its effort to prevent government contractors from obtaining reimbursement for costs incurred opposing union activity. He pleased the teachers unions by fighting hard against school choice "voucher" proposals. He twice backed increases in the minimum wage. And as the administration's point man on the politics of welfare reform, he reached a deal with labor permitting the federal government to hire ten thousand people recently removed from the welfare roles—but with assurances that they would not be hired as replacements for any union employees, that they would receive no benefits unavailable to federal workers in the lower grades, and that they would receive no preference in eligibility for child care services.

But the priority Gore attached to doing labor's bidding was most evident in an administration clash with Republican Governor George W. Bush of Texas over the latter's effort to streamline procedures for determining eligibility for welfare, food stamps, Medicaid, and other "safety net" type assistance programs. Texas had invited private companies to bid for the right to design a new system, including the possible substitution of private workers for government employees to administer the assistance.

"That's when the AFL-CIO got into the act," recalls one senior Texas official. "The feds had to approve our plan because so much of the programs involved getting federal funds. We had no problem with our federal colleagues and we were told that Donna Shalala [secretary of health and human services] had signed onto the plan. But the White House blocked it."

"This was a big deal for labor," recalls a former Gore aide. "They don't want to see their government jobs privatized. They came to Al and he went to the president." Clinton sat on the deal for months while Bush fired off angry letters to Washington. Finally the answer came: permission denied. Gore was again willing to sacrifice some of his reputation as a government reinvention devotee for the chance to woo at least a share of union support from Gephardt.

Gore also clashed with Gephardt over the balanced budget agreement, which could be chalked up as a major administration success, because it had been achieved almost painlessly.

In a paper of remarkable insight, former Congressional Budget Office chief Robert Reischauer noted that legislation eliminating many agricultural subsidies and reforming the welfare system—the only two laws passed with any significant impact on budgetary projections—were expected to cut the deficit in the year 2002 by only $2.1 billion and $12.6 billion respectively. "Most of the improved deficit outlook resulted from slightly stronger economic growth, lower inflation and interest rates, a greater than expected revenue yield, and a slowdown in the actual and projected growth of Medicaid and, to a lesser extent, Medicare spending."

According to Reischauer, the overall amount of deficit reduction achieved by virtue of the 1997 budget deal was only about one-quarter of what had been achieved by the budget packages adopted in 1990 or 1993. Still, the measure drew a sharp rebuke from House Minority Leader Richard Gephardt who charged it had "a deficit of principle, a deficit of fairness, a deficit of tax justice, and worst of all, a deficit of dollars." Gephardt was echoing those who charged that many of the cuts anticipated for future years would never be enacted into law. The White House had excluded Gephardt from the budget negotiations, presumably on the assumption that one set of adversaries at a time was sufficient. Now the minority leader led his fellow liberals in opposition. And once again, as with NAFTA and welfare reform, President Clinton passed one of the central items on his agenda with more Republican than Democratic support.

Gephardt also moved to attack the administration's approach to China, calling it "a bankrupt policy" disdainful of the nation's lack of commitment to human rights.

Gore fired back. In a May 8, 1997, speech to the New

Hampshire legislature, he recalled the evolution of New Hampshire's economy from the time when its biggest companies manufactured blankets, shoes, kegs and barrels, and milk bottle caps to today's businesses of cutting-edge computers, electronic systems and components, circuit boards, and avionic systems. "The Granite State is now also the Silicon State," he declared with a bow in the direction of his own administration's economic policies.

But, warned Gore, "Some people would like to snatch defeat from the jaws of victory." Gephardt was clearly in his sights. "There's still a fight whether this is the right plan for the new economy. Despite overwhelming evidence that each element of this strategy has worked, our plan still has its critics. It still faces opposition from organized foes who would push New Hampshire and the nation off course back to the past, back to the old economy, with the old hazards that we have worked so hard to escape."

Even by the standards of the perennial presidential campaign it was rather early for the smell of gunpowder to be in the air. This, of course, delighted the political press, which was euphoric over what promised to be a three-year battle between Gore and Gephardt for the soul of the Democratic Party, the winner capturing the presidential nomination in the year 2000. Political columnist David Broder, for example, could barely contain his joy, writing that "when important issues are at stake, it is an obligation for leaders—not selfish indulgence—to speak out boldly and clearly on their views. That is what Gephardt and Gore have done. Bravo to both."

His colleague, the thoughtful Dan Balz, saw the dispute as emblematic of a clash between two economies: "Gephardt has been nearly obsessed with the stagnant or declining wages of less-educated workers and the growing inequality between the upper class and the middle class that occurred throughout the 1980s and early 1990s. Gore, who coined the phrase 'information superhighway' two decades ago, has become an enthusiastic proponent of the information-based economy."

The reaction in the Clinton White House was less enthusiastic. The year 2000 campaign was going to be tough enough, even if Gore pranced happily through the primaries with little or no opposition. The Republicans had one or two potentially formidable challengers. The last thing Gore needed was some liberal bomb-thrower softening him up with a steady attack for the next three years.

That concern was underlined when Gephardt once again articulated a pointed critique of the administration's approach in an address at Harvard University. Calling upon an activist government to cure the problems of stagnant wages, inadequate health insurance coverage, poor schools, and sluggish growth, Gephardt all but accused Clinton and Gore of taking their cues from the Republicans:

> This is a different approach from some who now call themselves New Democrats, but who set their compass only off the direction of others, who talk about the political center, but fail to understand that if it is only defined by others, it lacks core values. And who too often market a political strategy masquerading as policy.

At this, the White House dispatched political gunslinger James Carville to the TV cameras. Carville responded not to Gephardt's policy arguments on the merits, but attacked the minority leader personally as a "phony" whose positions were once as moderate as the president's and Gore's, but who, during his campaign for the presidency a decade ago, had suddenly discovered an inner liberal self, just in time for the Iowa caucus and New Hampshire primary.

Gephardt got the point quickly. An administration that attacked him so directly was not beyond trying to undercut his leadership position in the House, opening up a second front that could threaten both his presidential and congressional leadership aspirations. Further, a brutal internecine battle could injure already slim Democratic chances of retaking the House in the 1998 elections, delaying, at least for another two years, Gephardt's opportunity to become Speaker again.

Gephardt realized too that with the exception of trade, the big issues that separated "Old" Democrats from "New" Democrats—the budget, welfare reform, anti-crime legislation—had been dealt with and were now off the table, at least for a while. What remained was a long list of items on which most Democrats could stand together. Clinton, Gore, Gephardt, and Minority Whip David Bonior could walk into a room and come out agreeing that campaign fundraising laws should be amended to eliminate soft money; that stringent anti-tobacco legislation should be passed; that a strong effort to adopt a "bill of rights" for HMO clients must be under-taken; that steps toward a "flat tax" must be opposed; that school choice "voucher" systems must be stopped in their tracks; that affir-mative action, including what opponents term "race preference pro-grams," must be preserved; that the minimum wage should be raised again; that abortion rights must be protected; and that "privatiza-tion" experiments with Social Security must be resisted.

Small wonder that Gephardt had been both an Old Democrat and a New Democrat simultaneously. Small wonder that Gore had "reinvented" government without changing it. Small wonder Bill Clinton talked of solving problems without ideological labeling. There had been differences between the moderate and liberal Democrats. There still were, and not all were over fringe issues. But at the core of the Democratic Party remained a belief in the right-ness of government intervention to protect the nonwinners against the results of the Darwinian struggle for survival and supremacy. And in a complex, sometimes bewildering world, these Democrats often saw government as the power of first resort.

Gephardt's retreat was so rapid, Patton's Third Army couldn't have caught up with him. One of the country's more loquacious politicians suddenly fell silent on subjects he had been addressing relentlessly. Within months, he and Gore were seen exchanging chummy grins and handshakes. In mid-January 1998 Gephardt and his wife Jane accepted an invitation to dine with the Gores at the vice president's Massachusetts Avenue residence. By the following summer, the attempted *rapprochement* between "Old" Democrats and "New" Democrats had become institutionalized with a White House gathering of the "Old" and the "New" put together by resident presidential propagandist Sidney Blumenthal and presided over by First Lady Hillary Rodham Clinton. The idea was to find common ground from which to battle the Republicans in the congressional campaign of 1998 and the presidential contest of 2000. The real *leitmotif*: getting Al Gore Jr. nominated without having to battle Richard Gephardt in the primaries.

That effort received yet another boost when the Democrats came close to toppling GOP control of the House in mid-term 1998 elections. With the carrot of a potential speakership now in view, as well as the stick of a White House mugging should he challenge Gore, Gephardt, on February 3, 1999, formally took himself out of the presidential race.

*　　　*　　　*

Among Democrats who have worked with both men, or had the opportunity to observe both closely and over a sustained period, there is no judgment more widely shared or deeply entrenched than that Bill Clinton is a marvelous working politician while Al Gore is, at best, a bit better than average when promoting himself, somewhat better than that when playing a supporting role. "Bill Clinton is our Ronald Reagan," says one who spent four years in a senior position on the Gore staff. "There will never be another one like him." Gore, on the other hand, can stay remarkably focused—"on message" is the term of art—when he is defending the president or campaigning for one of his programs.

While the similarities between Reagan and Clinton probably begin and end with their ability to connect with voters, Clinton and

Gore present fascinating contrasts. Clinton tends to think horizontally, leaping from issue to issue while never losing his political anchor. Gore is a more vertical thinker, digging deeper and deeper in search of fundamental truth. For better or for worse, *Earth in the Balance* shows the depth of Gore's thought processes. It is not the sort of book Bill Clinton could ever have written.

As working politicians, Clinton empathizes while Gore confronts. Clinton is smooth while Gore can be awkward. Clinton thinks on his feet while Gore takes refuge behind a fortress of facts or legalisms. Clinton is infinitely resilient while Gore is brittle. Clinton is the matador, graceful and artistic in political combat, while Gore tends to stagger when forced to abandon positions. Clinton is utterly without pretense, perfectly capable of lying, but what would you expect from a man wearing a slightly crushed derby and a polka dot tie and hawking wares from a patent medicine wagon? Gore is given to what Timothy Noah of the *Wall Street Journal* called "solemn, high-flown conceits." It was Noah who recounted four dinner parties at the vice presidential residence devoted to celebration of "the metaphor." Invited guests would arrive at 7 PM for drinks and were promptly escorted into a large room where gold-painted chairs were lined up in rows for a lecture to be delivered by an invited scholar. Gore explained that he was inspired by the notion that breakthroughs such as the discovery that the earth revolves around the sun created metaphors for other phenomena that people could discern in their lives. Now, alas, there is a metaphor gap. "The total amount of knowledge is doubling every four years," said Gore, "and the number of new discoveries that offer intriguing explanations of physical phenomena are a lot more plentiful today than in the early years of scientific revolution. But the number of such metaphors that migrate into the rest of the culture have slowed down." A number of guests conceded they had no idea what the evening had been about. Or the host.

Nowhere were the differences between the two more in evidence than on their respective travels to China, one year apart. In 1998 Clinton led a massive entourage to China, ignoring calls from influential Republicans that he postpone the visit. Clinton seemed unworried about a grand jury investigating his relationship with former White House intern Monica Lewinsky. He appeared equally unworried about charges that he had altered America's high-tech export policy—saving China years of research and development on advanced military systems—in exchange for massive campaign contributions.

And perhaps he was right to be unworried, because Clinton, in the end, would overwhelm his critics by turning his trip into a celebration of touring American values, drawing praise even from Republicans. Almost unnoticed amidst all this political brilliance was the fact that the visit amounted to little more than calculated appeasement to the Chinese on every issue of importance. Never before had any American president been as explicit and categorical in rejecting any special status for Taiwan. Nor was there precedent for Clinton's public adulation of Chairman Jiang, his acceptance of China as an "emerging" industrial power entitled to special treatment on entering the World Trade Organization, his willingness to enter into a "strategic partnership" with a Communist power, or half a dozen other actions that must have discouraged friends from Tokyo to New Delhi.

Of course, the underlying problem was that after six years in office the Clinton-Gore team had not managed to develop even the semblance of a China policy. "Engagement" is too amorphous a term to describe a relationship twenty-six years after Nixon's visit with Chairman Mao and twenty years after ambassadors were first exchanged. Dropping the linkage between trade and human rights merely involved dropping campaign rhetoric and continuing the policy that had *de facto* existed under the Bush administration. On the critical issues of the day—China's covert weapons dealings with Iran and Pakistan, the size and capability of its own nuclear arsenal, its effort to minimize U.S. influence in the Pacific, its obstruction-ism in the face of U.S. efforts to tame North Korean conduct and weapons programs, and its continuing failure to enforce agreed-upon rules for the conduct of international trade—the Clinton-Gore team had no coherent approach before, during, or after Clinton's visit.

Compared to Clinton, Gore's legal and political problems at the outset of his trip were fairly mild. The Buddhist Temple affair had been embarrassing, and his fundraising calls from the White House had provoked GOP demands for appointment of an inde-pendent counsel. Not the send-off he would have preferred, of course, but nothing to prevent a successful journey.

Still, Gore's China visit would be remembered as his poorest performance in an important assignment. It was characterized by the sort of idiotic, paranoid mistakes politicians and their staffs tend to make when trying too hard to control events.

En route to Beijing, reporters were barred from a speech Gore delivered to the Japanese Chamber of Commerce on the spurious grounds that the occasion was a "working meeting." The pattern continued at a number of Beijing events, allegedly because the Chinese wanted them closed—something totally contrary to their normal desire to trumpet every stop of a distinguished visitor to their country.

Gore's moment of consummate embarrassment came when his host, Prime Minister Li Peng—who in 1989 had declared martial law, leading to the Tiananmen Square massacre—suddenly pro-duced wine and champagne glasses and proposed a toast. Undoubtedly picturing future campaign ads showing him clinking glasses with the "Butcher of Tiananmen Square," Gore stumbled, spilled half his drink, and generally looked like a man who would rather be doing something more pleasant, like shoveling out the pig parlors on his father's farm.

Nor could Gore and his staff quite agree on whether he had

raised with Li the question of Chinese efforts to influence the U.S. election then being investigated. One aide said no. Another said yes. Ambassador Jim Sasser—Gore's longtime Tennessee ally—implied it had been mentioned but given short shrift. Part of the problem was simply bad staff work. Leon Fuerth, the vice president's veteran foreign policy advisor, added responsibility for press briefings to his China portfolio, perhaps preparing for the day when Gore would be president and he, the president's national security advisor. Undoubtedly a splendid idea, but one which might better have been implemented on a less demanding state visit, perhaps to Luxembourg.

In the months after his disastrous China trip and the Buddhist temple and White House fundraising scandles, Gore's standing in the polls slowly improved. Journalists covering the vice president looked for signs of a personal rebound, and Gore and his staff encouraged them, with Gore describing criticism of his performance in China as "a blessing in disguise." He had taken some hard shots, but nothing that suggested permanent damage. "I've picked up a lot of experience and I've picked up a lot of inexpensive lessons," he told one reporter.

But in the White House there was concern that Gore was becoming even more of a "control freak." "He has good political instincts, but he doesn't trust them," says one White House insider. "He wants to script every move he makes, to be standing just where he should be standing for each occasion, to say what his handlers tell him to say, and no more." There is, in short, not a man behind the robot, but quite possibly, a robot behind the man.

That tendency was made even clearer by the contrast with the ability of Bill Clinton—under far greater legal and political threat than Gore—to think on his feet, to charm audiences of all kinds, to trust his ability to read audiences, and to connect with constituencies at any time and under any conditions. "Bill Clinton is Teflon and Al Gore is Velcro," went one line of analysis. And here, not even Tipper provided much help.

"Tipper is great when it comes to making sure he has a private life—time with the family, vacations with the kids, that sort of thing," says one who knows the family well and who likes both Mr. and Mrs. Gore. "But when she sees Al under attack, she becomes the ultimate loyalist. She is angrier than he is and not in a position to give detached advice."

*   *   *

Save for those moments when either he or the president was on the road—or when he was presenting one of his relentless global warming mediafests—Gore was displayed like a prop at nearly every White House event and photo-op during the first year of the second Clinton term. Gore as "president-in-training" in 1998 had replaced "Prince Albert" of 1988. But Gore was as welcome inside the Oval Office as he was in the East Room or the Rose Garden. And sometimes the president's inclusiveness provided outsiders with a window on how Al Gore might perform if he were president.

One of those occasions occurred on December 19, 1997, when the president, as part of his dialogue on race, invited to the White House several distinguished opponents of racial preferences, including Ward Connerly of the California Board of Regents; Abigail Thernstrom of the Manhattan Institute; her husband, Stephen Thernstrom of Harvard; Linda Chavez of the Center for Equal Opportunity; Lynn Martin, the former Republican congresswoman and Labor secretary; Ellen Chao, formerly the head of the Asian Civil Rights Coalition; and Representative Charles Canady, Republican from Florida, whose Constitutional Rights subcommittee has been a center of anti-preference activity.

Clinton began by acknowledging that even as a supporter of affirmative action, he had concluded, "it works predominantly for people who are at least in a position for it to work. A lot of the people that I care most about are totally unaffected by it one way or another."

He asked for suggestions on how opportunity could be enhanced for those not reached by affirmative action. Connerly offered ways in which K to 12 education could be improved. "They're trying to do that in California by lowering classroom sizes. We're looking at testing. We're looking at the quality of teachers. We also have to start looking at ourselves. Are we telling our kids as parents that education is as important as it should be?"

Continuing along the same line, Linda Chavez related how the University of Maryland offers a specially structured program for freshmen whose parents never attended college, a program of disproportionate benefit to African American and other minority students but which avoids categorizing students on the basis of race. "[A]ffirmative action preferences are part of this debate because there's a whole world of people out there who believe that they're wrong and that they send the wrong signal from government; that so long as you've got government picking winners and losers on the basis of the color of their skin, that you can't get beyond racism, you can't get to the color-blind society."

When the subject turned to economic affirmative action, the president again said he believed such programs "did a profound amount of good for the people who got into the programs...." But he acknowledged that once in, those afforded the opportunity have had difficulty "graduating out," making it on their own without preferences. And while he disagreed in principle with preferring people on the basis of race, he continued supporting such programs, in part because "I really thought that the institutions were better off and the white majority, or whoever else, was better off if there was some intermixing because of the world they're going to live in."

In a discussion marked by civility and mutual respect, there were only two exceptions, both provoked by Gore interventions. First, the vice president structured a hypothetical community where

50 percent of the population was white and 50 percent black, but where the police force was 100 percent white, "and the problems of the kind we all deplore took place, and the community decided that the police force would be better able to do its job if blacks were much more represented on the police force, because the police force would have a much greater ability to relate to the community effectively and do its job...." Having built his straw man, Gore then wondered whether affirmative action would be justified to address the problem.

Linda Chavez replied, "I don't think you could find me a concrete example of such a place in urban America today." The first tool in making sure minorities are hired, she reminded the vice president, is vigorous enforcement of anti-discrimination laws. "And then you engage in outreach. You do create training programs. You do go into high schools and try and recruit people and get them ready so that they will be able to be prepared to take the test to become a police officer. Those are all things that you can do. And they are all things we approve of."

Late in the discussion, Gore said, "I think it is naive in the extreme to assert that there is no persistent vulnerability to prejudice—rooted in human nature, prejudice based on race and ethnicity—and other characteristics as well."

Gore then cited the ethnic hatred in Bosnia (where both sides are white), the approaching fiftieth anniversary of the rape of Shanghai (committed by Asians against Asians), and the near genocide in Rwanda of the Tutsis by the Hutus (where blacks slaughtered blacks). "I think that people are prone to be with people like themselves, to hire people who look like themselves, to live near people who look like themselves. And yet in our society when we have this increasing diversity, we have community value, a national interest in helping to overcome this inherent vulnerability to prejudice."

But the issue, the visitors reminded Gore, was not so much what society might do to repair the wounds of past discrimination, but the one thing it ought not try to do: impose new quotas or preferences that introduce new forms of discrimination on the basis of race or ethnicity. "Mr. Vice President," said Representative Canady, "none of us are suggesting that we stop all of these efforts. We believe in the outreach efforts that have gone on. We believe we should actually intensify those efforts. What we have a problem with is classifying people on the basis of their race and telling some people they're going to lose because they belong to a non-preferred group, and other people they're going to win because they belong to a preferred group."

It was an extraordinary session, agreed most of those who attended, where Clinton's reputation for empathy, analysis, and nuance was put on dazzling display, and where Gore's reputation for stiff-necked condescension was also very much in evidence.

Nor was the vice president finished. Exactly one month later, he spoke at Martin Luther King, Jr.'s, Ebenezer Baptist Church in Atlanta at the commemoration of the civil rights leader's birth. No longer, in Gore's view, as expressed in his speech, were opponents of racial preferences well-intentioned people with whom there was a difference of opinion. Like scientists who question global warming, they had become wicked heretics who merit excommunication from the church of the righteous.

"Yet now we hear voices in America arguing that Dr. King's struggle is over—that we've reached the promised land…. They use their color blind the way duck hunters use their duck blind. They hide behind the phrase and hope that we, like the ducks, won't be able to see through it.

"They're in favor of affirmative action if you can dunk the basketball or sink a three-point shot. But they're not in favor of it if you merely have the potential to be a leader of your community and bring people together, to teach people who are hungry for knowledge, to heal families who need medical care. So I say: we see through your color blind. Amazing Grace also save me; was color blind but now I see."

An instant later, Gore wondered aloud where opponents of affirmative action stood on "that heinous crime" in Jasper, Texas, where two white men beat and mutilated a black and dragged his body through the steets behind their vehicle; or how they felt about a 1997 Virginia incident where a black man "was doused with gasoline, burned alive, and decapitated by two white men"; or a scene in Lowell, Massachusetts, where white thugs attacked an interracial couple with baseball bats.

In the recent history of political oratory there has rarely been a more brazen example of arrogant demagoguery masquerading as principle. In fact, Gore's own rhetoric undermines his central argument. There is, of course, no affirmative action whatsoever in rewarding a university applicant who "can dunk the basketball or sink the three-point shot." To the contrary, people with those skills are awarded scholarships on the basis of their athletic merit, and no one complains when the result is a starting five composed entirely of black athletes. What those who oppose racial preferences or discrimination contend is that whatever the standard—academics, athletic skills, musical accomplishment, leadership potential, or any combination of the above—it should be applied without the tragic distortion of race as an element.

Gore's performance managed to repel a staff writer named Jeff Jacoby who works for that liberal northeastern bastion, the *Boston Globe*. Describing Gore as a man with a "mean mouth," Jacoby rejected the idea that those who oppose race preferences believe the country is already color blind. "What many of them do claim is that American law ought to be color blind and that affirmative action with its racial quotas, preferences, and plus factors is doing more harm than good."

As for Gore's thinly veiled linkage of opponents of affirmative action to the brutal racist attacks against black Americans, Jacoby had this to say: "Does Gore actually believe such rubbish? Who knows? What matters is that he is willing to say it, to inject, for political gain, the worst kind of racial poison into the national bloodstream. That is vileness of a very low order. Imagine anyone so sleazy becoming president."

In these examples, as in others, was one of the ironies of the Clinton-Gore administration. While Bill Clinton bobbed and weaved from scandal to scandal, ministering his political balsam, trying with amazing popular success to be all things to all people, it was stolid Albert Gore, Jr., who could well wind up needing protection from himself. Gore's zealotry, strangely juxtaposed with moderation on many issues, was less a platform around which the Democratic Party could rally than a plank leading to shark-infested political waters, where he might, if he wasn't careful, be torn to pieces by more intellectually supple opponents, or, during the heat of a political campaign, by the once adoring press. The operative question was, under the harsh spotlight of being the leading presidential contender in the country, would the pressurized, brittle, buttoned down Al Gore, Jr., implode?

CHAPTER TWENTY-ONE

MILLENNIUM MAN

GORE WAS WELL into his game of "shadow president" in January 1998 when the bombshell fell: charges that Clinton had conducted an affair with White House intern Monica Lewinsky, charges that he lied about it under oath, charges that he obstructed justice and suborned perjury.

Gore remained a loyalist and attempted to rally the spirits of congressional Democrats, who sensed impending doom. But while Gore defended the president, he tellingly never publicly affirmed Clinton's version of events or his defense strategy, saying only he was confident the president would respond persuasively at the appropriate time. Nevertheless, his public performance could be manic, as in a bizarre joint appearance with Clinton at the University of Illinois on January 25, 1998, days after the Lewinsky scandal broke.

"And I want to ask you now, every single one of you, to join me in supporting him and standing by his side. I give to you the president of the United States, William Jefferson Clinton." Gore delivered these pedestrian words in frantic screams, gesturing wildly as he spoke the lines. It reminded some observers of Gore's sometimes peculiar performances in the 1996 campaign. On one such occasion in Cleveland, near the close of the campaign, Clinton watched his shouting, gesticulating, putative successor with amusement, later telling the crowd, "I do not know what the vice president ate for breakfast this morning. But if he had two more bites of it, he would have blown the roof off."

When confronted with questions in a media studio, he could be more circumspect. In a lengthy interview with NBC's Clare Shipman on February 4, Gore offered a perfunctory endorsement of Clinton's denial of wrongdoing, saying, "Well the president has denied these charges and I believe him." But he declined to suggest that judging a president by his character was out of bounds, saying, "that's for the American people to decide." Nor would he endorse Hillary Rodham Clinton's charge of a right-wing conspiracy, saying only that "I respect her opinions and analysis," and that the attacks against Mr. Clinton had been "unprecedented." And as for the orchestrated White House attack against Independent Counsel Kenneth Starr, Gore took a pass, saying, "I'm not going to comment on Judge Starr. I'll leave that for—I'm just not going to make any comment on that."

Gore was in Hawaii vacationing with his family when Clinton followed his August 17 grand jury testimony with a brief television address to the nation. In a curious, hostile performance, Clinton admitted "a relationship with Miss Lewinsky that was not appropriate," and "wrong." His public statements had, he admitted, given "a false impression and misled people."

Gore responded by issuing a statement saying how "proud " he was to work for a "great president" like Bill Clinton. But once again, he did not echo the president's complaint that his "privacy" had been breached, nor did he endorse the president's attacks against Independent Counsel Kenneth Starr.

*   *   *

There were other problems confronting the administration. Japan was in deep recession. Other Asian economies suffered crippling deflation as overexposed investors cut back on their investments. Latin American countries were swept into the credit crunch. U.S. exports suffered a want of buyers, the stock market lost about 15 percent of its value, and the dollar fell dramatically in the currency markets.

It would soon rebound, but for Gore, the trouble was more than the economy. His leadership on foreign policy burdened him with other political baggage. The Mansour Kikhia affair is a case in point.

Kikhia was a former Libyan diplomat, U.S. resident, and husband of an American citizen. Seized by Libyan agents in Cairo in 1993, with the full, if covert, cooperation of Egypt, he was abducted to Tripoli and secretly executed. It was Egyptian President Hosni Mubarak's way of chalking up goodwill points with Libya's Muammar Qaddafi.

U.S. intelligence had the whole story. Armed with the truth, Clinton sent a low-key request to Egyptian authorities asking them to investigate the matter. They did next to nothing on the case.

In the summer of 1997 Secretary of State Madeleine Albright, frustrated by Egyptian intransigence, indicated she would go public with the details of the Kikhia case, which, obviously, would have been profoundly embarrassing to Mubarak. The White House, with Gore leading the way, told Albright to cool it. Al Gore would handle the matter through "quiet diplomacy"—which meant the administration would keep the issue buried.

"The Kikhia case is a moment of truth for the Clinton administration's commitment to deal more candidly and decently with American citizens and the public in such tragedies, even if sensitive intelligence is involved," wrote Jim Hoagland of the *Washington Post*. "So far, the end result of the changes made looks distressingly like diplomacy as usual."

Gore was also involved in White House deliberations regarding Iraq and signed onto a significant change in policy that would have gone unannounced and unknown had not Scott Ritter, Reserve Marine officer and a senior American member of the UN weapons inspection team, resigned in protest on August 26, 1998. Ritter claimed the administration had been impeding inspectors' work by refusing to permit them to conduct surprise inspections, capitulating to Iraqi objections. In one instance, Ritter believed his team was about to discover ballistic missile components. A second time the team was after evidence that biological weapons had been tested on live prisoners. "The illusion of arms control is more dangerous than no arms control at all," he said.

Ritter's charges were 100 percent true. Only six months earlier, during a crisis where Saddam Hussein allegedly backed down, Clinton had said that Saddam could not be allowed to defy inspectors or "he will conclude that the international community has lost its will. He will then conclude that he can go right on and do more to rebuild an arsenal of devastating destruction. And some day, some way, I guarantee you he'll use the arsenal." But, behind the scenes, the Clinton administration agreed to undercut the UN inspections.

Why the secret change in policy? Once it had done its best to quiet and then slander Ritter, the administration sought to justify its retreat by claiming a lack of UN Security Council support for military action to compel Iraqi inspection compliance. The *quid pro quo* was a *de facto* agreement by the Security Council to maintain an embargo on Iraq for as long as Saddam remained in power, though this was ensured anyway because any change in embargo policy was subject to America's Security Council veto.

True to form, Saddam continued to play his cat-and-mouse game with U.N. inspectors, leading the Clinton-Gore team, in one particularly bizarre episode, finally to order American bombers into the air to punish Saddam's intransigence, only to order the bombers back to their stations. Weeks later, as impeachment hung in the air, the president ordered the strikes carried out. The awkward and indecisive presidential display probably spelled the end of on-site weapons inspections, and, could well have marked the beginning of the end of the sanctions regime. Perhaps in the 2000 campaign, Gore, who was so vitriolic about George Bush's supposedly spineless—and even illegally corrupt—foreign policy, can offer some insights on his own administration.

Foreign failures aside, a surprising number of observers have suggested that of all the obstacles capable of wrecking the year 2000 candidacy of Al Gore, Jr., none poses a greater danger than the so-called "Millennium Bug" or "Y2K" glitch. On first impression, the very notion seems absurd. The country's number one techno-nerd done in by a computer glitch?

But on reflection it is Gore's very expertise in the field that makes his long silence and episodic interest appear so strange. There is no questioning the reality of the problem, the high national stakes, or the need for leadership. The only question is: where is Al Gore?

The coming Y2K problem was noted by computer engineers in the late 1980s. By the mid-1990s, it had become the subject of feature reports in leading newspapers and technical journals. Throughout 1997 various member of Congress—Representatives Steve Horn and Constance Morella, Senators Robert F. Bennett and Daniel Patrick Moynihan, among others—were sounding the alarm. And by mid-1998, as reported by the highly regarded *National Journal*, which devoted an entire issue to the subject, 70 percent of government and industry managers were predicting at least an economic slowdown caused by the glitch, 59 percent were predicting a mild recession, 35 percent, a deep recession and widespread bankruptcies, and 10 percent, a depression with sufficient social instability to require at least limited martial law.

As has been recounted *ad infinitum*, the glitch came into being because years ago software experts, corporate executives, and agency managers decided to save money by reducing storage space, identifying four digit years—1975, for example—by only two digits—75.

The problem is that vast numbers of computers will think that the year 2000 will be the year 1900, or simply fail to recognize the number 00 at all. The result could be chaos in banking and stock transactions, power outages, and computers that simply shut down. According to one estimate, half the nation's air fleet may have to be grounded because of possible computer malfunction.

The conservative, pro-defense Center for Security Policy says, "The indisputable fact is that disruptions will affect the operations of at least *some* of the mainframe computers responsible for vital services like the power grid, telecommunications, banking and control of air, train and ground transportation and at lease *some* of the microprocessors governing everything from elevators, nuclear power plants, military hardware and oil tankers and refineries." For safety's sake, the entire nuclear power generating industry may well be forced to shut down. That would cost the eastern United States 40 percent of its power supply. The potential legal liability of businesses that fail to mitigate the problem—to say nothing of their insurance carriers—boggles the mind.

Perhaps the most frightening situation is at the Pentagon, where the Number 2 man, John Hamre has described the glitch as "the mother of all security problems." At the Department of Defense only 29 percent of the mission-critical systems could meet Y2K standards, according to a mid-1998 Office of Management and Budget assessment. It is one of fourteen agencies not on track to fix its Millennium Bug problems by the year 2000. Representative Steve Horn, chairman of the House Subcommittee on Government Management, Information and Technology, has graded the military's preparation, "D." Many precision U.S. weapons and some early warning systems are, as of early 1999, still unprepared and could malfunction. According to a General Accounting Office report, the Global Command and Control System, which is "deployed at seven hundred sites worldwide and is used to generate a common operating picture of the battlefield for planning, executing and managing military operations" would not work. The General Accounting Office reported, "The U.S. and its allies... would be unable to orchestrate a Desert Storm-type engagement in the year 2000 if the problem is not corrected."

Even worse, the Pentagon worries about the reliance on far flimsier and less reliable systems by China and Russia. Testified Hamre:

> We're very concerned, for instance, that the military leadership in Russia right now is coping with serious funding constraints. They are increasingly falling back on nuclear weapons to safeguard their national security; and they don't have any program to deal with the year 2000.

According to the *National Journal*, "The Pentagon is belatedly developing a program to share early-warning data between nuclear command-and-control organizations around the world."

The cure for the Y2K glitch requires testing every system, rewriting billions of lines of software programs, then testing the system again to make sure it is truly fixed. That in turn will require an estimated $300 billion to $600 billion. But the biggest problems are the running clock and the shortage of experts able to fix the deficient systems. Those far down the economic food chain may not be able to get the required help. Franklin D. Raines, the former Office of Management and Budget chief, called the glitch the "Number 1" problem facing small business.

Yet Vice President Gore, who claims paternity of the term "information superhighway," who receives and sends up to one hundred e-mails a day on his IBM 560 lap-top computer, who seems to regard Silicon Valley as his political home away from home, had nothing to say during the first five-and-a-half years of his vice presidency about the biggest problem in the history of high-tech America.

Dr. Edward Yardini, chief economist of Deutsche Bank Securities (North America) Morgan Grenfell has said, "We need to alarm the public. You can alarm the public and then the public can pressure the politicians and the business leaders to do everything in their power to fix this problem. If we don't let the public in on the problem, then they will panic sometime in the next year."

"The government should use the soapbox of the bully pulpit to get the word out," said Stephen Roach of Morgan Stanley Dean Whitter & Co. A more pessimistic Dennis Grabow, who founded a Chicago-based Y2K consulting company, Millennium Corporation, offered this prescription for government action: "In our view, the die is cast, and we need to plan for disruptions in the economy, especially in many of the basic infrastructure areas of water, electricity, telecommunications, and transportation."

By executive order early in 1998, President Clinton established a Year 2000 Council to coordinate government efforts in dealing with the Millennium Bug. To head the group, he named John Koskinen, at the time a retired former Office of Management and Budget official. Critics immediately labeled Koskinen a "fall guy," while the Center for Security Policy charged, "The Year 2000 Council has no authority to act, allocate funds, or force an agency to do anything. It is a figurehead organization with monitoring or oversight responsibilities, and little else."

Gore's lack of personal involvement was widely noted and widely criticized. Liberal Republican Congresswoman Constance Morella asked Gore early in 1998 to lead the nation's repair effort. Morella told the *National Journal* that Gore replied that the effort would take too much of his time. Then, after a pause, he suggested, "Maybe you should to it," a remark his press secretary, Lawrence J. Haas, described as "tongue in cheek."

When the *Washington Post* undertook an assessment of Gore's

mysterious nonrole, Haas said that the "vice president receives regular briefings on the government's progress in fixing Year 2000
computer problems, has personally directed the cabinet to make the
fixes a high priority, and has spoken about the potential crisis to the
President's Management Council, a group of senior political
appointees." The *Post* reported: "But when asked to point out the
speeches in which Gore has talked about the so-called millennium
bug, Haas could not identify *one.*" This contrasts sharply with the
eleven trips Gore made to California between Election Day 1996
and June 1998, many on speaking and fundraising excursions to
Silicon Valley.

Republicans speculated that Gore's silence may have had
something to do with his not wishing to undermine the "peace and
prosperity" theme essential to Democratic hopes in regaining control of the House in the November 1998 elections.

Andrew L. Shapiro, at the time a fellow at the Berkman Center
for Internet and Society at Harvard, was probably closer to the mark
when he said, "It's very much a factor in his positioning for the 2000
race. Al doesn't want it to be Al's mess." Of course, had the administration acted in timely fashion in 1993 or 1994 when both the time
and the human resources were there to correct the problem, it
would have been "Al's success" rather than "Al's mess."

The president and vice president finally addressed the issue in
mid-July 1998. At a time when surveys showed that half the small
businesses that knew about their computer problem intended to do
nothing about it, Clinton reflected, "All told, the worldwide cost will
run into the tens, perhaps the hundreds of billions of dollars, and
that's the cost of fixing the problem, not the cost if something actually goes wrong."

Gore described four levels of the problem: the federal government with its approximately seven thousand critical systems; state
and local government that use computers to run everything from
Medicaid to water treatment plants; the private sector with its mil-

lions of noncompliant computers; and then the problem of international compliance.

"When you have that many of them," said Gore of computers, "if only a small percentage of them don't accurately read the date, then the world has a problem. And unless the old lines of code are fixed, the problems, of course, will be serious."

Said Representative Steve Horn of the Clinton-Gore statements, "The denial phase is over."

Gore had finally decided that his silence was a bigger political risk than speaking out on the issue. Still, if both government and industry fail to meet the challenge of Y2K, the *wunderkind* of high-tech politics will likely take a fall. The juxtaposition is inevitable: obsessed with the highly speculative "crisis" of global warming, Gore suffered a failure of perspective. Faced with the real crisis of Y2K, he suffered a failure of nerve.

*   *   *

On a gray, chilly day in Nashville in early December 1998, Al Gore, Jr., buried his father, who had died at the age of 91, and eulogized him. "Of all the lessons he taught me as a father, perhaps the most powerful is the way he loved my mother," the younger man said. "When I was growing up, it never once occurred to me that the foundation upon which my security depended would ever shake." Perhaps, as one reporter suggested, he was already into the "subtext" of the next campaign, "as candidates affirm their steadfastness in reaction to Mr. Clinton's sex scandal." Or perhaps this was striking one final blow in the long-running debate as to whether the elder Gore's love, or his aloofness, was principly responsible for the development of Al Gore, Jr.'s, personality.

Of Albert Gore, Sr.'s, political legacy, there was less debate. When the elder Gore came off a struggling farm during the Depression, he had compassion in his heart for hard-working people who couldn't feed their families, educate their children, or provide medical help for their sick. He spent little time thinking abstractly about the appropriate role for government. He saw acute needs, and he saw government as a means to meet them. Never in his speeches or writings did he display any concern about the moral underpinnings of income redistribution, or the economic wisdom of high marginal tax rates. To the contrary, Albert, Gore Sr., merely saw government as a tool the exploited many could wield against the well-off few.

On matters of principle, like civil rights and Vietnam—the latter cause unmentioned in the vice president's eulogy—Albert Gore, Sr., believed he was elected to vote his conscience. Friends sometimes thought of him as stuffy and unyielding. Even his wife, Pauline LaFon Gore, once suggested he had failed to learn the basic lesson, "If there's no chance of victory, there's no sense in bloodying yourself." When he lost his Senate seat, some said he was out of touch with the voters of Tennessee. Actually, he was *untouchable* by those voters. He knew how his constituents felt about race and the war in Vietnam. He simply disagreed with them, and when the choice had to be made, he voted his conscience rather than theirs. Maybe he would have been a different kind of senator had he come home to hold bipartisan "town meetings" every week. Maybe he would have conducted himself more shrewdly had his use of sampling devices and "focus groups" been more sophisticated. Maybe, but maybe not.

Unlike his father, Al Gore, Jr., was a child of government and a student of government who grew up to be a man of government. He has had no life to speak of outside government save for a few years on a Nashville newspaper—where he covered government.

Like his father, Al Gore, Jr., is a liberal. But he is a chastened liberal. He harbors no illusions about government curing all social ills. But if he has altered his father's goals, he remains committed to the *process*. Craft the right bill and a sick woman in Pittsburgh will get the kidney transplant she needs to survive. Come up with the right formula and cable, satellite, and telephone companies will be forced to compete in the public interest. With the right government program, we can protect people from greedy HMOs, raise the financial cost of bad habits like smoking, and put more teachers in the schools. And we can even "reinvent government" so that it employs rational processes for purchasing goods and services, and better responds to the needs and conveniences of its customers and clients.

When he turns out the lights in his office and goes home, Gore is a good and decent family man. He would seem an unlikely fellow to turn the Oval Office into a pornographic playpen. One has difficulty seeing Gore's UN ambassador interviewing a Monica Lewinsky for employment based on the sort of credentials the original Monica brought to the task. Gore vacations with his wife and kids, ran marathons because his daughters dared him to get into the kind of physical shape needed to go twenty-six miles, performed fatherly duties like driving the baby-sitter home safely, and rarely let Tennessee politics make him miss the flight back to Virginia for Sunday church. "Gore's weekly schedule always had blocs of time—two to three hours in the middle of the afternoon—that were left blank," recalls a former senior aide. "If it had been Clinton we'd have wondered. But with Gore we knew what it was: a daughter's field hockey game, or in the spring, lacrosse. That's right. The vice president of the United States watching an afternoon girl's high school field hockey game in the middle of the week."

Gore's attitude of "family first" became part of the ethic of his office. "I can remember Lorraine Volles [Gore's former press secretary] walking out of business meetings with the vice president at - 5:45 PM saying, 'I've got to go, my day care runs out in fifteen minutes,'" recalls a former senior Gore aide. "Somebody always seemed to be bringing a kid to the office."

The most serious Gore family "scandal" involved the 1996 suspension of Albert III from St. Albans after getting caught smoking and drinking in a wooded area near the school with a handful of classmates and National Cathedral School girls. The Gores resented the treatment their son had received and complained to headmaster Mark Mullin. Unsatisfied with his response, they withdrew the boy from St. Albans, enrolling him in the equally posh Sidwell Friends school, where the vice president would spend a number of Saturday afternoons in the fall of 1997 and 1998 watching his son play football. Following the transfer, according to the *Washingtonian*, Tipper Gore angrily instructed St. Albans "to expunge the family from all school mailing lists—including the alumni list that her husband had once so proudly graced."

Friends describe Gore as a man who can be counted on. He spoke at a testimonial dinner in Nashville, raising $50,000 for an old *Tennessean* colleague who is battling cancer. Passing through Detroit, he has called his old army buddy, Mike O'Hara, at odd hours, just to get together for a hug and a beer at the city's airport. Unlike some on Capitol Hill who treat staff like depreciable office furniture, Gore has kept the nucleus of his staff together for years. They remain loyal, ready to come together on the next Gore campaign, believing their man to be among the more able and principled figures on the political scene.

But Gore is no longer the Eagle Scout of American politics. That image dissolved at a Buddhist temple in Hacienda Heights; in the White House, where Gore put the heavy hand on fat-cat contributors; in former Chief-of-Staff Peter Knight's dealings in the Molten Metal and Portals contracts; in the vice president's studied ignorance of the background of big contributor Howard Glicken; and, inevitably, in Gore's loyal defense of the second president in American history to be impeached by Congress—a president accused of perjury and obstruction of justice.

To his critics, Gore's stiffness is less innate gravity than flagrant pomposity; and Gore's distinction from any other old pol is minimized by an apparent chronic hypocrisy. The Gore who told a political convention that he would battle Big Tobacco because of his sister's early death is matched with the Gore who waxed lyrical over the satisfactions of tobacco farming—four years after Nancy Gore Hunger breathed her last. The Gore who rushed to aid Champion Paper, the Pigeon River polluter, when it served his political purpose to do so is matched with the Gore who risked putting the same company out of business when the political costs and benefits changed. The Gore who repudiated George Bush's foreign policy for "coddling" dictators has served an administration that has done more than any other to appease China and North Korea, while dealing far more ineptly with Iraqi dictator Saddam Hussein than George Bush did on his worst day.

But the most profound concern may not be that Gore pretends to be what he is not, but that he is exactly what he purports to be. Running as Clinton's second fiddle in 1992 and 1996, Gore escaped the kind of media scrutiny he will get when he runs for president. That scrutiny will reveal that Gore is less a hypocrite, than a moderate with a strange streak of extremism in him, a man who, in his wilder moments, is not running so much against the Republicans as he is against the Enlightenment, the internal combustion engine, and the idea that there are legitimate opinions aside from his own.

As to the man behind the impenetrable facade, the strong likelihood is that there is not much of a facade there at all. "With Al, what you see is what you get," says a long-serving former member of his staff. "He's not much different in a small group with friends. He'll joke a bit more, sure. But he is a private person. He is deadly serious. He's not a grandstander. He doesn't perform. He's in love with work."

And he knows where he must do that work to meet the expectations set for him, just as he had to fulfill the educational aspirations of his father, or plow the dangerous hillside on the Carthage farm.

INDEX